Safe as houses

Manchester University Press

The *Manchester Capitalism* book series

Manchester Capitalism is a series of books which follows the trail of money and power across the systems of our failing capitalism. The books make powerful interventions about who gets what and why in a research-based and solidly argued way that is accessible for the concerned citizen. They go beyond critique of neoliberalism and its satellite knowledges to re-frame our problems and offer solutions about what is to be done.

Manchester was the city of Engels and Free Trade where the twin philosophies of collectivism and free market liberalism were elaborated. It is now the home of this venture in radical thinking that challenges self-serving elites. We see the provincial radicalism rooted here as the ideal place from which to cast a cold light on the big issues of economic renewal, financial reform and political mobilisation.

General editor: Julie Froud

Already published:

The end of the experiment: From competition to the foundational economy

What a waste: Outsourcing and how it goes wrong

Licensed larceny: Infrastructure, financial extraction and the global South

The econocracy: The perils of leaving economics to the experts

Reckless opportunists: Elites at the end of the establishment

Foundational economy: The infrastructure of everyday life

Forthcoming:

Systems city: A new politics of provision for an urbanized planet

Safe as houses

Private greed, political negligence and
housing policy after Grenfell

Stuart Hodkinson

Manchester University Press

Published by Manchester University Press
Altrincham Street, Manchester M1 7JA

www.manchesteruniversitypress.co.uk

British Library Cataloguing-in-Publication Data
A catalogue record for this book is available from the British Library

ISBN 978 1 5261 4186 6 hardback

ISBN 978 1 5261 2998 7 paperback

First published 2019

Typeset in Sabon and Trade Gothic
by R. J. Footring Ltd, Derby
Printed in Great Britain
by Bell & Bain Ltd, Glasgow

This book is dedicated to the 72 people who died and the 255 survivors of the Grenfell Tower fire of 14 June 2017. They are forever in our hearts.

Contents

Boxes, figures and tables

Acknowledgements

Until the Grenfell disaster, I had struggled for years to write up my own research on unsafe and unjust regeneration schemes. Each of the human stories I had encountered deserved their own book to do justice to the magnitude of both their suffering and their dignified resistance. But as so many people have said, Grenfell changed everything. I realised I was sitting on damning evidence from 'other Grenfells in waiting' that pointed to exactly why this had happened, evidence that could help campaigners in their struggles to prevent another Grenfell happening again. So began the daunting process of sifting through over a decade of research to try to craft a clear account of why unsafe regeneration happens, who or what is to blame, and what can be done about it. Although I take responsibility for the book's argument, errors and omissions, it simply would not exist without the contributions of countless people.

My heartfelt thanks and respect are due in equal measure to the residents in Islington, Camden, Lambeth, Manchester, Kirklees, Leeds, Ashford, Lewisham, Reading, Salford and north-east Derbyshire who agreed to participate in the research. I will never forget your resolve, courage, humanity, solidarity with your neighbours and dignity in the face of appalling treatment from both the PFI companies and local authority landlords. The following people went to enormous lengths to assist me: Eugen Hockenjos, Thomas Cooper, Nigel Rumble, Simon Morris, Uzoamaka Okafor, Jacqui Dyer, Steve Hack and Jeanne Cornillon, to name but a few. Thanks also to the civil servants, former ministers, councillors, officers and private sector actors who agreed to be interviewed, and to the former employees of PFI companies who turned whistle-blowers for having the courage and the compassion to speak out.

I am immensely grateful to the British Academy (ref. PDF/2007/75) and the Economic and Social Research Council (ESRC) (ref. RES-061–25–0536) for funding the main research underpinning this book. I have also received incredible support over the years from a number of academics, experts and campaigners. I am indebted to Paul Chatterton and Jenny Pickerill, who gave me my first academic job in a research project that kick-started my interest in housing regeneration, and to Chris Essen, who worked with me from 2012 to 2015 to document much of the evidence in this book. Many other colleagues and former students in the School of Geography at the University of Leeds were integral to the success of the research, especially Paul Waley, Rachel Homer, Andy Turner, David Bell, Izzy Hawkins, Richard Goulding, Joe Beswick, Hannah Biggs, Hannah Smith, Shannon Lennon-Smith, Kate Honey, Gloria Dawson and Martin Gaskin. I was especially helped along the way by Ruth London (Fuel Poverty Action), Charlotte Johnson, Colin Nickless, Zoe Williams, Stephen Mackenzie, Phil Murphy, Ryan Powell, Ian Cole, Stewart Smyth, Sid Ryan, Chris Allen, Lee Crookes, Antonia Layard, Sarah Blandy, Anna Minton, John Grayson, Sarah Glynn, Simon Murray, Kofi Mawuli Klu, John Davies and Richard Whittell of Corporate Watch.

Special thanks go to: Sara Gonzalez, Helen Mercer, Hugo Radice, Pilgrim Tucker, Megan Waugh, Paul Watt, Tom Slater, Joel Benjamin, Dexter Whitfield, John Ward, Steve Hodkinson, Ralph Footring, Amaka and Eugen, who all read and provided remarkable advice on the draft manuscript; Tom Dark and Karel Williams at Manchester University Press, who were extraordinarily patient, helpful and supportive editors; my friends Stuey 1, Joseph, John, Sai and Megan; and finally, to my pan-European family, for all your unconditional love and support over the years. Kathryn, Moira, Steve, Rosa, Mariano, my incredible partner, Sara, and our crazy kids, Diego and Oihana – I could not have done this without you.

Abbreviations

ACM	aluminium composite material
ALMO	arm's-length management organisation
CCT	compulsory competitive tendering
CFOA	Chief Fire Officers Association
ESSU	European Services Strategy Unit
EU	European Union
EY	Ernst and Young
FFT	Faithorn Farrell Timms
FITA	Federation of Islington Tenants Associations
FRA	fire risk assessment
GDP	gross domestic product
HHSRS	Housing Health and Safety Rating System
HRA	housing revenue account
HSE	Health and Safety Executive
IC	independent certifier
ICO	Information Commissioner's Office
ITA	independent tenant advisor
JCA	Joint Competent Authority
JLIF	John Laing Infrastructure Fund
KCTMO	Kensington and Chelsea Tenant Management Organisation
KPI	key performance indicator
LSVT	large-scale voluntary transfer
MFN	Myatts Field North
MFN RAMB	Myatts Field North Residents Association and PFI Monitoring Board
NHS	National Health Service
PFI	Private Finance Initiative

PPP   public–private partnership
PSC   public sector comparator
PUK   Partnerships UK
PwC   PricewaterhouseCoopers
RBS   Royal Bank of Scotland
RRFSO   Regulatory Reform (Fire Safety) Order 2005
RSL   registered social landlord
RTB   right to buy
SMBC   Sumitomo Mitsui Banking Corporation
SPV   special purpose vehicle
TCA   The Consulting Association
TMO   tenant management organisation
VFM   value for money

Introduction: Grenfell and the return of 'social murder'

At around 12.54 a.m. on 14 June 2017, an exploding fridge freezer set fire to a flat on the fourth floor of Grenfell Tower, a 24-storey public housing block of flats in the west London borough of Kensington and Chelsea. Ten minutes later, firefighters were on the scene, handling what appeared to be a routine job – post-war high-rises like Grenfell had been designed to contain fires within separate flats and the residents had been told to 'stay put' rather than evacuate. But the fire did not behave as expected. Within 15 minutes, a column of flames had rapidly climbed up the outside of the tower block to the uppermost storey, and shortly after the whole building was ablaze. Survivors and emergency service workers would later recount the sheer horror of human carnage that took place, which they were helpless to prevent. As people leapt from the tower, others trapped inside climbed to the upper floors and roof, some trying to make ropes from sheets, others making phone calls and video messages to their loved ones, begging for help or saying goodbye. Those who survived did so in large part by ignoring the official fire safety advice to 'stay put' in their flats. It would take 250 firefighters, 70 fire engines and 60 hours to extinguish the fire that eventually claimed the lives of 72 people in one of Britain's most deadly infernos since the Great Fire of London of 1666.[1]

While the architectural and construction quality of tower blocks has attracted long-standing critique, Grenfell Tower was a beacon of the high building standards brought in after the 1968 Ronan Point disaster in east London that killed four people when a new tower block partially collapsed following a gas explosion. The original architect involved in Grenfell's construction in 1974 had stated a year prior to the fire that its design and solid concrete construction meant it 'could last another 100 years'[2] – so what went wrong on 14 June 2017? It is now known that the devastating speed with which the fire spread and the high death toll were primarily caused by the Tower's flawed £9 million refurbishment in 2014–16. Flames from the originating flat travelled up the building's new external cladding, apparently fuelled by the low fire resistance of the aluminium panels and the ultra-combustible plastic core. Subsequent tests showed that the Grenfell cladding succumbed to flames less than 9 minutes into what should have been 40 minutes of resistance.[3] In a cruel twist, it was revealed that a non-combustible cladding originally chosen for Grenfell had been decided against in favour of a cheaper and more incendiary substitute due to cost-cutting pressures on the local authority from the austerity policies of the Coalition and Conservative governments since 2010.[4]

The poor quality of workmanship and materials used during this outsourced regeneration project fatally compromised the building's original fire-resistant structure and both the central fire alarm and emergency fire escape lights failed on the night of the fire.[5] Despite this, the Grenfell refurbishment passed all building control inspections by the local authority. It has since been revealed that Grenfell residents repeatedly raised concerns about fire safety and the standards of works by the main private contractor, Rydon Maintenance Ltd, before, during and after the renovation work. However, they were largely ignored by the Conservative-controlled Kensington and Chelsea council, and its arm's-length management organisation, Kensington and Chelsea Tenant Management Organisation (KCTMO). Incredibly, several residents were even threatened with legal action over making their claims public.[6] In November 2016 an online blog by residents who were members of the Grenfell Action Group made this chilling prophecy about their future:

> It is a truly terrifying thought, but the Grenfell Action Group firmly believe that only a catastrophic event will expose the ineptitude and incompetence of our landlord, the KCTMO, and bring an end to the dangerous living conditions and neglect of health and safety legislation that they inflict upon their tenants and leaseholders....

> It is our conviction that a serious fire ... is the most likely reason that those who wield power at the KCTMO will be found out and brought to justice![7]

Grenfell residents were not alone – other canaries in the mine were also being ignored. The disaster was foretold in the seven major fires and 11 deaths in high-rise council tower blocks since 1986 linked to flammable cladding across the UK (see box I.1). Each fire generated the same demand by a coalition of campaigners, the fire service, coroners, architects and parliamentary committees for

---

Box I.1 Grenfell foretold

In 1986, despite warnings from safety campaigners, a 24-storey block of flats at Royston Hill in Glasgow, clad with polystyrene panels and aluminium sheeting, caught fire. In April 1991, a major fire at the 11-storey Knowsley Heights in Huyton, Liverpool, was linked to the absence of fire breaks in the gap between the cladding and the block's walls. In June 1999, a 55-year-old disabled man died in a fire in the 14-storey Garnock Court in Irvine, Scotland, after the fire spread via the combustible plastic cladding. Three people were killed, two of them firefighters, in the 17-storey Harrow Court fire in February 2005, in Stevenage, Hertfordshire, when a fire developed and spread from the fourteenth floor up the outside of the building to higher floors. In July 2009, six people were killed and at least 20 injured in the 14-storey Lakanal House fire in Southwark, London, when a fire from a faulty television spread with unexpected speed, the exterior cladding panels burning through in just four and a half minutes. In April 2010, two fire-fighters were killed while attending to a fire in a 15-storey council block, Shirley Towers in Southampton, being overcome by heat after getting trapped by falling plastic cables. In August 2016, at the 17-storey Shepherd's Court, in Hammersmith and Fulham, a faulty tumble-dryer caught fire on the seventh floor and flames spread up six floors on the outside of the building; the London fire brigade blamed the cladding.

Source: O. Wainwright and P. Walker, '"Disaster waiting to happen": fire expert slams UK tower blocks', *Guardian*, 14 June 2017, at https://www.theguardian.com/uk-news/2017/jun/14/disaster-waiting-to-happen-fire-expert-slams-uk-tower-blocks (accessed 12 October 2018).

government to revise building regulations so as to require sprinkler systems in all new and existing high-rise blocks, and ensure that cladding was non-combustible and actively resistant to the spread of fire.[8] While governments in Scotland and Wales have taken steps to address some of these issues under their devolved powers, the UK government in England has consistently refused to act.

Since Grenfell, safety inspections continue to expose the enormous scale of the safety time bomb in our midst. Nine days after the fire, five high-rise tower blocks containing 800 flats and 4,000 residents on the Chalcots Estate in Camden, London, were evacuated over multiple fire safety concerns. The tower blocks had been refurbished and re-clad by Rydon between 2006 and 2009 under a controversial £153 million Private Finance Initiative (PFI) scheme to which I will return later in this book.[9] At the time of writing, 468 high-rise buildings had been officially identified as having combustible cladding, with the majority in the private sector, as well as a number of schools and hospitals built under PFI.[10] But the issues go beyond cladding. Checks in Greater Manchester found that 367 tower blocks – 75 per cent of the total – failed to meet safety standards, with only 117 of those surveyed 'broadly compliant' with fire safety legislation.[11] Two London council estates – the Ledbury Estate in Southwark and the Broadwater Farm Estate in Haringey – built using the defective 'large panel system' designs implicated in the 1968 Ronan Point disaster that were never strengthened, had to be evacuated for emergency work or demolition. The problem of construction defects extends far beyond housing to encompass other public and private buildings. In April 2016, 17 schools built and managed by Edinburgh Schools Partnership – a consortium of Miller Construction, Amey and the Bank of Scotland – had to be closed following the partial collapse of a wall at a primary school. Construction defects were later found in an additional 80 PFI schools in Scotland.[12]

Social murder

As this book will reveal through damning evidence from other botched public housing regeneration schemes in England under similar outsourcing arrangements, the Grenfell disaster was neither an accident nor a one-off event but instead an act of what German industrialist and socialist Friedrich Engels called 'social murder'.[13] Engels used the term in his classic text *The Condition of the Working Class in England in 1844*, to capture the mass immiseration and premature deaths of the industrial working class from starvation, disease and injury at the hands of unsafe working conditions and insanitary slum housing provided by private landlords. Social murder, he argued, was the result of unregulated private greed, in which a capitalist class knowingly forced people to work and live in deadly conditions and ignored all calls to improve those conditions despite mounting evidence of their murderous nature:

> when society places hundreds of proletarians in such a position that they inevitably meet a too early and an unnatural death, one which is quite as much a death by violence as that by the sword or bullet; when it deprives thousands of the necessaries of life, places them under conditions in which they cannot live – forces them, through the strong arm of the law, to remain in such conditions until that death ensues which is the inevitable consequence – knows that these thousands of victims must perish, and yet permits these conditions to remain, its deed is murder just as surely as the deed of the single individual … social murder.[14]

Over the 19th and 20th centuries, working-class struggle against social murder saw local authorities gradually empowered to clear the slums left behind by the unregulated capitalism of the Victorian era and build high-quality, decent, affordable, secure and safe public housing for rent, reaching a third of the UK's total housing stock by 1979. At face value, therefore, the link between the contemporary society that produced the Grenfell disaster and the dangerous working and housing conditions of the mid-19th century appears misplaced. However, the disaster exposed a much deeper neoliberal fault-line in the governance of housing safety, from decades of so-called 'free market' policies aimed at boosting capitalist profitability and in particular feeding the voracious returns demanded by an increasingly dominant global financial investor class.[15] Successive governments of all political persuasions rolled back state provision and social protections through privatisation, outsourcing and deregulation across every sphere of society. When we focus on the dangerous effects of these policies on housing, and the 'institutional indifference'[16] of those in power to the safety warnings of campaigners and those affected, the charge that Grenfell was social murder strikes at the heart of this abhorrent tragedy and its wider political relevance.

Safe as houses?

Nowhere has this neoliberal agenda been more fervently pursued than in the realm of housing. Thatcherism flipped the post-war model on its head, aiming to shrink the state's housing role to an 'ambulance service' for the genuinely 'weak'[17] and instead to establish a 'property-owning democracy' in which the vast majority of people would be encouraged to act like 'little capitalists' in the housing market, treating shelter as a financial asset by speculating on house price inflation and passing on the spoils to their children. One route to this end was, and still is, the privatisation of public housing; since 1980, 2.5 million homes have been sold off to tenants at large discounts under the 'right to buy', the vast majority of which have never been replaced. This laid the basis for the UK's crisis of housing insecurity, a crisis made worse since 2010 by years of cruel Conservative austerity policies that have hit the poorest households and communities hardest. In this book, however, I will contend that it is a less well known part of this privatisation story – the *demunicipalisation* of public housing – that can help us to understand more fully the issues raised by the Grenfell disaster. Instead of allowing local authorities to invest directly in repairing and modernising their remaining housing stock, both Conservative and Labour governments since 1979 have sought to make such funding conditional on local authorities agreeing to sell off or outsource to commercial actors the management, maintenance and even regeneration of public housing.

Accompanying privatisation and outsourcing has been a dangerous game of deregulation in which both the *legal standards* governing building and housing safety and their *enforcement* have been fundamentally weakened. While the government has declared the Grenfell cladding to be unlawful, experts believe the watering down of building regulations in 2006 at the behest of the insulation industry created a legal route through which combinations of previously outlawed combustible materials as used on Grenfell could be used on buildings over 18 metres high.[18] A more flexible regulatory framework has gone hand in hand with the rise of 'self-regulation', with an estimated 85 per cent of all building work previously requiring third-party inspection now being self-certified.[19] Meanwhile, local authority building control teams, previously the police force of quality control, must now compete in a liberalised market with private sector companies for contracts to inspect building work, making speedy approval a priority over rigorous checking of compliance. This perhaps explains why Rydon's chief executive officer, Robert Bond, could so confidently declare after the Grenfell fire that its work 'met all required building regulations – as well as fire regulation and Health & Safety standards'.[20]

For social housing residents, demunicipalisation and deregulation have transformed what used to be a clearer and more democratic line of landlord accountability into a highly fragmented set of often conflictual relationships between multiple actors all chasing the bottom line. Residents find themselves routinely fobbed off and passed around their landlord and its contractors, and then frequently rebuffed by their local councillors, MPs, government departments and various regulatory bodies who all claim not to be responsible for dealing with residents' concerns. They are also increasingly locked out of the legal system due to the gradual dilution of tenants' statutory rights to repair, as well as cuts to legal aid. This is especially the case for council tenants, as local authorities' environmental health officers are legally prevented from using their health and safety enforcement and prosecution powers on their own housing department or any management company or subsidiary acting on its behalf.[21] It was this legal quagmire that Grenfell residents faced when trying to challenge what they saw as the health and safety risks posed by the refurbishment.[22] Parliamentary efforts to change this situation and protect all tenants from dangerous housing conditions in England were defeated by Conservative MPs in 2016, when the official government line was that they would 'result in unnecessary regulation and cost to landlords'.[23]

It took the Grenfell disaster and intense political pressure in its aftermath for the government finally to give in and support new safety regulations on landlords and to appoint Dame Judith Hackitt, former chair of the Health and Safety Executive, to undertake a review of building regulations and fire safety in high-rise buildings. Combustible cladding has now been banned on all new residential and public buildings over 18 metres high, and borrowing controls on local authority housing departments have been relaxed – but this is too little, too late for the residents of Grenfell Tower.

About this book

Safe as Houses provides the first comprehensive account of the disastrous safety implications of the privatised model of commercial outsourcing and self-regulation that has come to dominate social housing and the wider built environment and that has left in its wake what Grenfell residents called an 'accountability vacuum' for ordinary people.[24] The book recounts the frustrated efforts of residents, whistle-blowers and even academics since the early 2000s to make social landlords and other public bodies listen to their concerns and evidence about how this outsourcing model was putting lives at risk. Instead of their concerns being listened to and properly investigated, local authorities and other public bodies have not only sided with the private companies, but have done everything in their power to ignore, deflect and even silence those who speak out. I know this because, as I will discuss in chapter 5, I too was targeted after I published evidence about dangerous work being carried out under the guise of regeneration. These experiences are now part and parcel of an ever-increasingly privatised state. By outsourcing regeneration to private companies whose social responsibilities have been progressively reduced over recent decades, politicians have ensured that the most important risks in regeneration – the health and well-being of residents – are moved away from the companies and state bodies involved and ultimately placed onto the public. In the process, residents' safety has been sacrificed in pursuit of profit.

The book evidences this argument through an in-depth focus on public housing regeneration schemes in England since 1999 carried out under PFI, arguably the leading edge of outsourcing and deregulation in the UK. PFI has been the preferred means by which governments since 1992 have invested in building new or maintaining existing public infrastructure like hospitals, schools, roads, prisons, street lighting, leisure centres and social housing – as of end March 2017, there were 715 PFI schemes operating across the UK, worth at least £308.46 billion in committed public spending up to 2050 (see chapter 2). I will show how PFI is in reality *outsourcing on steroids*, handing over the *entire process* of financing, building, managing and maintaining public buildings and assets to 'special purpose vehicles' (SPVs) – typically a subsidiary company that represents the interests of private developers, banks and investors – through highly lucrative, long-term contracts that provide a guaranteed stream of taxpayer-funded, inflation-proof payments. Proponents of PFI promised that this far more expensive route for financing public infrastructure was worthwhile because it would guarantee greater 'value for money' through the private sector's apparent 'superior' management of risk and a 'payment by results' contract that supposedly made profit conditional on performance. However, such claims amount to what the former head of the Financial Services Authority and current Royal Bank of Scotland (RBS) chairman, Sir Howard Davies, has called 'a fraud on the people'.[25] Not only were the claimed efficiencies hugely exaggerated but, as I show in this book, PFI takes the regime of self-regulation to its ultimate extreme by effectively allowing the private companies to monitor and certify their own compliance with building and fire regulations, contractual standards and key performance indicators, leading to poor-quality work and services that are almost always rewarded with handsome profits. Three original case studies of public housing PFI regeneration are presented in chapters 3 and 4:

- The refurbishment, maintenance and management since 2003 of some 6,500 homes in nearly 3,000 Georgian and Victorian 'street properties' in the London Borough of Islington that were municipalised – that is, purchased from private owners – by the local authority during the 1960s and 1970s and turned into council housing. The council has signed two contracts (one for 30 years in 2003 and another for 16 years in 2006) with a combined value of over £721 million, with Partners for Improvement in Islington Ltd, an SPV representing a consortium of United House, Hyde Housing Association and the Bank of Scotland, with Rydon providing responsive repairs and cyclical maintenance.

- The renovation and repair of five tower blocks built in the late 1960s on the Chalcots Estate in the London Borough of Camden. A 15-year contract worth £153 million was signed in 2006 with Partners for Improvement in Camden Ltd, an SPV representing United House and the Bank of Scotland, with Rydon once again involved, this time as the main contractor. The scheme included a new cladding system similar to that used at Grenfell and later found to be combustible, forcing the council to step in to procure remedial works worth a staggering £92.9 million. In 2018 the PFI was terminated, three years earlier than planned, after Camden stopped paying the SPV.

- The comprehensive regeneration of Myatts Field North (MFN) estate in the London Borough of Lambeth, originally built in the mid-1970s as part of a slum clearance and area improvement plan, with the provision of 477 homes. After years of delays and uncertainty, in 2012 Lambeth signed a £272.4 million contract for 25 years with Regenter Myatts Field North Ltd, a joint venture between Pinnacle Regeneration Group and John Laing Investments Ltd, to carry out the demolition and replacement of approximately 300 homes, to refurbish the remainder (again by Rydon), to provide new community facilities and green spaces, to build 503 new private flats outside of the PFI contract, and to connect all new and existing homes to a district heating system run by the energy giant E.ON.

The book shows how this form of privatised regeneration works in practice, who the main actors are, how the law and public bodies empower them to evade accountability and act with impunity, and how much they profit in the process. The evidence presented is a damning indictment of what happens when public housing is outsourced to private companies that are empowered to squeeze every ounce of profit out of an estate by cutting corners and doing poor-quality and unsafe work. At the heart of the problem is the illogical notion that fire safety and building quality should be left to the voluntary action of profit-seeking capitalists rather than remaining a state-enforced requirement. The book concludes with policy proposals and campaign ideas needed to end the era of unsafe regeneration and housing provision in the outsourced state. We should all hope that if Grenfell was a disaster foretold, it will also represent the moment in history when political negligence and private greed were tamed, and the place we call home finally can become as safe as houses.

Chapter 1 charts the life and death of public housing, from its emergence as part of a wider collective resistance to the social murder of unregulated capitalism to its planned demise under neoliberal policies of privatisation, demunicipalisation, deregulation and austerity. It argues that public housing rep-resented both the partial decommodification of shelter and the protection of residents' health and safety through a wider system of building regulation and control. These qualities made public housing a target for privatisation and demunicipalisation policies that have recommodified and financialised housing and land for profit-seeking corporate interests. It was in this context that the 'outsourced regeneration' under PFI described in this book was born, with the launch in 2000 of New Labour's Decent Homes programme, which sought to bring all social housing in England up to a minimum decent standard by 2010. The chapter ends with an explanation of how the assault on public housing was accompanied by the rolling back of building regulations and the rolling out of self-regulation that have weakened building safety and residents' ability to hold their landlords to account.

Chapter 2 introduces the contested politics of PFI and regenera-tion under New Labour. It begins by outlining the basic workings of a PFI scheme before exploring the origins of this model as part of the wider corporate takeover and financialisation of public services. It then debunks official claims that the inflated cost of private finance is justified by the superior 'value for money' delivered through PFI's supposed 'risk transfer' and 'payment by results' model. This is followed by an overview of the origins and evolution of PFI as the 'only game in town' for local authorities during the 2000s that wanted to retain ownership of public housing and access the desperately needed finance for home and estates in need of major regeneration and refurbishment. The chapter describes 20 PFI schemes across England eventually selected by the government, covering some 20,000 homes with a combined contract value of £5.58 billion, and explains how under PFI every aspect of housing regeneration – including the up-front financing – is contracted out to private companies. Finally, the chapter examines the controversy on the ground that met the undemocratic imposition of housing PFI schemes – sometimes in the face of resident opposition and the problems that engulfed the procurement of these contracts.

Chapters 3 and 4 present evidence gathered from the three case studies in Islington, Camden and Lambeth that arguably represent the most controversial PFI housing regeneration schemes in England. Chapter 3 recounts the experiences of residents in Islington's street properties and Camden's Chalcots Estate under the near-identical 'Partners for Improvement' consortia, while chapter 4 focuses exclusively on the MFN regeneration under Regenter. After setting out the origins of each scheme as well as the promises made to residents in each of them, the chapters illustrate in painstaking detail how residents experienced the kind of 'regeneration from hell' now synonymous with Grenfell. These chapters document the extraordinary number of problems that have plagued every aspect of these schemes, with information gathered through residents' testimonies and complaints over defective works and services in both new-build and refurbished properties. The chapters also detail the shocking safety defects discovered during post-Grenfell inspections.

Chapter 5 focuses on a particularly sinister side of the out-sourced state under PFI that was clearly present in the Grenfell disaster – the 'accountability vacuum'. It draws on interviews with professionals in both the public and the private sectors, residents involved in PFI schemes and whistle-blowers to illuminate with specific examples three aspects of this deficit: first, the lack of public or regulatory scrutiny of PFI works and services under an extreme form of self-regulation and self-certified performance reporting; second, the role of poorly written contracts that set largely meaningless key performance indicators (KPIs) and result in minimal financial penalties for demonstrable failings; third, the local authority's prioritisation of protecting long-term partnerships with private companies over genuine resident involvement and empowerment. I argue that all of this is compounded by the absence of genuinely independent and powerful regulatory bodies, as well as by an absence of legal routes that residents could use to get redress, meaning that those who do speak out are routinely ignored and sometimes actively silenced.

Chapter 6 turns to the bottom line of outsourced regeneration and self-regulation – the colossal financial riches made from these PFI contracts at the expense of residents and the taxpayer, and shows who benefits and by how much. The chapter maps out the intricate value-extraction chain of companies, and follows the money from government to the companies directly involved and then through to their ultimate owners, often offshored in tax havens. It shows how PFI enables a variety of commercial actors to capture an array of taxpayer-funded or otherwise underwritten income streams that would simply not be possible if regeneration was financed and procured directly through the public sector. This includes the complex yet lucrative financial deals done to raise the upfront investment that provides private banks, financial market traders and PFI investors with enormous risk-free profits, the generous profit margins commanded by the construction and maintenance firms from the lack of genuine competition in the procurement process, the conflicts of interest for the global accountancy firms that both advise the contracting companies and audit the schemes, and the huge windfalls on offer from the transfer of public land to the private companies involved through the development and sale of private housing.

Chapter 7 concludes by setting out a vision of immediate and gradual reforms needed for ending the era of unsafe regeneration and housing provision in the outsourced state. This means ending the disastrous regime of self-regulation by strengthening all building and fire safety laws for all homes and buildings, whether existing or in the pipeline, and creating new enforcement agencies that are independent of government and industry, with legal powers to inspect and enforce regulations. It also means ending PFI and similar models of outsourcing to bring back democratic control and accountability of public services and ensure the safety of our buildings. But re-regulation and nationalisation alone will not be enough. We must start to put in place a longer-term plan to end the financialisation of home and place based on a new model of public housing that treats the provision of shelter as a social service democratically accountable to its residents.

About the research

The evidence presented in this book stems from research carried out between 2007 and 2018 under different funded research projects and subsequent updates. From 2007 to 2011, I was funded by the British Academy Postdoctoral Fellowship scheme (ref. PDF/2007/75) to explore housing regeneration and PFI as part of a wider investigation entitled 'The new enclosures: council housing privatisation in contemporary Britain'. I conducted a number of interviews with former government ministers, civil servants, local councillors, local authority housing officers and individuals working on social housing and PFI in the private sector. I also began to document some of the many emerging problems in PFI housing schemes at both the national policy level and at the local project scale, meeting residents affected by some of the early PFI regeneration contracts in Manchester, Reading and Leeds.

What I saw and heard was so shocking that I decided to focus the next stage of my research on evidencing residents' experiences of PFI. This led to a three-year project, between 2011 and 2014, funded by the Economic and Social Research Council (ESRC) (ref. RES-061–25–0536) entitled 'Public housing regeneration under the Private Finance Initiative: a study about people, place and local governance'.[26] I wanted to understand how PFI transformed public housing as a place, a residential community and a democratically governed public service and, above all, what residents' 'lived experiences' of PFI were. Three case studies were chosen, in Islington, Camden and Lambeth. Part of the methodology involved using a 'participatory action research' approach that brought the affected residents' interests into the heart of the research design and implementation so that it became about both documenting and seeking to redress the poor accountability for construction and management failures under PFI.

A list of key interviews from these projects is presented in the appendix to this book, and these and other primary and secondary sources, including data disclosed under the 2000 Freedom of Information Act, are fully referenced in the chapters. This evidence base (and the book more generally) draws on the following peer-reviewed journal articles, though with updates and much new material: S. Hodkinson and C. Essen, 'Grounding accumulation by dispossession in everyday life: the unjust geographies of urban regeneration under the Private Finance Initiative', *International Journal of Law in the Built Environment*, 7:1 (2015), 72–91; S. Hodkinson, 'The new urban enclosures', *City: Analysis of Urban Trends, Culture, Theory, Politics, Action*, 16:5 (2012), 500–518; S. Hodkinson, 'The Private Finance Initiative in English council housing regeneration: a privatisation too far?', *Housing Studies*, 26:6 (2011), 911–932; S. Hodkinson, 'Housing regeneration and the Private Finance Initiative in England: unstitching the neoliberal urban straitjacket', *Antipode* 43:2 (2011), 358–383. The book also draws on and updates the research presented in a number of reports co-written with residents that are referenced in chapters 3, 4 and 5. The evidence in chapter 6 is based on my own analysis of PFI companies' annual accounts and the methodology is fully explained in the chapter.

Notes

1 P. Apps, 'Grenfell: the paper trail', *Inside Housing*, 11 August 2017, at http://www.insidehousing.co.uk/home/home/grenfell-the-paper-trail-51907 (accessed 12 October 2018); Architects for Social Housing, 'The truth about Grenfell Tower', Architects for Social Housing blogsite, 21 July 2017, at https://architectsforsocialhousing.wordpress.com/2017/07/21/the-truth-about-grenfell-tower-a-report-by-architects-for-social-housing (accessed 12 October 2018).

2   C. Gras, 'Lancaster West Estate – an ideal for living?', Constantine Gras website, 3 June 2016, at https://www.grasart.com/blog/lancaster-west-estate-an-ideal-for-living (accessed 12 October 2018).

3   BRE Global Ltd, 'BRE Global client report: BS 8414–1:2015 + A1:2017 test referred to as DCLG test 1' (Watford: BRE, 27 July 2017), at https://www.gov.uk/government/uploads/system/uploads/attachment_data/file/648789/DCLGtest1_BS_8414_Part_1_test_report_Issue1.2.pdf (accessed 12 October 2018).

4   S. O'Neill and F. Karim, 'Keep costs of cladding down, Grenfell Tower experts told', *The Times*, 30 June 2017, at https://www.thetimes.co.uk/article/keep-costs-of-cladding-down-grenfell-tower-experts-told-6qrhmwzxv (accessed 12 October 2018).

5   P. Apps, 'Grenfell fire doors provided only 15 minutes resistance to flames, police reveal', *Inside Housing*, 15 March 2018, at http://www.insidehousing.co.uk/news/news/grenfell-fire-doors-provided-only-15-minutes-resistance-to-flames-police-reveal-55285 (accessed 12 October 2018); The Construction Index, 'BRE report catalogues Grenfell refurb errors', *Construction Index*, 17 April 2018, at https://www.theconstructionindex.co.uk/news/view/bre-report-catalogues-grenfell-refurb-errors (accessed 12 October 2018).

6   N. Fifield, 'Two women feared dead in Grenfell Tower tragedy were threatened with legal action – after raising alarm about fire safety', *Mirror*, 17 June 2017, at http://www.mirror.co.uk/news/politics/two-women-feared-dead-grenfell-10640944 (accessed 12 October 2018).

7   Grenfell Action Group, 'KCTMO – playing with fire!', Grenfell Action Group blogsite, 20 November 2016, at https://grenfellactiongroup.wordpress.com/2016/11/20/kctmo-playing-with-fire (accessed 12 October 2018).

8   S. Webb, 'New government fire safety advice is sensible and proportionate', *Inside Housing*, 6 October 2017, at https://www.insidehousing.co.uk/comment/comment/new-government-fire-safety-advice-is-sensible-and-proportionate-52700 (accessed 12 October 2018).

9   In the London Borough of Sutton, poor performance cost Rydon an entire project when a five-year contract worth over £12 million to carry out repairs and maintain the council's 6,000 properties was cancelled after only one year because Rydon failed to meet 'minimum acceptable performance' in the quality and timeliness of repairs and maintenances. J. Evans and N. Rovnick, 'Rydon under scrutiny in Grenfell Tower tragedy', *Financial Times*, 23 June 2017, at https://www.ft.com/content/9096dde8-5826-11e7-80b6-9bfa4c1f83d2 (accessed 12 October 2018).

10 Ministry of Housing, Communities and Local Government, 'Building safety programme monthly data release', 20 September 2018, at https://assets.publishing.service.gov.uk/government/uploads/system/uploads/attachment_data/file/741971/Building_Safety_Data_Release_September_2018.pdf (accessed 12 October 2018).

11 M. Rose, 'Manchester: 367 tower blocks failed to meet fire standards after Grenfell', *Guardian*, 19 March 2018, at https://www.theguardian.com/

uk-news/2018/mar/19/manchester-367-tower-blocks-failed-fire-tests-grenfell-tower-disaster (accessed 12 October 2018).

12 J. Benjamin 'The price of PFI? – Debt, fire unsafe hospitals and collapsing schools', People Vs PFI website, 5 July 2016, http://peoplevspfi.org.uk/2016/07/05/the-price-of-pfi-debt-fire-unsafe-hospitals-and-collapsing-schools (accessed 12 October 2018).

13 The charge of social murder over Grenfell was led by *Guardian* columnist Aditya Chakrabortty in a searing article published a week after the disaster: A. Chakrabortty, 'Over 170 years after Engels, Britain is still a country that murders its poor', *Guardian*, 20 June 2017, at https://www.theguardian.com/commentisfree/2017/jun/20/engels-britain-murders-poor-grenfell-tower (accessed 12 October 2018). It was then used by Labour's Shadow Chancellor, John McDonnell MP, who told a fringe meeting at the Glastonbury Festival that those killed in the fire 'were murdered by political decisions that were taken over recent decades', including cuts to local government and the fire services under austerity: J. McDonnell, 'Grenfell victims "murdered by political decisions"', BBC News website, 26 June 2017, at https://www.bbc.co.uk/news/uk-politics-40401314 (accessed 12 October 2018).

14 F. Engels, *The Condition of the Working Class in England in 1844* (New York: Cosimo Classics, 2008 [1845]), p. 95.

15 D. Harvey, *A Brief History of Neoliberalism* (Oxford: Oxford University Press, 2005).

16 Grenfell residents began using the phrase 'institutional indifference' just weeks after the fire: R. Wearmouth, M. Thurlow, 'Grenfell Tower fire: in their own words, residents reveal their pain and anger four weeks after blaze', *Huffington Post*, 12 July 2017, at https://www.huffingtonpost.co.uk/entry/grenfell-tower-fire-residents-forgotten_uk_596642c0e4b03f144e2fccc7? (accessed 11 December 2018).

17 M. Harloe, 'The green paper on housing policy', in M. Brown and S. Baldwin (eds), *The Year Book of Social Policy in Britain 1977* (London: Routledge and Kegan Paul, 1978).

18 P. Apps, 'Was the cladding legal?', in P. Apps, S. Barnes and L. Barratt, 'The paper trail: the failure of building regulations', *Inside Housing*, Shorthand Social website, 23 March 2018, https://social.shorthand.com/insidehousing/3CWytp9tQj/the-failure-of-building-regulations-the-paper-trail (accessed 13 October 2018).

19 S. Tombs, *Social Protection After the Crisis: Regulation Without Enforcement* (Bristol: Policy Press, 2016); Department for Communities and Local Government, 'Competent person scheme – current schemes and how schemes are authorised', 4 April 2013, last updated 12 March 2018, at https://www.gov.uk/guidance/competent-person-scheme-current-schemes-and-how-schemes-are-authorised#types-of-building-work (accessed 16 October 2018).

20 ITV News, 'Statement from Rydon after public inquiry announcement', ITV News, 15 June 2017, at https://www.itv.com/news/meridian/update/2017-06-15/statement-from-rydon-after-public-inquiry-announcement (accessed 13 October 2018).

21 G. Peaker, J. Bates and K. Buck, 'Improving fire safety under housing legislation', Legal Action Group website, 17 July 2017, at https://www.lag.org.uk/article/201773/improving-fire-safety-under-housing-legislation (accessed 13 October 2018).

22 T. Huckle, 'Grenfell Tower – a different perspective', *New Law Journal*, 7753 (2017), 9–10, at https://www.newlawjournal.co.uk/content/grenfell-tower-different-perspective (accessed 13 October 2018).

23 M. Jones, 'Housing and Planning Bill', *House of Commons Debates*, 12 January 2016, column 763, at https://publications.parliament.uk/pa/cm201516/cmhansrd/cm160112/debtext/160112-0003.htm (accessed 13 October 2018).

24 S. Hodkinson, 'Grenfell foretold: a very neoliberal tragedy', in C. Needham, E. Heins and J. Rees (eds), *Social Policy Review 30: Analysis and Debate in Social Policy* (Bristol: Policy Press, 2018).

25 BBC News, 'RBS chairman: PFI has been a fraud', *BBC News* website, 18 January 2018, at https://www.bbc.co.uk/news/av/uk-politics-42741079/rbs-chairman-pfi-has-been-a-fraud (accessed 13 October 2018).

26 See the ESRC website, https://www.researchcatalogue.esrc.ac.uk/grants/RES-061-25-0536/read (accessed 18 October 2018).

1 Privatisation and the death of public housing

In the emotional aftermath of the Grenfell Tower fire, some commentators from across the political spectrum were quick to paint the disaster as the ultimate failure of post-war public housing rather than a result of decades of neoliberal policies promoting private greed over safety. Simon Jenkins of the *Guardian* saw in Grenfell a salutary reminder of the more general failure of high-rise housing: 'How many times should we say it? Don't build residential towers.... They are antisocial, high-maintenance, disempowering, unnecessary, mostly ugly, and they can never be truly safe.'[1] The *Daily Mail*'s notorious right-wing commentator Richard Littlejohn claimed that Grenfell Tower represented 'all that is wrong with our social housing stock in microcosm ... a dumping ground for problem families and recent immigrants'.[2] Even Sadiq Khan, the Labour Mayor of London who hailed from a south London council estate, stated that the 'defining outcome of this tragedy [may well be] that the worst mistakes of the 1960s and 1970s are systematically torn down'.[3]

In reality, public housing has not only been the most decent, secure and affordable housing for working-class people, but it has also encompassed some of Britain's finest housing design and planning.[4] Indeed, surviving residents' testimonies of their love for their lost homes and close-knit community bore no resemblance to the stigmatised assumptions about life in a tower block.[5] Yet the enemies of public housing have continually used some of its failings to attack its historical legacy and contemporary relevance. This chapter will argue that such portrayals blind us to the origins of public housing as part of a wider collective resistance to the social murder and class robbery of unregulated capitalism. Public housing represented both the partial decommodification of shelter and the protection of residents' health and safety through a wider system of building regulation and control. These qualities are precisely why this public housing model has been targeted for re-privatisation since the 1970s under neoliberalism and financialised capitalism. The chapter will explain how this neoliberal project has unfolded, focusing on the policies of privatisation, demunicipalisation and deregulation that have recommodified and financialised housing and land for profit-seeking corporate interests, compromised building safety and undermined residents' ability to hold their landlords to account.

Resisting social murder and exploitation: the origins of public housing

The origins of British public housing – rented homes designed, built, managed and maintained by principally local municipal authorities – were forged in the 19th-century slums of unregulated capitalism in which social murder rampaged. Friedrich Engels vividly captured the horrors of Victorian urban life in his documented visits to towns across England during the early 1840s:

> Every great city has one or more slums, where the working-class is crowded together.... These slums are pretty equally arranged in all the great towns of England, the worst houses in the worst quarters of the towns; usually one- or two-storied cottages in long rows, perhaps with cellars used as dwellings, almost always irregularly built.... The streets are generally unpaved, rough, dirty, filled with vegetable and animal refuse, without sewers or gutters, but supplied with foul, stagnant pools instead ... ventilation is impeded by the bad, confused method of building of the whole quarter.... Scarcely a whole window-pane can be found, the walls are crumbling, door-posts and window-frames loose and broken, doors of old boards nailed together, or altogether wanting in this thieves' quarter, where no doors are needed, there being nothing to steal.[6]

These 'cattle-sheds for human beings', as Engels called them, marked by high rents, overcrowding and eviction, were disastrous to the health and safety of millions of working-class people, who were ravaged by cholera epidemics from poor sanitation and rising rates of building fires.[7] This was a housing crisis founded upon a rapidly growing urban population, swelled by uprooted rural and European migrants, private land ownership and industrial capitalism's unquenched thirst for cheap, casual labour living near to factories. But, above all, it was a crisis rooted in the parasitical and socially destructive role of *rentier* capitalists – those living off unearned income from their monopolistic ownership or other control of assets or resources – in this case a relatively small class of private landlords on whom 90 per cent of the population depended for shelter by the end of the 19th century. In the context of negligible state regulation, the worst of these landlords freely converted uninhabitable damp cellars into overcrowded dwellings in ever more populous areas. These slums were periodically torn down for redevelopment to feed the urban commercial property boom, displacing families into new slum areas in a continuous race to the bottom.[8]

The birth and early years of public housing

Social murder led to the growing politicisation of 19th-century city dwellers, with a militant labour movement demanding decent, affordable, secure and *safe* housing as a universal social right, not a class privilege. This pressure from below won a succession of public health reforms that by the late 1860s had seen the first municipally built housing in Liverpool, and that in 1875 compelled municipalities to clear sewage and rubbish and provide clean water. At the same time, enlightened factory owners like George Cadbury, Joseph Rowntree, Titus Salt and Robert Owen built high-quality homes in model villages for their workforce. Middle-class social reformers and wealthy philanthropists like Octavia Hill and George Peabody directly intervened in the housing market by setting up charitable trusts to buy existing housing and build affordable homes at modest rates of return for investors. However, these voluntaristic small-scale efforts were imbued with a paternalistic ethos in which elites drilled upward mobility and self-reliance into their working-class tenants while excluding the so-called 'undeserving', 'feckless' and 'idle poor'.[9]

The failures of both the private market and philanthropy to meet mass housing need gradually forced the state to intervene directly in the provision of working-class housing. The combined effect of World War I (1914–18) and the 1917 Russian Revolution recast public housing as a political solution to the collapse of private house building and fears that worsening housing conditions could fuel a Bolshevik-inspired revolutionary movement. A key trigger was the 1915 Glasgow Rent Strike, when 25,000 households resisted private landlords' rent rises in a militant campaign that threatened to spill over into the naval docks and munitions factories and undermine the war effort,[10] which forced the state to immediately freeze rent levels and mortgage rates. This was followed by the 1919 Housing, Town Planning Act, which promised to build 'homes fit for heroes' through an unprecedented public house building programme in which local authorities were *obliged* to build new housing for rent, supported by a generous financial subsidy, at standards previously the preserve of the middle class.

Arguably the heyday of public housing and state provision came under the 1945–51 Labour government. Its main champion, the left-wing Minister of Health, Nye Bevan, opposed speculative house building and in a much-quoted speech he made to Parliament in 1949 envisaged public housing for all social classes as part of his famous vision of a mixed community 'where the doctor, the grocer, the butcher and the farm labourer all lived in the same street'.[11] Far less quoted was his observation in the same speech that 'one of the reasons why modern nations have not been able to solve their housing problems is that they have looked upon houses as commodities to be bought and sold and not as a social service to be provided'.[12] Labour built over 1 million high-quality public homes by the time of its 1951 electoral defeat and created green belts of countryside around cities and towns to prevent urban sprawl. It should also be remembered that, in the 1960s and 1970s, a small but significant portion of public housing came from the compulsory purchase by some local authorities, usually run by Labour councils, of empty or dilapidated houses from private

owners and landlords; these were then renovated and often converted into multiple council homes and flats. As historian David
Ellis argues, such municipalisation in inner London was also an
effective response to the gentrification of working-class areas by
middle-class professionals purchasing 19th-century properties for
conversion into family homes, and so helped to maintain a degree
of social and ethnic mix where the local working-class population
would otherwise have been displaced.[13]

Although private homeownership was politically prioritised to
become the dominant form of tenure over time, and the commitment to public housing wavered especially under Conservative
governments, a post-war house-building 'arms race' between ruling political parties meant that by 1979, public housing had grown
to 6.6 million homes. This represented a third of the UK's total
housing stock and was supplemented by an additional 400,000
social homes rented from charitable housing associations which
themselves received public funding to build housing for rent after
1974.[14] Public housing was the cornerstone of a wider post-war
housing welfare 'deal' in which the state committed itself to
meeting housing need. This resulted in the regulation of the private
rented sector through rent controls and security of tenure, enshrined in the 1977 Rent Act, and the right of the most vulnerable
homeless groups to secure social housing tenancies, under 1977
Homeless Persons Act. Overall, state intervention ensured that
over 40 per cent of households had a secure tenancy.

Public housing's murkier past

However, public housing also had a darker side that Grenfell
exhumed. One problem has been the 'feudal relationship' between
landlords and tenants in some places, something that continues
today, as we shall see in later chapters. In a series of books
and articles spanning the 1960s to the early 1980s, the famous
anarchist architect and planner Colin Ward provided evidence of
the council tenants' experience, calling it 'municipal serfdom'. He
showed how, in some cities, tenants were victims of authoritarian
council managers, living in segregated and substandard housing

that people did not want to live in, and that state officials had no desire or incentive to save or improve.[15] Alongside this residential disempowerment has been the legacy of physical defects. The Labour government's failure to nationalise land and the building industry after 1945 meant that the supply of public housing has remained at the mercy of the private construction sector and landowner class. In contrast to the often rose-tinted portrayals of the post-war consensus, Conservative governments always treated public housing as a short-term solution to temporary market failure and, despite building more council houses than Labour, they did so by dramatically reducing their quality. From the late 1950s, the growing scarcity and high cost of urban land and an endemic shortage of skilled labour in the construction industry saw subsidies offered by all governments increasingly chasing 'more with less'. This favoured greater *densification*; that is, building more homes per square metre, at reduced space standards, often in high-rise tower blocks, which in turn opened the door to the corrupting influence of major building companies promoting cheaper but highly profitable industrialised systems of *prefabrication* using concrete and industrialised off-site methods of production. Between 1955 and 1975 some 440,000 flats were built in public tower blocks, the vast majority in inner urban areas.[16]

While this included some magnificent examples of modernist architecture inspired by Le Corbusier's ideas of 'streets in the sky' and 'machine living', significant numbers of council and private tower blocks were built using 'untried and under-researched tech- niques ... as a short-cut to cheap and accelerated output'.[17] One such untried prefabrication method – 'large panel system' designs, comprising factory-made pre-cast concrete floor and wall panels assembled with the aid of a crane – had deadly consequences. On 16 May 1968, just over 50 years before Grenfell, a brand new 22-storey council tower block at Ronan Point in Canning Town, east London, partially collapsed after a gas explosion from a faulty cooker blew out the supporting walls, killing four people. The Ronan Point disaster highlighted the endemic problems of the time of poor design, unskilled labour, and inadequate building regulations and enforcement systems. Many tower blocks were left with a 'legacy of decay, premature obsolescence and, in some cases, early demolition'.[18]

Beyond bricks and mortar: decommodification, security and safety

Nevertheless, we must not throw the baby out with the bathwater. It is important to remember that public housing went beyond bricks and mortar, to embody a collective intervention against the exploitation by private slum landlords that significantly decommodified access to shelter and provided a foundation for working-class social reproduction.[19] Over the course of the 20th century, public housing became the most affordable form of tenure, due to the combination of government subsidy, councils' capacity to borrow at much cheaper rates of interest than private developers, the collective pooling of tenants' rental income to meet the combined 'historic costs' of building the local housing stock and the not-for-profit ethos of the public landlord. Public housing offered tenants far greater security and protection from cut-throat private landlordism, and its municipal provision meant the landlord could be democratically held to account at local elections. We should not forget that Grenfell Tower itself represented a dramatic improvement for residents in an area of west London once synonymous with 'Rachmanism' – the exploitation, harassment and unlawful eviction of tenants, especially West Indian immigrants, by the notorious private slum-lord of the 1950s and early 1960s, Peter Rachman. More broadly, public housing in its various national forms was an important pillar of the post-World War II social democratic consensus in Western societies that sought to regulate the worst excesses of capitalism and imperialist state competition that had fuelled the rise of fascism and war. Public housing became a key institution of 'collective consumption', alongside free public healthcare and education, and social security systems ('the welfare state'). This decommodification agenda was also part of a concerted effort to ward against the socially destructive effects of rentier capitalism on the productive economy.

Above all, public housing was born out of a bottom-up movement against social murder and for safer housing, safer workplaces and safer cities. When conceived in this expansive way, public housing arguably began not in 1890 but in 1189, the date of Britain's first recorded municipal building regulations, drawn up by the City of London. With Grenfell in mind, it is no coincidence that these regulations began and developed over time primarily as a municipal response to the horrors of fire that haunted medieval and early modern urban Britain. Nearly 600 'major fires' were recorded between 1500 and 1900,[20] the most devastating being the 1666 Great Fire of London, which destroyed over 13,000 homes. This led to the 1667 Rebuilding of London Act, which outlawed flammable construction materials of wood and thatch, and required all houses to be built of brick, stone, slate or tile, and party walls between houses to be thick enough to withstand two hours of fire. Anyone flouting the new rules would have their house pulled down by a new body of municipal surveyors. By the 18th century, most British cities had adopted their own building control systems, significantly reducing the number of major multi-dwelling fires. Local building rules had been brought together as a single body of national building regulations by the mid-1960s, which enshrined in law highly detailed minimum standards of design and building work, to safeguard the health and safety of the occupiers and users. Local authority building control teams operated as a 'policing service' to ensure strict application of the regulations, complemented by a municipal health and safety inspectorate that used its statutory powers to outlaw the letting of properties unfit for human habitation. They were complemented by local authority 'direct labour organisations' – in-house building and maintenance teams run as a separate business units – that first emerged towards the end of the 1890s in London as a response by town halls to evidence of price-fixing rings and corruption in letting public contracts to private building companies, and the shortage of housing.[21] By 1978 direct labour organisations employed around 173,000 workers – 12 per cent of the national construction workforce – in construction and repair work on highways, parks, housing and other public buildings. They too played a vital role in improving health and safety and offered more secure employment while retaining experienced older workers and employing more apprentices.[22] Although far from perfect, by the late 1970s national regulations combined with municipal production and enforcement helped to control the activities of builders, developers and landlords and ensure that all existing and new housing was generally safe to live in, irrespective of tenure.

Today, as the Grenfell disaster has made clear, much of this protective shield that public housing embodied has been dismantled. To understand how this happened and why, we need to retrace the emergence of the neoliberal project in the 1970s and its malign influence on housing policy and practice.

Neoliberalism, financialisation and the re-privatisation of housing

From the late 1960s to the 1970s, Western capitalism experienced a crisis of profitability amid rising international competition, inflation and economic stagnation that signalled the end of the post-war boom. The relentless pressure on corporate profits sparked the rise of the 'shareholder value' movement within big business that would pave the way for greater *financialisation* of the global economy, namely 'the transformation of work, services, land or other forms of exchange into financial instruments ... that can be traded on financial markets'.[23] Capitalists sought to restore profitability by ending the post-war social democratic class compromise with labour, so as to lower the wage and corporate tax bill and restructure workplaces in the interests of becoming more competitive. While manufacturing companies increasingly shifted production to places like Mexico and China to take advantage of cheaper labour, firms in general began to shift their business model away from making particular products through long-term investment and towards *making money from money* in the short term, through the speculative buying and selling of financial commodities – stocks, shares, bonds, property assets, currencies and derivatives.[24]

It was in this context that the economic philosophy of free market individualism, promoted by thinkers like Friedrich Hayek and Milton Friedman – better known as neoliberalism – was seized on by capitalist interests to justify a broad assault on labour and state intervention. They argued that the so-called 'stagflation crisis' of the 1970s was the result of too much state ownership, regulation and trade union power, which collectively stifled competition and private enterprise. Instead, neoliberalism conjured a beguiling fantasy of a self-regulating market economy in which competition between private firms and consumer choice would always produce the most efficient allocation of economic wealth. Free marketeers implored governments to privatise and deregulate as much as possible and morph into a 'night-watchman state'. In reality, rolling back the state was also about providing new profitable opportunities for financialised capital through the privatisation of state industries, utilities and public services.

Armed with this blueprint, successive UK governments since 1979 have set about systematically privatising the economy and the state. This neoliberal turn was initially driven by the Conservatives under Thatcherism (1979–97), embraced and extended in different ways by New Labour (1997–2010) and aggressively recharged by the austerity policies of three Conservative-led governments since 2010, under the pretext of cutting government debt incurred by the state bail-out of the banking sector after the global financial crisis of 2007–08. Over these past four decades, hundreds of state-owned enterprises, utilities and major infrastructure assets have been privatised, within the UK's oil, gas, coal, steel, water, electricity, ship-building, telecommunications and car-making industries, as well as within the country's transport sector, such as the port authorities and railways. Although promoted by Margaret Thatcher as expanding economic ownership to the masses under 'popular capitalism', privatisation actually did the reverse: much of the estimated £200 billion[25] raised was handed to the rich in tax cuts, while the portion of shares held by individuals in UK companies actually fell from 40 per cent before 1979 to less than 12 per cent by the time of Thatcher's death in 2013, with more than half of all UK company shares owned by a list of foreign entities dominated by global investors and other national governments.[26]

Alongside this great asset sale has been the outsourcing of public works and services to private companies. First under the Conservatives' 'compulsory competitive tendering' (CCT) regime but then more seriously under New Labour's drive to get 'best value' from public services through marketisation and 'public–private partnerships' (PPPs) (of which more in chapter 2), large swathes of national infrastructure and municipal provision were contracted out – including the construction, management, repair and cleaning of public buildings and an array of regulatory and safety functions. Direct labour organisations were forced to compete with private contractors on highly unequal terms and were vastly reduced in size and number. Far from bringing better value for money or improved services for the public, outsourcing has seen not-for-profit public monopolies replaced by profit-seeking private cartels that have cut quality and casualised workforces.[27] It has also driven the enormous growth in the use by both public and private sector bodies of expensive private sector consultants, dominated by the big four accountancy firms – KPMG, PwC (PricewaterhouseCoopers), Deloitte, and EY (Ernst and Young) – to advise on how to restructure, commodify and commercialise public services to serve corporate interests. Today, the UK public sector is the second largest single outsourcing market after the United States, with an estimated value of £101 billion in 2014–15, or around half of total government spending on goods and services.[28] As I will discuss later in this chapter, as the private sector has ballooned in size, it has been simultaneously unburdened of its social and environmental responsibilities through deregulation or what advocates have dishonestly labelled the 'war on red tape'.

The privatisation project in housing

Within this wider context of privatisation, the world of public housing has been transformed beyond recognition under a pro-active project to recommodify the social relations of housing *per se* and thus create new opportunities for both private owners and interest-bearing capital to extract wealth from housing and land. In practice, housing privatisation has simultaneously scaled multiple fronts. The first wave, from 1979, focused on rolling back the existing public housing stock in favour of expanding homeownership and rebooting the private landlord sector. This was spearheaded by giving tenants a statutory 'right to buy' (RTB) their council homes at large discounts on the market value, which had reached 60 per cent for houses and 70 per cent for flats by 1989.[29] The 1985 deregulation of mortgage finance saw new lenders – often subsidiaries of foreign banks – enter the market, enabling existing and first-time buyers, including for the first time lower-income households, to access cheap credit; this flood of property investment stimulated a boom in the housing market.

The RTB was accompanied by a more Machiavellian strategy of financially straitjacketing local authorities to prevent them from either spending the capital receipts raised from RTB sales or borrowing to repair existing homes and build new ones. Between 1979 and 1994, total public expenditure on housing decreased in real terms by 60 per cent, starving many councils of the resources they needed to even carry out basic repairs.[30] Government subsidy was instead gradually switched to housing associations, but these built only modest amounts of social rented housing compared with councils. This austerity was in part designed to make the purchase of their council property more attractive to those tenants financially able to take over the responsibility for maintaining and improving their homes. It also served to reduce the supply of new housing, which served to further inflate the price of existing housing and land, stimulating both speculation and more RTB sales.

Running alongside this was what academic Norman Ginsburg called 'Rachmanism with tax breaks' – a systematic rolling back of rent and tenancy protections for private tenants under the 1988 Housing Act (England and Wales) alongside financial incentives to attract new investment into the private rental sector.[31] Private landlords were now able to evict their tenants at will, without having to show any grounds, and tenancies could be as short as six months. In 1996, banks agreed to create specific buy-to-let mortgage products at much lower rates of interest than previously available for private landlords who agreed to have their properties managed by approved lettings agents, stimulating a buy-to-let boom. This was followed by the tearing up of rights for the homeless under the 1996 Housing Act, which replaced their legal right to *permanent* accommodation with a right to only *temporary* housing for up to two years in either hostels or specially leased accommodation in the private rental sector, and which narrowed the eligibility criteria by removing the rights of those judged to be what is termed 'intentionally homeless', though this can include being evicted because the person could not afford the rent, and also by barring asylum seekers altogether.

Privatisation through the back door: demunicipalisation meets regeneration

Despite its popularity, the RTB could never fully privatise the public housing stock due to a combination of tenant poverty and the system-built defects affecting many council estates and tower blocks that prevented sales. An alternative privatisation front was therefore opened up from the mid-1980s, known as *demunicipalisation*, which sought to transfer the management, repair and ownership of public housing to non-public landlords and contractors. Councils' legal duty to directly meet new housing need was ended and they were given new freedoms to sell off their housing, including blocks or whole estates, to alternative providers. The tenants' movement, though, successfully resisted government attempts to impose an array of estate privatisation schemes and after 1988 won an important statutory right to have a binding majority 'yes/no' ballot over proposals to transfer their homes to a different landlord. However, during the late 1980s a small number of mainly Conservative-led rural authorities in southern England began selling off their housing to existing and specially formed housing associations, after convincing their tenants to vote yes, often by blackmailing them with threats of disinvestment. These local initiatives were turned into a national programme of 'large scale voluntary transfer' (LSVT) – better known as 'stock transfer' – that by 1997 had sold off around 300,000 public housing dwellings (with their households in residence) to the housing association sector, which after 1988 was itself increasingly commercialised and deregulated. The Conservatives also expanded compulsory outsourcing to council housing management in 1996 and brought in new powers for tenants to have greater involvement in the management of their homes through tenant management organisations (TMO). It was in this context that the management of Grenfell Tower was initially transferred in 1996 to KCTMO, with tenants elected to the company board.[32]

When New Labour took power in 1997, it inherited an appalling legacy, with public house building virtually eliminated, a quarter of the existing stock now owned by former council tenants, and a toxic mix of physical disrepair and social despair on thousands of council estates across the country. The Chartered Institute of Housing estimated for England an immediate £10 billion repair backlog, with an additional £10 billion needed to modernise homes lacking central heating and double glazing, replace kitchens and bathrooms over 20 years old, and renew vital structural elements such as roofs.[33] Over 220,000 council homes (around 7 per cent of 3.2 million) were deemed unfit for human habitation and another 300,000 were categorised as in substantial disrepair or requiring essential modernisation.[34] With mass unemployment in the 1980s and 1990s leading to abject poverty in some working-class communities, the RTB had contributed to a rising social apartheid, with wealthier working-class tenants buying up semi-detached houses in suburban areas, leaving behind 'a residual housing sector increasingly occupied by the poorest sections of society ... living in less desirable locations in inner city areas or on socially stigmatised "hard-to-let" estates'.[35]

In the face of this urban decay, New Labour promised a programme of regeneration. This was symbolised by Tony Blair's decision to make his first major speech as Prime Minister at the Aylesbury Estate in south London, at the time reputed to be the largest public housing estate in Europe and a media by-word for urban despair. Blair promised that there would be no more 'forgotten people' under his government.[36] Following the 1998 launch of its New Deal for Communities to fund area-based neighbourhood renewal initiatives in 39 of England's most deprived neighbourhoods, in 2000 New Labour unveiled its Decent Homes programme, which required local authorities and housing associations to bring their social housing stock up to a minimum 'decent' (in fact minimal) standard by 2010.[37] It was initially estimated that 1.6 million homes in the social rented sector – 38 per cent of its stock – failed the standard.[38]

After 18 years of Conservative constraint on the public housing sector, the Decent Homes programme was a welcome policy shift that would eventually unlock over £20 billion in investment to repair and modernise over 2.5 million homes. I met many tenants who were ecstatic about their new kitchen and bathroom suites, double-glazed windows and modern electrics. While Decent Homes was accompanied by a new 'major repairs allowance' that gave councils a more generous budget to maintain homes in their present condition, New Labour's Decent Homes target came with a fairly large catch: government steadfastly refused to allow local authorities the financial freedoms to borrow to build new homes and repair their existing stock, and largely maintained the strict financial straitjacket imposed under Thatcherism. Instead, government would help local authorities access the necessary finance to meet the Decent Homes target only if they opted for one or more of three demunicipalisation 'options':

- Option 1 was stock transfer. The local authority would sell off its entire stock or specific estates either to a housing association or to a newly created local housing company, collectively rebranded as 'registered social landlords' (RSLs).
- Option 2 was arm's-length management organisations (ALMOs). High-performing councils would be given greater borrowing freedoms to repair their homes as long as they transferred the day-to-day management to an ALMO (wholly owned by the council) to run the council's housing and improvement programme on a commercial basis, with a chief executive and management board able to procure its own goods and services.
- Option 3 was PFI. Where a stock transfer or ALMO was politically or financially unfeasible for housing stock that needed major investment beyond meeting the Decent Homes standards, the government made the PFI route available for specific estates, neighbourhoods or types of housing. This involved the local authority contracting out the design and delivery of the short-term regeneration work, along with the long-term maintenance (cleaning, repair, renewal) and management of the housing and estate, to a private sector consortium for up to 30 years – I will return to PFI in chapter 2.

There would be no 'fourth option' – despite demands for it from campaigners – of direct investment by councils through borrowing supported by government subsidy. In 2010, I interviewed two former New Labour Housing Ministers – Nick Raynsford (Housing Minister 1999–2001) and Keith Hill (Housing and Planning Minister 2004–05) – who separately headed the Decent Homes programme throughout the 2000s. Both made it clear that the decision to offer this Hobson's choice to councils and tenants was based on New Labour's ideological opprobrium for municipal landlordism. As Hill explained, in their experience as constituency MPs, residents' poor experiences were not simply the result of Thatcherite cuts, but rooted in the nature of the municipal beast:

> it wasn't just money that was the problem with council landlords. It was inefficiency, it was prioritising staff rather than tenants, it was a lack of commitment to delivering a service…. Council officers do not come under a great deal of scrutiny during the day-to-day delivery of the service … what was the incentive to raise their game … if you just handed them the money?[39]

Raynsford saw Decent Homes as a vehicle to 'create different structures not under the direct control of councils that were capable of focusing on the delivery of a decent housing service and make the landlord organisation much more responsive to tenants'.[40] The ordering of the three types of investment vehicle was not accidental. Labour wanted as many councils as possible to sign up to stock transfer with a target of demunicipalising up to 200,000 homes and promised to write off any 'overhanging debt' linked to the stock to enable RSLs to raise private finance to invest in the modernisation of homes and estates.

However, stock transfer had been vehemently opposed by many Labour councils and the tenants' movement as part of a Decent Council Housing campaign, with 'no votes' in 40 areas by 2000. This was a major factor behind the creation in England of the ALMO and PFI options, as they offered a neat way around tenant opposition to privatisation because the council remained the landlord, meaning tenants and residents had no legal right to a ballot. To sweeten the pill, Labour insisted that a third of ALMO boards be made up of resident representatives, to make them accountable to tenants and local areas, while providing those councils taking the PFI route with a generous subsidy to cover the capital costs of the regeneration scheme. Despite Labour Party conferences annually passing motion after motion backing Defend Council Housing's campaign supporting the above fourth option, New Labour refused to budge.[41]

Overall, Labour's Decent Homes programme and its Scottish and Welsh equivalents resulted in more than 1 million homes being sold off to RSLs, and just over 1 million homes being 'temporarily' transferred out of direct local authority control and into ALMOs and PFI SPV companies. The refusal to allow councils to build social housing – now the sole preserve of RSLs – gave New Labour the shameful record of building less council housing over its 13 years in power than the Conservatives built in Thatcher's final year in office. Not only was social housing further residualised as a tenure of last resort for those in dire need, but it was steadily marketised and financialised. From 2002, social rents were increased above inflation to converge towards the private market average by 2016. With greater freedom to charge market rents, evict tenants and build private housing, RSLs became the main constructors and providers of social housing. More broadly, having retained and deepened the deregulation of mortgage finance, New Labour's priority was to expand homeownership even further and encourage more people to engage in 'asset-based welfare' by investing a booming housing market. Although it trimmed the excesses of the RTB by reducing discounts and lengthening qualifying and re-sale periods,[42] by the mid-2000s the failure to ensure sufficient supply of new homes of all types of tenure contributed to a growing affordability crisis that saw unsustainable increases in house prices and mortgage debt, which contributed to the global financial crash in 2008 and the subsequent collapse of new housing supply to its lowest peacetime levels since the 1920s.

Completing the privatisation project under austerity

While the 2008 financial crisis saw New Labour suddenly willing to give local authorities a more direct role in filling the supply vacuum, the election of Conservative-led governments since 2010 has seen the radical resuscitation of Thatcher's privatisation project. The RTB has been relaunched and expanded to most housing association tenants, and in September 2018 the maximum cash discount on the market value was raised from £38,000 under New Labour to £108,000 in London and £80,900 elsewhere, set to rise annually in line with consumer price inflation.[43] Subsidy for building new social rented housing has been diverted to the construction of new 'affordable rent' homes, but there are a lot fewer of these and they have fixed-term (rather than lifetime) tenancies and higher rents (as high as 80 per cent of local market rents). The 2011 Localism Act ended the statutory right to a secure lifetime tenancy for new social housing tenants in England from April 2012, as it allows local authorities and housing associations to offer so-called 'flexible tenancies' with a minimum term of two years. It also ended the statutory right to secure social housing for those found to be unintentionally homeless, who can now be housed in the private sector for a minimum of 12 months, ending the local authority's duty to support them. Provisions were included in the 2016 Housing and Planning Act to make it mandatory for local authorities to grant only fixed-term tenancies of 2–10 years, although these have now been paused. In 2015, the government gave social landlords the power to charge market rents to households with an income of over £60,000. At the same time, major cuts to welfare support for housing and other living costs since 2010 will total £27 billion a year by 2021 – equivalent to £690 a year for every working-age adult.[44] Social tenants deemed to be under-occupying their homes – even though most have no choice – have been hit by the so-called 'bedroom tax', while housing benefit cuts for private renters have drastically shrunk the choice of accommodation available to low-income households, and created a growing gap between benefit payments and rents.[45]

The death of public housing and the growing housing crisis

Overall, public housing had declined from its post-war peak of 32 per cent of the housing stock to under 8 per cent by 2018 due to the staggering net loss of 4.5 million homes since 1979. The RTB has to date accounted for the sale of over 2.5 million of these homes across the UK, representing the most lucrative of all privatisations since 1979, raising £50 billion in capital receipts (although far more if valued in today's prices).[46] More than 85 per cent of these homes sold were not replaced, as the financial restraints imposed by successive governments prevented the council construction of housing.[47] Of the remaining 2 million homes lost to the municipal sector, 1.4 million have been transferred to RSLs and the remainder presumably demolished. An additional 750,000 social rented homes have been built UK-wide by RSLs, but these are on average let at higher rents than public housing. Over time, the ever-fragmented social housing sector has been increasingly corporatised, with both providers and tenants further exposed to market forces by commercial organisations where board members are legally obliged to act in the interests of the company, not the wider resident body. At the same time, governments have reduced the level of grant subsidy per new home built by RSLs, increasing their reliance on commercial borrowing and raising finance from bond markets and in turn putting upward pressure on rents and the development of homes for sale.[48] With welfare cuts leading to growing rent arrears among social housing tenants, the greater financial risks facing RSLs account for the growing pace of mergers, whereby the top 30 housing association groups accounted for around 59 per cent of the social housing sector in 2018, compared with 41 per cent in 2015. [49] Corporatisation and centralisation of the social housing sector is moving landlord accountability further away from tenants, councillors and local communities.

The privatisation of public housing amid the wider financialisation of housing and land has contributed to a new housing crisis of dwindling supply, rampant unaffordability and growing insecurity.[50] Over time, the house-building sector has become ever more concentrated into fewer, larger national firms operating a business model that focuses on controlling and trading land in high-demand areas and restricting housing supply so as to increase the price. Priced out of homeownership and unable to access social housing, today's 'generation rent' is driving the remarkable resurgence of the private landlord sector, from less than 9 per cent of the housing stock in 1986 to owning one in five UK homes in 2016. Privatisation of public housing has played a fundamental role in the return of the rentier, with some 40 per cent of council homes sold to tenants in England under the RTB now in the hands of private landlords.[51] As rising rents are now being combined with welfare cuts, housing insecurity is rising again: homelessness increased by nearly 60 per cent between 2009 and 2017, to 236,000 people across Britain, pushing over 120,000 children into temporary accommodation.[52] This crisis is most acute in London, in part due to extreme house price growth and land values that have made it the second most over-valued property market in the world and a target for increased demand from profit-seeking investors.[53] Almost 40 per cent of all evictions take place here, and tens of thousands of homeless households are being moved to other local authority areas each year, most within London, but a growing proportion to other cities and regions, including Newcastle upon Tyne.[54] It was this housing crisis that explains the shocking failure of the Grenfell survivors to be adequately rehoused by Kensington and Chelsea council after the fire: a total of 181 households made homeless were still living in temporary accommodation more than 12 months after the disaster.[55] In reality, there were plenty of empty homes in Kensington and Chelsea – 1,652 to be precise – scandalously left vacant by distant owners seeking to capitalise on the highest property prices in the UK, where in some streets mansions of the super-rich sell for over £50 million.[56]

As we will see in later chapters, displacement in and from London is also being driven by so-called urban regeneration schemes that began under Decent Homes, with demolition and re-development of estate stock transferred or outsourced under PFI. With slashed council budgets insufficient to meet high real estate values, many London local authorities are now seeking, through demolition and the redevelopment, to expand luxury private housing, largely to raise finance for services other than housing, at the expense of affordable and secure housing.[57] This assault on council estates was ratcheted up under the Conservative govern-ment's policy proposal in 2016 to pump-prime the demolition and redevelopment of what it called the UK's 'worst 100 estates'.

Profit before housing safety: the rise of self-regulation

As the Grenfell disaster revealed, the management, repair and regeneration of social housing have not simply been 'contracted out' by the state to private companies, but have been moved into a very different regulatory environment, one that has elevated profit-making above residents' safety. This particular story began in the 1980s under the Conservatives' Deregulation Initiative, which created a Deregulation Unit in every government department; those units were charged with systematically reviewing, removing or weakening regulations on the private sector. New Labour may have rebranded deregulation as 'Better Regulation', but beneath the spin, its appointment in 2004 of the then Sainsbury's chairman Philip Hampton would lead to what academic Steve Tombs calls the institutionalisation of 'regulation without enforcement'.[58] The number of national regulatory bodies was reduced through mergers and cuts, with only businesses deemed most likely to evade compliance with health and safety regulations now targeted for inspection. In other words, big business was empowered to take more risks with safety in the knowledge that the chances of being caught were now dramatically reduced. Since 2010, the Conservative-led governments have ratcheted up the de-regulation game – former Prime Minister David Cameron declared it his personal mission to kill off for good 'the over-the-top health and safety culture' in a bonfire of regulations.[59] The Coalition government introduced a 'one-in, two-out' rule in July 2013 whereby for every pound of additional net cost imposed on business by new regulations, government departments had to cut other regulation by two pounds.[60] Regulatory oversight has been further reduced through real-terms government funding cuts of 49.1 per cent to local authorities (2010–11 to 2018–19) and similar-sized cuts to the budget of the Health and Safety Executive (HSE).[61] At the same time, a new business-friendly regulatory enforcement regime is being rolled out for companies and franchises operating across more than one local authority area, called the 'primary authority' scheme. This involves firms paying one local or public authority to regulate all of its sites nationally, helping to ensure the 'absence of inspectorial enforcement in the vast majority of its outlets'.[62] Overall, research has found that there has been a long-term downward trend in enforcement activity on the part of statutory regulators, with the average workplace expected to see an inspector 'once every 50 years'.[63] As we will now see, this deregulation agenda has been particularly strong in the building industry and housing sector.

Deregulating the building industry

The battle to protect the health and safety of both construction workers and users of the resulting built environment against the profit-driven greed of building companies and developers has a long and controversial history. It is common knowledge that for more than a century many workers who joined trade unions or who organised for better working conditions and safety on con- struction sites found themselves blacklisted from being allowed to work in the private sector. In his remarkable autobiographical account of working as a shop steward in local authority direct labour organisations, Tony O'Brien recounts numerous incidents of being suddenly dismissed from jobs and chased off site, only to find it near impossible to get another job with the same or different building firm anywhere in London.[64] In the mid-2000s, following a campaign by unionised electricians in Manchester who found themselves repeatedly sacked from construction sites, the Information Commissioner's Office (ICO) raided the offices of an organisation called The Consulting Association (TCA). In 2009, the ICO released a report showing the industrial scale of blacklisting operated by TCA on behalf of 44 of the UK's largest building contractors – including Carillion, Balfour Beatty, McAlpine, G. Wimpey, Laing O'Rourke, Lovell, Miller, Morrison, Kier, Mowlem and Willmott Dixon. They used a centralised database holding personal information on 3,213 workers provided by senior managers of the main contractors that had been shared covertly among these companies. When people applied for work on building sites, companies would fax their names to TCA to see if they matched, paying them £2.20 per name check.[65] As a result, trade unionists were blocked from working on an industrial scale, and this played a key role in the deterioration of construction and safety standards.

Since the 1980s, the casualisation of the construction work-force as part of this dirty war against trade unionists has gone hand in hand with the deregulation of the building industry. The 1984 Building Act 'swept away 306 pages of building regulations and replaced them with just 24',[66] turning a mountain of pre-scribed inputs and proscribed materials into generic statements outlining the broad standards of performance that buildings were expected to achieve. This flexibilisation empowered industry to interpret how these standards could be met and to suggest alternative – usually cheaper – ways of complying. Corporate interests have also been allowed to take control of safety testing and certification, especially since the privatisation in 1997 of the Building Research Establishment – now BRE. It had been founded in 1921 as the Building Research Group to pioneer research into building materials and methods of construction, with a key focus on safety, and in 1972 was amalgamated with the Fire Research Station to conduct large-scale fire testing of building materials, including cladding. After privatisation, BRE became one of the main industry bodies for testing, certifying and approving building products and systems. Although owned by a trust with charitable status, BRE is today a highly commercial organisation embedded in the private building and materials industry. Its board of trustees reads as a roll-call of diverse corporate interests, and is chaired by James Wates, the chairman of private construction firm Wates Group, which incidentally is a key beneficiary of PFI contracts.

Decades of building deregulation with the shift to more flexible interpretation of standards are a major cause of the use of combustible cladding on Grenfell Tower and 468 buildings to date. Prior to 2006, approved Document B of the UK's Building Regulations clearly banned combustible cladding and insulation in buildings over 18 metres high. But many commentators argue that this ban was relaxed in 2006 as a result of regulatory changes ostensibly designed to fulfil the UK's promise to reduce carbon dioxide emissions under the 1997 Kyoto Agreement. Following Kyoto, the European Union (EU) issued a new European Directive on Energy Performance of Buildings in 2002 that tasked member

states such as the UK with improving the overall energy efficiency
of new and existing buildings, primarily through better insulation.
Due in part to the enormous cost of insulating millions of homes
with more expensive non-combustible materials, the building
regulations were subtly changed in 2006 to create an alternative
legal route through which combinations of combustible materials
previously outlawed could be used. The changes were linked to a
closed-door industry consultation run by the privatised BRE, which
included representatives of the combustible insulation industry
previously locked out of supplying high-rise developments. In
2014, the Building Control Alliance (BCA), which represents
building control officials, agreed to formalise the approval of this
cladding without it even being fire-tested as a system, through the
use of 'desktop study reports' based on existing test data supplied
by government-accredited testing bodies, including BRE.[67]

The use of combustible cladding underlines another regulatory
controversy in England – the weak rules governing the fitting of
sprinkler systems to high-rise blocks. Sprinklers are required only
in new-build residential tower blocks over 30 metres high and
there is no requirement for retrospective action. This is despite
the All-Party Parliamentary Fire Safety and Rescue Group of MPs
privately warning four government ministers about the need for
urgent action following the deadly 2009 Lakanal House fire in
Southwark.[68] In contrast, since 2005, in Scotland sprinklers have
had to be fitted to any new building above 18 metres and in Wales
all new or refurbished residential buildings have had to have
them. The government's anti-regulation, free market stance was
illustrated in comments made by the then Minister of Housing and
Planning, Brandon Lewis MP, during a parliamentary debate in
Fire Sprinklers Week, February 2014: 'We should intervene only if
it is entirely necessary, and only as a last resort ... it is the responsibility of the fire industry, rather than the Government, to market
fire sprinkler systems effectively and to encourage their wider
installation'.[69] Sprinklers would have undoubtedly saved lives in
Grenfell Tower: as the Chief Fire Officers Association (CFOA)
has stated, sprinklers have almost eliminated fire deaths and have
massively reduced damage to health and property by controlling a
fire after five minutes, and reducing smoke density and toxicity.[70]

A more flexible regulatory framework has gone hand in hand with the gradual outsourcing and liberalisation of building control services previously the preserve of municipalities. The first company to gain approval to compete with local authorities was the National House Building Council Ltd in 1985, which held the private sector monopoly until the Conservatives' full liberalisation of building control services in 1997. Building control is the only local authority regulatory service in direct competition with the private sector – an estimated 35 per cent of all building control work is now done by private sector companies.[71] The advent of competition has seen building control become a highly commercialised and performance-managed industry in which winning and maintaining clients, especially the high-value construction firms, is king. The legal minimum requirement for building control inspection has been reduced to a final site inspection following an application for a completion certificate, and any interim site inspections are at the contracted building officer's discretion.[72] Due to the need to focus their available resources, building inspectors will check only those aspects considered the highest risk, such as foundations, fire-stopping and drainage, and will generally not inspect structural elements or perform intrusive or disruptive inspections, such as looking behind walls and in concealed parts of buildings, to check work has been done properly with the correct materials. This kind of ongoing and on-site scrutiny is carried out by a clerk of works or equivalent employed either by the contractor or by the client; it is something that many companies and local authorities have cut back on. Academic research suggests that the need to secure income has led building control teams to 'avoid any [regulatory] behaviour that might upset their client base'[73] – in other words, to offer a speedy service in which building work can proceed with minimal friction so as to maximise profits for construction firms and developers. Under austerity, funding cuts to non-ring-fenced local services like building control have created additional pressures on local authority teams to become even more developer-friendly, to win more contracts against private companies, so as to plug financial holes.[74] A growing number of local authorities are outsourcing their regulatory functions altogether. For example, in 2013, the London Borough of Barnet outsourced all of its back-office services, including planning and regeneration, to Capita and Capita Symonds in 10-year contracts worth £480 million in total. In 2015, environmental and regulatory services accounted for the second largest proportion of public spending on external contractors.[75] Overall, this has diluted the quality of inspection and enforcement, and thus the built environment, and there have been rising numbers of complaints about private sector building inspectors.[76]

Quality control has been further undermined by the roll-out of self-certification. Before deregulation, anyone carrying out building work had to notify the local authority in advance and pay a charge for council inspectors to check plans and construction work for regulatory compliance. The 1991 Building Regulations Act introduced a new fast-track route for gas heating appliance installers approved by their professional body, to self-certify their work and simply to notify the local authority within 30 days of completion, for authority records, without charge. New Labour gradually expanded self-certification from 2002 to 10 main areas of building work under these so-called 'competent person schemes' run by government-approved professional bodies. To qualify for self-certification, a firm or individual must typically have one example of work per area inspected and approved by the relevant professional body, with a re-assessment every three years. Once assessed as competent, a firm's conformity with building regulations is largely unknown and unaudited. The removal of regulatory oversight is breath-taking: an estimated 85 per cent of all building work that requires the notification of building control bodies – around 3 million jobs – is now self-certified.[77] That means most electrical, plumbing and construction work being conducted by companies in people's homes is no longer subject to any external inspection. The government itself acknowledged in 2012 that some self-certification schemes were 'not complying fully with their conditions of authorisation or achieving a sufficiently high level of compliance with the Building Regulations'.[78] This means that, as a rule, the regulators of safety in the built environment increasingly have to take the word of the relevant contractor that behind the façade of a shiny new building everything has been built to safe and legal standards.

Empowering landlords, neutering tenants

The final piece of the self-regulation jigsaw concerns the damaging changes to the governance of health, safety and fire standards for rented housing introduced by New Labour. The 2004 Housing Act introduced a new risk-assessment approach called the Housing Health and Safety Rating System (HHSRS), under which the landlord or owner of the building is responsible for identifying and removing hazards to health and safety. Under the 2005 Regulatory Reform (Fire Safety) Order (RRFSO), landlords and building owners are also now obliged to evaluate the risk to people from fires occurring in the common areas of multi-occupancy buildings, including whether additional safety measures are necessary, with the local fire and rescue authority legally empowered to carry out inspections and serve enforcement notices in the event of non-compliance. While appearing stronger on paper, the new laws have in practice served to reduce hugely the enforcement powers available to regulatory bodies. The HHSRS effectively abolished the previous minimum legal fitness standard for rented housing in England, replacing a black-and-white 'pass/fail' approach with a more flexible set of standards not always backed by statutory obligation and open to greater interpretation by landlords and local authority enforcement teams, based on the assessment of risks. The RRFSO, meanwhile, has led to a radical reduction in fire safety checks, as the previous annual inspection and certification regime operated by the fire brigade has been replaced by third-party fire risk assessors employed by landlords or the building owners to conduct fire risk assessments (FRAs). However, there is no legal requirement on landlord or owners to employ qualified or professionally accredited fire risk assessors, and no legal timeframe for the assessment. Phil Murphy, a former fire-fighter and health and safety compliance manager turned housing safety activist in Greater Manchester, explained to me how the new laws impacted on fire safety:

> Before the Regulatory Reform Order, every non-single-household domestic dwelling with the exception of HMOs [houses of multiple occupancy], and other public and commercial buildings like offices

had to have a valid fire safety certificate following an annual inspection by the fire brigade. If we found non-compliance, we would write warning letters with links to the relevant legal sections. As soon as the new regulations came in, the government slashed the number of fire safety officers in the fire brigade, so the frequency of visits was reduced. Fire safety inspections are now in the hands of the fire risk assessors but what are their professional qualifications and experience? They might do a three-day online course. I went on two residential courses each lasting six weeks. Fire risk assessors also have an incentive to say that all is good to their 'client' so as to get the job the next year and they can hide behind poor inspections with no legal requirement to disclose the FRAs. The cuts to the fire service along with the cuts to local authority building control mean that the regulatory system has lost so much vital knowledge and experience that we now have people who don't what they are checking or why.[79]

After Grenfell, the Fire Protection Association revealed that just under two-thirds – 500 – of the 800 fire risk assessors operating in the UK were not registered with accredited bodies and in 2013 the fire service discovered that 14 per cent of risk assessments, across all types of property, were non-compliant.[80] These fire safety failings have been exacerbated by austerity, with the number of fire safety inspections in tower blocks falling by 25 per cent in the five years up to 2017 following huge cuts to stand-alone fire and rescue authorities.[81]

Meanwhile, tenants' ability to take action against rogue landlords has also suffered. For private tenants, complaints about housing conditions can now lead to so-called 'revenge evictions' whereby landlords exploit the no-fault repossession route provided by section 21 of the 1988 Housing Act to evict their residents after a six-month tenancy has expired without giving a reason. Homeless charity Shelter estimated that in 2013/14 alone, some 213,000 private tenants were evicted by landlords after asking for repairs to be carried out or after complaining to the local authority about their housing conditions, and over 850,000 private tenants had not asked for repairs or complained for fear of eviction.[82] Local authority environmental health officers do have powers to inspect and prosecute private landlords and housing associations under the HHSRS. However, local authorities are generally unable or reluctant to prosecute private landlords because of cuts to inspection teams and because they have come to depend on them for housing the homeless as a result of the shortage of social housing. There is evidence that local authority inspections and prosecutions of private landlords are falling. About 50 per cent of councils had served no or only one enforcement notice in 2014/15, with just one London council serving 50 per cent of notices nationally and 70 per cent of those in London.[83]

Since 2015, the Conservative government has legislated to try to prevent revenge evictions by making section 21 notices invalid if the landlord has not provided tenants with an energy performance or gas safety certificate, or if issued within six months of the landlord being served an improvement notice or emergency remedial action notice by the council. In practice, the process remains extremely time-consuming and fraught with risk: if the landlord issues a section 21 notice after receiving the tenant's initial complaint and the court hearing happens before the council has inspected the property and issued a notice, the tenant has no defence and is likely to be evicted. Given the stretched financial circumstances of local authority environmental health services, it can take months for an inspection to take place. Added to this, environmental health officers often work informally with landlords to encourage them to undertake repairs without the need for an inspection, thus preventing the tenants from protection against revenge eviction.[84]

While social housing tenants with secure tenancies have strong legal protections against eviction, their rights and regulatory protections have also been eroded since 2004. In 2012, the Coalition government abolished the Tenant Services Authority (TSA), which was set up in 2008 to regulate 'consumer' standards in social housing. Council tenants in particular find it increasingly difficult, if not impossible, to take action against disrepair and unsafe housing. This is because local authorities cannot prosecute themselves, which means that the only way in which council tenants can seek to have basic fitness standards enforced, including fire safety, is by bringing their own private prosecution. But this is possible only if the hazards are caused by disrepair or relate to a relevant tenancy condition.[85] Furthermore, bringing legal claims of any sort has been made far more difficult and daunting for all since April 2013 following cuts to legal aid, and legal aid is now available only to tenants who can prove that disrepair poses a serious risk to residents' health and safety.[86]

Conclusion

In this chapter I have explained how the Grenfell disaster and the discovery of other Grenfells in waiting is rooted in neoliberal policies of housing privatisation and deregulation rolled out since 1979. Public housing – its homes, tenure, affordability and security, as well as its wider regulatory system of municipal building control and health and safety regulation – made a remarkable contribution to driving up the quality and safety of working-class housing over the 20th century. The neoliberal turn, however, led to the rise of outsourced regeneration in a dangerous self-regulatory environment geared towards maximising profit. We can gain a powerful insight into the destructive combination of outsourced regeneration and self-regulation responsible for the Grenfell disaster through an in-depth focus on housing regeneration and management under PFI, to which we now turn.

Notes

1   S. Jenkins, 'The lesson from Grenfell is simple: stop building residential towers', *Guardian*, 15 June 2017, at https://www.theguardian.com/commentisfree/2017/jun/15/lessons-grenfell-tower-safer-cladding-tower-blocks (accessed 13 October 2018).
2   R. Littlejohn, 'Awkward questions no one will answer about Grenfell Tower', *Daily Mail*, 21 July 2017, at http://www.dailymail.co.uk/debate/article-4673612/Awkward-questions-no-one-answer-Grenfell-Tower.html#ixzz5AxALhCsc (accessed 13 October 2018).
3   S. Khan, 'We owe it to the Grenfell Tower victims to establish the full truth', *Guardian*, 18 June 2017, at https://www.theguardian.com/commentisfree/2017/jun/18/sadiq-khan-grenfell-tower-tragedy-establish-full-truth (accessed 15 October 2018).
4   J. Boughton, *Municipal Dreams: The Rise and Fall of Council Housing* (London: Verso, 2018).

5 K. Razzall, S. Moralioglu and N. Menzies, 'The 21st floor', BBC News
   website, 28 September 2017, at https://www.bbc.co.uk/news/resources/
   idt-sh/Grenfell_21st_floor (accessed 13 October 2018).
6 F. Engels, *The Condition of the Working Class in England in 1844* (New
   York: Cosimo Classics, 2008 [1845]), p. 27.
7 S. Ewen, 'The problem of fire in nineteenth century British cities: the
   case of Glasgow', *Proceedings of the Second International Congress on
   Construction History*, 1 (2006), 1061–1074, at https://www.arct.cam.
   ac.uk/Downloads/ichs/vol-1-1061-1074-ewen.pdf (accessed 13 October
   2018).
8 D. Englander, *Landlord and Tenant in Urban Britain, 1838–1918* (Oxford:
   Clarendon Press, 1983), p. x.
9 R. Whelan (ed.), *Octavia Hill and the Social Housing Debate: Essays and
   Letters* (London: Civitas, 1998), at http://www.civitas.org.uk/pdf/rr3.pdf
   (accessed 13 October 2018).
10 N. Gray (ed.), *Rent and Its Discontents: A Century of Housing* (London:
   Rowman & Littlefield International, 2018).
11 Aneurin Bevan introducing the 1949 Housing Bill, in *House of Commons
   Debates*, vol. 462, cc. 2121–2231 (1949), at https://api.parliament.uk/
   historic-hansard/commons/1949/mar/16/housing-bill (accessed 13 October
   2018).
12 *Ibid.*
13 D. Ellis, 'After Grenfell, what can we learn from the housing policies of
   the 1970s', History and Policy website, 27 June 2017, at http://www.
   historyandpolicy.org/opinion-articles/articles/after-grenfell-what-can-
   we-learn-from-the-housing-policies-of-the-1970s (accessed 13 October
   2018).
14 Ministry of Housing, Communities and Local Government, 'Live table
   101: dwelling stock: by tenure, United Kingdom (historical series)', UK
   government website, 2018, at https://www.gov.uk/government/uploads/
   system/uploads/attachment_data/file/710181/Discontinued_LT_101.xls
   (accessed 13 October 2018).
15 C. Ward, *Tenants Take Over* (London: Architectural Press, 1974).
16 P. Dunleavy, *The Politics of Mass Housing in Britain, 1945–1975: A
   Study of Corporate Power and Professional Influence in the Welfare State*
   (Oxford: Oxford University Press, 1981).
17 I. Cole and R. Furbey, *The Eclipse of Council Housing* (London:
   Routledge, 1994), p. 103. Embodying the corruption of the day, the high-
   rise experiment was led by Keith Joseph, then Conservative Minister for
   Housing, while he was also a director and major shareholder in Bovis, his
   own family's construction company. In 1963 he announced a programme
   to system-build 400,000 houses a year, a programme that was continued
   by the Labour government when it came to power in the following year.
18 *Ibid.*, p. 104.
19 D. Madden and P. Marcuse, *In Defense of Housing: The Politics of Crisis*
   (London: Verso, 2016).
20 E. L. Jones, S. Porter and M. Turner, *A Gazetteer of English Urban Fire
   Disasters, 1500– 1900* (Norwich: Geo Books, 1984).

21 N. Flynn, 'Direct labour organisations', *Local Government Studies*, 7:2 (1981), 56–59.

22 L. Clarke, 'Building by direct labour: the significance of direct labour organisations (DLOs) in the provision of public housing in the UK 1890–1980', in J. W. P. Campbell, W. Andrews, N. Bill, K. Draper, P. Fleming and Y. Pan (eds), *Proceedings of the First Conference of the Construction History Society, Queens' College Cambridge, 11–12 April 2014* (Cambridge: Construction History Society, 2015), pp. 81–90.

23 J. Ryan-Collins, T. Lloyd and L. Macfarlane, *Rethinking the Economics of Land and Housing* (London: Zed Books, 2017).

24 H. Radice, 'Confronting the crisis: a class analysis', in L. Panitch, G. Albo and V. Chibber (eds), *Social Register 2011: The Crisis This Time* (London: Merlin Press, 2010), pp. 21–43.

25 The figure comes from my own updating of the following source: 'Privatisation', House of Commons Library Research Paper 14/61, 20 November 2014, at https://researchbriefings.files.parliament.uk/documents/RP14-61/RP14-61.pdf (accessed 15 October 2018).

26 J. Meek, *Private Island: Why Britain Now Belongs to Someone Else* (London: Verso, 2016).

27 D. Whitfield, *Public Services or Corporate Welfare: Rethinking the Nation State in the Global Economy* (London: Pluto Press, 2001). The 1980 Local Government, Planning and Land Act introduced CCT for local councils' construction, maintenance and highways works. This spread to blue- and white-collar services under the 1988 Local Government Act. New Labour scrapped CCT in favour of 'Best Value' under the 1999 Local Government Act. Best Value re-opened the door to municipal provision but within a marketised environment that in fact expanded the commercialisation of public services by introducing an elaborate market-testing and target-setting exercise in which council services that failed to improve were forcibly taken over by private or voluntary sector providers.

28 Trades Union Congress and New Economics Foundation, *Outsourcing Public Services* (London: Trades Union Congress, 2015).

29 A. Murie, 'The Right to Buy: History and Prospect' *History and Policy* (11 November 2015), at http://www.historyandpolicy.org/policy-papers/papers/the-right-to-buy-history-and-prospect (accessed 13 October 2018).

30 P. Balchin, 'The United Kingdom', in P. N. Balchin (ed.), *Housing Policy in Europe* (London: Routledge, 1996), p. 211.

31 N. Ginsburg, 'The Housing Act, 1988 and its policy context: a critical commentary', *Critical Social Policy*, 9:25 (1989), 56–81.

32 P. Apps, 'Grenfell: the paper trail', *Inside Housing*, 11 August 2017, at http://www.insidehousing.co.uk/home/home/grenfell-the-paper-trail-51907 (accessed 12 October 2018).

33 Chartered Institute of Housing and Graham Moody Associates, *Council Housing – Financing the Future. Final Report* (Coventry: CIH, 1998).

34 Department for Communities and Local Government, *English House Condition Survey 1996: Summary*, UK Data Archive Study Number 6101

(London: Department for Communities and Local Government, 2006), at https://doc.ukdataservice.ac.uk/doc/6101/mrdoc/pdf/6101ehcs_1996_summary.pdf (accessed 13 October 2018).

35 D. Hughes and S. Lowe, *Social Housing Law and Policy* (London: Butterworths, 1995), p. 60.

36 BBC News, 'Blair's speech: single mothers won't be forced to take work', BBC News website, 2 June 1997, at https://www.bbc.co.uk/news/special/politics97/news/06/0602/blair.shtml (accessed 13 October 2018).

37 Department of Environment, Transport and the Regions, *Quality and Choice: A Decent Home for All*, Housing Green Paper (London: The Stationery Office, 2000). To be classed as 'decent', homes had to pass the standard for legal minimum fitness for human habitation, be in a reasonable state of repair, have reasonably modern facilities and services – such as a kitchen not older than 20 years and a bathroom not older than 30 years – and provide a reasonable degree of thermal comfort through effective insulation and efficient heating. In 2002, the government expanded the programme to vulnerable households in private sector accommodation.

38 Department for Transport, Local Government and the Regions, *A Decent Home – The Revised Definition and Guidance for Implementation* (London: The Stationery Office, 2002).

39 Interview with former Labour MP and Housing Minister Keith Hill, 18 March 2010.

40 Interview with former Labour MP and Housing Minister Nick Raynsford, 16 February 2010.

41 The position was made clear by Keith Hill in January 2004 to a House of Commons Select Committee: 'There will be no so-called fourth way. The cavalry will not come over the hill with alternatives.... We do not want to force tenants into accepting changes they do not want ... but we are not going to provide an alternative option'. See Select Committee on Office of the Deputy Prime Minister: Housing, Planning, Local Government and the Regions, Examination of Witnesses, Questions 479–499, 28 January 2004, at https://publications.parliament.uk/pa/cm200304/cmselect/cmodpm/46/4012805.htm (accessed 13 October 2018).

42 Labour reduced the maximum RTB discount to £38,000 in London and empowered councils to lower this further to £16,000 in high-pressure areas of southern England. New tenants also had to wait five years instead of the previous three before they could qualify for the RTB and/or sell their homes without having to repay their discount.

43 The RTB was abolished in Scotland in 2016 and in Wales in 2017. In England, discounts are currently worth up to 70 per cent of market value with a generous cash limit of over £100,000 in London. Plans to require English local authorities to sell any empty council house deemed to be 'high value' under the 2016 Housing and Planning Act – threatening 24,000 homes a year – were abandoned in August 2018.

44 C. Beatty, and S. Fothergill, *The Uneven Impact of Welfare Reform: The Financial Losses to Places and People* (Sheffield: Sheffield Hallam University, 2016).

45 R. Powell, 'Housing benefit reform and the private rented sector in the UK: on the deleterious effects of short-term, ideological "knowledge"', *Housing, Theory and Society*, 32:3 (2015), 320–345.

46 Figures taken from the UK Housing Review 2017, available at https://www.ukhousingreview.org.uk/ukhr17/index.html (accessed 16 October 2018). See also A. Murie, 'The right to buy: history and prospect', History and Policy website, 11 November 2015, at http://www.historyandpolicy.org/policy-papers/papers/the-right-to-buy-history-and-prospect (accessed 13 October 2018).

47 Ministry of Housing, Communities and Local Government, 'Live Table 101: Dwelling stock: by tenure, United Kingdom (historical series)', 2018, at https://www.gov.uk/government/uploads/system/uploads/attachment_data/file/710181/Discontinued_LT_101.xls (accessed 13 October 2018).

48 See R. Goulding, 'Governing risk and uncertainty: financialisation and the regulatory framework of housing associations', in H. Carr, B. Edgeworth and C. Hunter (eds), *Law and the Precarious Home: Socio-Legal Perspectives on the Home in Insecure Times* (Oxford: Hart Publishing, 2018).

49 'UK social housing sector worth around £11.4bn in 2017', Planning and Building Control Today website, 9 March 2017, at https://www.pbctoday.co.uk/news/planning-construction-news/uk-social-housing-market-worth-around-11-4bn-in-2017/39316 (accessed 15 October 2018).

50 J. Ryan-Collins et al., *Rethinking the Economics of Land and Housing*.

51 N. Barker, 'Revealed: the scale of ex-RTB home conversions to private rent', *Inside Housing*, 7 December 2017, at https://www.insidehousing.co.uk/insight/insight/revealed-the-scale-of-ex-rtb-home-conversions-to-private-rent-53525 (accessed 16 October 2018).

52 Shelter, *Shut Out: Households at Put at Risk of Homelessness by the Housing Benefit Freeze* (London: Shelter, 2017), at https://england.shelter.org.uk/__data/assets/pdf_file/0005/1391675/LHA_analysis_note_FINAL.pdf (accessed 16 October 2018).

53 A. Minton, *Big Capital: Who Is London For?* (London: Penguin, 2017).

54 P. Watt, '"This pain of moving, moving, moving": evictions, displacement and logics of expulsion in London', *L'Année Sociologique*, 68:1 (2018), 67–100.

55 A. Gentleman, 'Four out of five Grenfell families still need homes, says support group', *Guardian*, 7 December 2017, at https://www.theguardian.com/uk-news/2017/dec/07/grenfell-families-need-home-support-group (accessed 13 October 2018); Letter by Nick Hurd MP, Minister for Grenfell Victims, at https://www.parliament.uk/documents/commons-committees/communities-and-local-government/2017-19-Correspondence/Letter-from-Nick-Hurd-MP-response-to-23-July-2018-letter-Grenfell-Tower-fire-30-July-2018.pdf (accessed 13 October 2018).

56 D. Batty, M. McIntyre, D. Pegg and A. Asthana, 'Grenfell: names of wealthy empty-home owners in borough revealed', *Guardian*, 1 August 2017, at https://www.theguardian.com/society/2017/aug/01/names-of-wealthy-empty-home-owners-in-grenfell-borough-revealed (accessed 13 October 2018).

57 J. Beswick and J. Penny, 'Demolishing the present to sell-off the future? The emergence of "financialized municipal entrepreneurialism" in London', *International Journal of Urban and Regional Research*, 42:4 (2018), 612–632.

58 S. Tombs, *Social Protection After the Crisis: Regulation Without Enforcement* (Bristol: Policy Press, 2017); see also P. Hampton, *Reducing Administrative Burdens: Effective Inspection and Enforcement. The Hampton Review – Final Report* (London: HM Treasury, 2005).

59 D. Cameron, 'Reducing the burden and impact of health and safety', Conservative Party speech, 1 December 2009, at https://conservative-speeches.sayit.mysociety.org/speech/601227 (accessed 13 October 2018).

60 House of Lords, *Deregulation: Government Policy Since* (London: House of Lords Library, 1997), p. 9, at https://researchbriefings.files.parliament.uk/documents/LLN-2017-0041/LLN-2017-0041.pdf (accessed 13 October 2018).

61 National Audit Office, *Financial Sustainability of Local Authorities 2018*, Report by the Comptroller and Auditor General HC 834, 8 March (London: National Audit Office, 2018), at https://www.nao.org.uk/wp-content/uploads/2018/03/Financial-sustainabilty-of-local-authorites-2018.pdf (accessed 13 October 2018).

62 S. Tombs, 'Making better regulation, making regulation better?', *Policy Studies*, 37:4 (2016), 332–349, p. 344.

63 S. Tombs and D. Whyte, 'But not just in housing: one law for the poor at Grenfell Tower', Open Democracy website, 21 June 2017, at https://opendemocracy.net/uk/steve-tombs-and-david-whyte/on-grenfell-one-law-for-rich-one-poor (accessed 13 October 2018).

64 T. O'Brien, *Tackling the Housing Crisis with Publicly Owned Construction Direct Labour Organisations* (self-published, 2018).

65 D. Smith with A. Just, *Blacklisting: The Need for a Public Inquiry* (Liverpool: Institute of Employment Rights, 2017).

66 P. Apps, 'Was the cladding legal?', in P. Apps, S. Barnes and L. Barratt, 'The paper trail: the failure of building regulations', *Inside Housing*, Shorthand Social website, 23 March 2018, at https://social.shorthand.com/insidehousing/3CWytp9tQj/the-failure-of-building-regulations-the-paper-trail (accessed 13 October 2018).

67 *Ibid.*

68 BBC News, 'Four ministers were warned about tower block fire risks', BBC News website, 21 June 2017, at https://www.bbc.co.uk/news/uk-40330789 (accessed 13 October 2018).

69 *House of Commons Debates*, 6 February 2014, column 188WH, at https://publications.parliament.uk/pa/cm201314/cmhansrd/cm140206/halltext/140206h0002.htm (accessed 13 October 2018).

70 Chief Fire Officers Association (CFOA), *The Business Case for Sprinklers* (Tamworth: CFOA Publications Ltd, 2013), at https://www.cfoa.org.uk/download/38472 (accessed 16 October 2018).

71 Local Authority Building Control, 'Submission to the All-Party Parliamentary Group for Excellence in the Built Environment', 31 October 2015, at http://cic.org.uk/admin/resources/labc-1.pdf (accessed 18 October 2018).

72 J. Cole, *Report of the Independent Inquiry into the Construction of Edinburgh Schools*, February 2017, at http://www.edinburgh.gov.uk/download/meetings/id/53239/report_of_the_independent_inquiry_into_the_construction_of_edinburgh_schools (accessed 13 October 2018).

73 R. Hawkesworth and R. Imrie, 'Organisational change in systems of building regulation and control: illustrations from the English context', *Environment and Planning B – Urban Analytics and City Science*, 36: 3 (2009), 552–567, at https://dx.doi.org/10.1068/b34036 (accessed 13 October 2018).

74 London Fire and Emergency Planning Authority, *Structural Fire Safety in New and Refurbished Buildings* (London: Strategy Committee, FEP 2265, 11 July 2014), at http://moderngov.london-fire.gov.uk/mgconvert2pdf.aspx?id=3106 (accessed 13 October 2018).

75 Trades Union Congress and the New Economics Foundation, *Outsourcing Public Services*, p. 59.

76 Local Authority Building Control, 'Submission to the All-Party Parliamentary Group'.

77 Department for Communities and Local Government, *Changes to the Conditions of Authorisation for Building Regulations Competent Person Self-certification Schemes. Final Impact Assessment* (London: Department for Communities and Local Government, June 2012), at https://www.gov.uk/government/uploads/system/uploads/attachment_data/file/8405/2157372.pdf (accessed 13 October 2018).

78 *Ibid.*, p. 5.

79 Interview with Phil Murphy, former firefighter, 17 September 2018.

80 L. Barratt, 'Hundreds of unregistered fire risk assessors operating in UK, warns FPA', *Inside Housing*, 6 February 2018, at https://www.insidehousing.co.uk/home/home/hundreds-of-unregistered-fire-risk-assessors-operating-in-uk-warns-fpa-54443 (accessed 13 October 2018); S. Barnes, 'Experts slam fire risk assessments process', *Inside Housing*, 22 June 2017, at https://www.insidehousing.co.uk/news/news/experts-slam-fire-risk-assessments-process-51090 (accessed 13 October 2018).

81 National Audit Office, *Local Government: Impact of Funding Reductions on Fire and Rescue Services*, Report by the Comptroller and Auditor General (London: National Audit Office, 2015), at https://www.nao.org.uk/wp-content/uploads/2015/11/Impact-of-funding-reductions-on-fire-and-rescue-services-A.pdf (accessed 13 October 2018); Tombs and Whyte, 'But not just in housing'.

82 Shelter, 'True scale of revenge evictions exposed by Shelter investigation', Shelter Media Centre website, 2014, http://media.shelter.org.uk/home/press_releases/true_scale_of_revenge_evictions_exposed_by_shelter_investigation (accessed 16 October 2018).

83 K. Buck and S. Battersby, *The Challenge of Tackling Unsafe and Unhealthy Housing. Report of a Survey of Local Authorities for Karen Buck MP* (privately published, December 2015), at http://sabattersby.co.uk/documents/KBReport2.pdf (accessed 16 October 2018).

84 *Ibid.*

85 G. Peaker, 'Homes (Fitness for Human Habitation and Liability for Housing Standards) Bill – Karen Buck MP', Nearly Legal specialist housing law website, November 2017, at https://nearlylegal.co.uk/wp-content/uploads/2017/11/FitnessBillBriefing.pdf (accessed 16 October 2018).
86 T. Huckle, 'Grenfell Tower – a different perspective', *New Law Journal*, 7753 (2017) 9–10, at https://www.newlawjournal.co.uk/content/grenfell-tower-different-perspective (accessed 13 October 2018).

2 Outsourcing on steroids: regeneration meets the Private Finance Initiative

Following the Grenfell disaster, an astonishing revelation was made by the London Metropolitan Police Service: it had identified at least 60 companies and bodies involved in the tower's 2014–16 refurbishment, part of a total of 383 organisations connected with its original construction or subsequent management and maintenance.[1] This scale of splintered governance is indicative of what has happened to public housing under decades of privatisation and demunicipalisation. This chapter introduces the controversial background and evolution of the PFI model in housing regeneration – what I call *outsourcing on steroids*. There are many different variations of PFI both in the UK and globally but, in simple terms, it involves outsourcing the design, capital financing, construction or renewal and operation of public infrastructure – such as hospitals, schools and social housing – to private companies in long-term contracts – typically lasting 30 years.

The chapter begins by outlining the basic workings of a PFI scheme before exploring the origins of this model as part of the wider corporate takeover and financialisation of public services outlined in chapter 1. The second section unpacks official claims that the inflated cost to the public purse of using private finance over direct government borrowing is justified by the superior 'value for money' delivered through PFI's 'risk transfer' and 'payment by results' model. I show that such claims amount to an accounting trick that exaggerates public sector inefficiency and private sector risk-taking while ignoring the greater social costs of using PFI. The third section provides an overview of the 20 public housing PFI regeneration schemes operational in England as of 2018, and introduces the three London local authority case studies which form the evidence base of the book: Islington's street properties, Camden's Chalcots Estate and Lambeth's MFN estate. The fourth section reveals the controversy on the ground that met the undemocratic imposition of many housing PFI schemes – sometimes in the face of resident opposition – and the problems that engulfed the procurement of these contracts.

PFI: no ordinary kind of outsourcing

While PFI shares many of the hallmarks of public service out-sourcing outlined in chapter 1, it takes them to new extremes – it is *outsourcing on steroids*. The public sector enters into a relationship with a special purpose vehicle (SPV), a company that represents a consortium of the main companies involved – usually a major con-struction firm, a facilities management firm and a multinational bank. The SPV then sub-contracts all of the works and services specified by the public authority in the PFI contract to the prin-cipal contractors it has chosen to deliver the construction project and the subsequent long-term management and maintenance of the new or renewed public infrastructure. These companies then further sub-contract different aspects of their individual contracts with the SPV to a small army of private sub-contractors, who in turn do the same. It is also common for the SPV and the main sub-contractors to employ private contractors to perform building control and other forms of quality compliance monitoring on the dozens of different sub-contractors working on site at the same time.

What sets PFI further apart from ordinary outsourcing is that even the up-front *financing* needed to undertake the construction is outsourced. Instead of the government directly borrowing the funds to pay the builders, this task is also contracted to the SPV, which raises the finance through commercial borrowing. This is the main reason for the inclusion of major multinational banks in PFI consortia, as they normally provide the vast majority (90 per cent) of the capital needed. Over time, the SPV will repay this loan and the interest accruing on it out of the monthly contract payments it receives from the public sector – called the unitary charge – which also covers the SPV's fees for providing management and maintenance services. In other words, the 'private finance' part of PFI is completely misleading, as every penny invested ultimately comes from the public purse. However, by outsourcing the up-front capital financing to the private sector, PFI allows governments effectively to hide these long-term liabilities – public debt – with only the annual service payments appearing in the public accounts as current expenditure.

As we will see below, privately financing public infrastructure is always more expensive than traditional public procurement using government borrowing. However, despite this additional cost, PFI is justified as offering better 'value for money' overall because of the private sector's apparent 'superior' management of risk relative to the public sector. The PFI contractor is supposedly incentivised to perform well, through a contractual mechanism that links payment to results. In theory, the SPV's ability to repay its private creditors and provide profits to its owners is put at risk. This risk is contractualised in three main ways: a construction timetable with target dates and long-stop (absolute) deadlines for different parts of the project to be completed and deemed 'available' to use; an 'output specification' that prescribes hundreds of 'availability standards' for design and construction; and a list of KPIs reflecting required service standards that the SPV must meet.

As key availability milestones and performance targets are achieved, the SPV is entitled to invoice the public authority for larger monthly payments, up to a maximum threshold. Once all of the construction is complete and the new hospital, school or housing is signed off as 'available', the contract moves from construction to operational mode. The SPV must then maintain these public assets at the required standards through repairs and programmed maintenance over the remaining decades of the contract. Where the SPV fails to meet its targets or where the infrastructure is no longer deemed to meet one or more availability standards, the contract's payment mechanism sets out the required financial deductions to the monthly invoice; continued failure triggers a 'ratchet mechanism' of higher and higher financial penalties until the problems have been rectified. The SPV's sub-contracts should ensure that these financial risks are passed on to the responsible sub-contractor. According to the magic mantra of 'payment by results', this financial risk will incentivise the PFI consortium to honour the promised construction and service standards, something that, so the privateers argue, the public sector has historically struggled to do. This philosophy was laid down to me by a civil servant formerly responsible for the housing PFI programme who had previously worked for local authorities and a major PFI contractor:

> You say to the private sector, 'If you don't get your design, costings, tendering or build management right, or if you need more staff than planned to deliver the KPIs, it's all your risk and it doesn't cost the public sector any more'.[2]

But the theory works in practice only if the works and services are properly monitored to ensure compliance and this is where PFI takes outsourcing to its ultimate logic: instead of the public authority monitoring and financially penalising non-compliance, the SPV itself is paid as part of the PFI contract to monitor and enforce the contract on its behalf. There is a well-known expression that you should not let a fox guard a henhouse, but in PFI that is exactly what happens. At the end of each month, the SPV sends an invoice to the public authority requesting payment of the applicable unitary charge based on its own self-declared availability and KPI scores, including any financial deductions for self-declared unavailability and under-performance in previous months. As we shall see over the course of this book, this system of self-regulation falls down spectacularly. To understand how such a disastrous idea took hold, we first need to retrace the origins of PFI in the wider financialisation of public services.

The origins of PFI

The ability of PFI to help politicians to remove long-term financial liabilities of public investment from the official figures for UK government borrowing and debt was a key factor behind its emergence in the early 1990s under the Conservative government.

PFI was presented as a way of addressing the long-standing under-investment in the UK's crumbling infrastructure at a time of fiscal constraint required under the EU's 1992 Maastricht Treaty convergence criteria for future economic and monetary union. Member states were barred from allowing their annual borrowing to exceed 3 per cent of gross domestic product (GDP), and their gross public sector debt to exceed 60 per cent of GDP. This financial straitjacket was tightened even further under New Labour's controversial 'sustainable investment rule' and 'golden rule' introduced in 1998 that restricted public sector net debt to 40 per cent of GDP and promised to eliminate budget deficits over the business cycle. PFI helped to by-pass these fiscal controls by reclassifying public debt as private debt. Yet behind this apparent pragmatism, both the financial straitjacket on government borrowing and the invention of PFI were a core part of the neoliberal agenda, outlined in chapter 1, to enable private companies and financiers to profit from public services. Fiscal constraint became an opportunity for a new kind of outsourcing that would bring the logics of markets and money further into the governance of public services while providing a new outlet for capital accumulation. PFI did this by redefining public services as something that could 'remain publicly financed but privately delivered in privately managed buildings'.[3]

It took a while for PFI to break through 'the barriers of Whitehall' due to its incredible complexity, the inadequacy of the existing statutory framework and Treasury concerns about losing control of public spending.[4] The private sector was also hesitant: while the big accountancy firms in the City of London licked their lips, banks and construction firms were initially put off by the government's insistence that PFI could be used only if the private sector took all of the financial risk. Although the Conservatives initiated 150 PFI projects after 1990, only 19 contracts were signed before they lost power in 1997. But during this time, the state was gradually transforming itself to enable PFI to take off. Bankers were seconded into the Treasury to help manage the PFI programme, and 15 senior representatives of the City, industry and the civil service, including leading corporate executives from companies that would benefit from PFI contracts, like General Electric,

Tarmac, Scottish Power, Serco and pension fund manager Hermes, were appointed to the government's Private Finance Panel, which had an agenda to 'introduce private finance into all aspects of the public sector'.[5] In 1995, the predecessors to the Local Government Association – the representative body of English and Welsh local authorities – set up a specialist procurement arm called Public Private Partnerships Programme Limited, known as 4Ps, with more private sector interests on the board, to promote PFI among councils, provide free advice and help central government to remove the legal and financial obstacles to its use.

Having made electoral capital out of the unpopularity of privatisation in opposition, in government New Labour enthusiastically embraced PFI as the 'cornerstone' of its so-called 'modernisation' agenda for public services. It appointed Malcolm Bates, former Private Finance Panel member and then chairman of private insurer, Pearl Assurance, to review PFI, supported by the UK arm of the US accountancy firm Arthur Andersen. Bates's recommendations led to the Private Finance Panel being replaced by a Treasury task force, divided into a policy arm run by civil servants and a projects section employing eight private sector executives led by Adrian Montague, a merchant banker from Dresdner Kleinwort previously involved in the Eurotunnel project.[6] In 1998 PricewaterhouseCoopers (PwC) was contracted to train certain civil servants and Capita Group PLC was awarded a contract for the provision of a PFI conference programme to share best practice.[7] New policy guidance was issued that reduced the risks to the private sector in PFI schemes. As Chancellor the Exchequer Gordon Brown told investors in 2000:

> These are core services ... which the government is statutorily bound to provide and for which demand is virtually insatiable. Your revenue stream is ultimately backed by the government. Where else can you get a long-term business opportunity like that?[8]

In 2000, the projects arm of the Treasury task force was rebranded as Partnerships UK (PUK) and part-privatised, with 51 per cent owned by the following private sector shareholders: Bank of Scotland, Prudential Assurance, Abbey National (now Santander), Sun Life Assurance, Barclays, RBS, Serco, Global Solutions Limited (now Group 4) and British Land Company.[9] By the time it left office in 2010, Labour had signed off more than 620 PFI schemes; as of March 2017, there were 715 PFI projects operating with a capital value of £59.06 billion and future contract payments totalling £308.46 billion through to 2050. By far the largest target of PFI has been the health service, in the form of new hospitals and other facilities, amounting to a quarter of total PFI expenditure.[10] As we will see in chapter 6, there is also a clear similarity between the corporate interests that advised and promoted the PFI model in partnership with government listed above, and the banks, contractors and advisors that went on to become directly involved in financing schemes and winning contracts.

Why private finance always costs more

By placing this investment 'off the books', PFI's accounting trick has enabled the state to renew some of the UK's neglected public infrastructure without officially increasing public sector borrowing or debt.[11] But there is a major downside to this arrangement – the exorbitant cost of PFI compared with traditional public borrowing.[12] As economist Ann Pettifor has brilliantly demonstrated, the reason for this is simple: as governments almost never go bankrupt due to their tax-raising powers, they can borrow far more cheaply than private companies. UK governments have for centuries utilised this low-risk status to access cheap public finance for investment by issuing bonds in the gilts market.[13] A gilt is a promise to pay the purchaser the original amount borrowed with interest, issued in sterling and listed on the London Stock Exchange. Its name derives from its reputation as a gold-coated investment due to its steady and guaranteed returns. In contrast, private firms, like individuals, are seen as much riskier borrowers, which is why banks and other financiers charge them a 'risk premium'.

Yet in PFI schemes, this logic is flipped on its head, with the private sector raising investment finance for the public sector. About 90 per cent of the capital needed for any PFI scheme is normally borrowed as 'senior debt'[14] from commercial banks – the very same banks that from the outset have been involved in promoting PFI, such as Barclays, HSBC, Bank of Scotland, Lloyds TSB and RBS. Over the years, studies have consistently put the implied interest rate of PFI senior debt as double that of government borrowing, at 6–8 per cent for PFI compared with 2–4 per cent for government.[15] In many PFI schemes this huge additional cost is partly caused by the need to purchase a financial derivative known as a 'swap deal' that turns the *variable* rates of interest and inflation at which senior debt is lent into a higher fixed interest rate. This is to give both public authorities and PFI consortia certainty about the long-term cost so they can budget accordingly. This additional cost falls onto the public purse yet it is completely unnecessary, as government gilts already offer fixed interest rates. The National Audit Office estimated in 2015 that swap liabilities across the entire PFI programme were around £6 billion and reported that it cost Northumbria Healthcare NHS Foundation Trust £24 million in swap breakage costs alone to buy out a PFI contract in 2014.[16]

The other main driver of PFI's inflated cost – and where the label 'rampant profiteering' can be used without fear of contradiction – are the returns on offer to the owners of the SPV, which are usually investment arms of the banks and construction firms involved in the PFI project. For example, as well as providing the senior debt financing to dozens of PFI schemes, the Bank of Scotland invested in the corresponding SPVs through its private equity firm, Uberior Investments Ltd. These investors normally provide the remaining 10 per cent of the up-front capital needed by investing equity in the company (purchasing shares) and providing an unsecured 'subordinate loan' at very high rates of interest. The value of their investment is further boosted at the public's expense through the indexing of unitary charge payments to the retail price index after the first year of the contract to counter the devaluing effects of inflation. In many contracts, this indexation extends to some of the project's capital costs, even though the PFI consortium's actual cost of finance is falling over time.[17] In other words, investors are guaranteed inflation-proof revenue streams for up to 30 years. Formally, PFI contracts typically include internal rates of return to equity of between 14 and 18 per cent – which is already an excellent deal, but, as we will see in chapter 6, they can prove to be much higher. On top of this are the unnecessarily higher costs of outsourcing management and maintenance services for 20 to 30 years to companies commanding generous profit margins. The costs are inflated even further by the need for public and private sector partners to employ special third-party corporate advisors to help them master the complexity of PFI contracts. These lawyers, accountants and other consultants charge eye-watering fees that form the vast majority of the procurement cost, and are dominated by the so-called 'big four' global accountancy firms – PwC, KPMG, EY and Deloitte.

PFI's magic wand: turning expensive financing into 'value for money'

In the early years of PFI, these higher costs clashed with the Treasury's own rule that private finance could be used only when it could demonstrate better value for money (VFM) than traditional procurement. So the whizz-kid financial brains in the PFI lobby came up with an array of a very dubious 'discount rates' to ensure that PFI would always come out looking cheaper than a hypothetical alternative known as the 'public sector comparator' (PSC). One such discount was to counter the so-called 'optimism bias' within public sector costing of conventional procurement by assuming that the private sector would always deliver construction projects on time and on budget. Another assumption was that the private sector was always more efficient than the public sector, meaning lower whole-life costs for disrepair and depreciation. It is notable that the private sector's assumed greater efficiency was based on a single study of 50 large procurement projects compiled for the Treasury by none other than Mott MacDonald, a major global consultancy firm involved in more than 200 PPP projects worldwide with a vested interest in promoting the PFI/PPP model.[18] Despite clear evidence of the enormous transaction costs for PFI contracts, they were assumed to be identical to traditional public procurement in the VFM analysis. An adjustment was also made to account for estimated corporation tax receipts from the SPV on the assumption that around a quarter of all contract payments received from the public sector would become profit subject to the tax rates at the time of contract signature. Finally, the financial benefits of any risks transferred from the public to the private sector in PFI deals were added to the cost of the PSC.[19]

Surprise, surprise: after applying these discount rates, PFI schemes up and down the country went from being often tens of millions of pounds more expensive than the PSC to costing magically less. However, as this book will show, the VFM exercise is a complete sham, with the assumptions behind these discount rates simply not playing out in the real world. For instance, some PFI contracts may well deliver on time and to budget once a contract is signed, but this ignores the additional and unnecessary financial and social costs incurred by the frequent delays that beset schemes in procurement due to PFI's complexity. These higher costs have led to 'affordability gaps' in PFI schemes, forcing service rationalisation, cutting down on the quality of materials and standards, or including public land in the deal to generate the missing finance. Moreover, because they are prohibitively expensive to break, PFI contracts prevent the public sector from getting a better deal over those 30 years. The PFI contractors become the long-term monopoly provider of works and services, many contracts contain exclusivity clauses that allow the contractor to be offered additional works and services outside of the negotiated contract; and to receive very high returns for accepting to undertake them. This is why we hear shocking stories of PFI schools being charged by their outsourced maintenance contractor £333 to change a light bulb, £500 to move a noticeboard and £180 to drill a hole.[20] Then there are the higher than expected costs of public sector monitoring once the contract begins. For example, Lambeth council had originally expected its monitoring costs to total £4.6 million over 25 years for its MFN scheme (see chapter 4), but the annual inspection of Lambeth's accounts for 2012/13 and 2013/14 showed that these costs had already reached £835,127 in the first two years alone. At this rate, the authority's monitoring costs by 2037 will be more than double the original forecast. Nor has the assumed financial benefit of PFI from corporation tax receipts played out in reality, due to the 11 percentage point reduction in corporate tax rates since 2011, which has benefited 87 per cent of all PFI contractors. And this is before we even broach the subject of systematic tax avoidance.[21]

But it is the financialisation and transfer of risk under PFI that are the most controversial aspects of the VFM analysis. Risk transfer under PFI in effect involves the public sector taking out a very expensive insurance policy with a private consortium to cover potential events occurring over the 30-year contract. However, as a leading advisor to housing associations involved in PFI told me, risk pricing is not 'as scientific as we might all like to think' and usually involves the private sector bundling up a lot of different things and offering an overall price to take those risks away from the public sector. Should these things not occur, or cost far less than the public sector has paid to have the risk transferred, then the assumed VFM is lost:

> What you do is you look at the picture overall and you say, well, 'we reckon a million pounds worth of pricing risk in there'. It's not ... I don't think it's desperately scientific. I think a lot of it comes down to commercial judgment and gut feel so that's why usually clients will say 'we're not going to give the council what they want'; we're not going to say ... 'we'll knock £50,000 off our bid if you delete that clause'.... There are some where you might be able to price it because you could point to something specific. So, for example, contamination risk: you could say, 'well we'll get some analysis done and we'll get them to analyse what a worst-case scenario is in terms of what might be in the ground and then we'll price that'.... I remember one deal where it was £8 million ... then you say to the council, 'if you don't retain that risk we will put £8 million into our bid price'. If you take that risk, £8 million straight off ... really poor value for money ... all the guidance tells you that you should only transfer risk where it is value for money to do so. That gets lost when you start talking to a council. [22]

Many fundamental social risks that are hard to quantify are not even included in the VFM exercise, such as the detrimental financial impact of a costly PFI project – which takes priority in public budgets – on the public sector's ability to maintain non-PFI buildings and other services. Nor does the VFM model calculate the future costs from the temporary or permanent loss of public buildings and land. While the new or renewed infrastructure is normally handed back to the public sector at the end of the contract, in some schemes, such as the Edinburgh Royal Infirmary, the land and/or the buildings will remain with the contractor. Also omitted are the risks from the formidable contract breakage costs from interest rate swap deals that make it far more difficult for public bodies to make savings from refinancing when interest rates fall, or to terminate contracts in the future. The combination of PFI's huge cost burden and its inflexibility has had devastating consequences in the National Health Service (NHS). Affordability problems in the first 10 NHS hospital PFI schemes were variously met by raiding hospital budgets, selling off hospital land and assets at below market value to PFI companies, mergers and closures, and reducing hospital capacity so as to cut both capital and operating costs.[23] Signed in 2006, the UK's largest PFI hospital contract, at Barts Health NHS Trust in east London, will eventually cost £7.1 billion by its planned end in 2048, or 11 per cent of the trust's annual budget. As a result, the trust ran into financial crisis in 2016 with the largest budget overspend in the NHS's history, resulting in hundreds of redundancies, cuts to services and the closure and sale of the London Chest Hospital site for new housing.[24] In other words, PFI projects can appear cost-effective on an accountant's balance sheet and yet be unaffordable to the public sector. Finally, as box 2.1 shows with the example of the London Underground, the most important risk of all – that of a public service failing – remains with the public sector and ultimately the public: should a consortium default on its contractual obligations, the social liabilities are assumed by the taxpayer.

These examples underline the reality that PFI contracts are negotiated, financed and written with a view to insulate the banks as well as the investors who own the SPV from all potential risks. The government effectively promises 30 years of inflation-proofed finance at fixed interest rates, and contractors rarely assume any demand risk because of the social need for the public infrastructure. This guaranteed tap of public finance has led to refinancing scandals where PFI consortia have agreed more favourable lending terms with banks once construction risks have diminished but have continued to receive payments from the public sector at the original higher interest rates. This has created windfall profits that public bodies have struggled to share in. The refinancing of 12 PFI projects between 1999 and 2005 resulted in a £142.6 million

Box 2.1 The London Underground PFI fiasco

Arguably the most high-profile example of PFI failure involved the London Underground. The scheme was launched in 2003, against the opposition of then London Mayor Ken Livingstone. It involved outsourcing the maintenance and renewal of London Underground's deteriorating infrastructure (including rolling stock) to two PFI consortia – Metronet and Tube Lines – for 30 years. Not only did the time and cost of forming the contracts prove far higher than originally anticipated, but the guarantee of risk transfer proved illusory when Metronet, which ran two-thirds of the Underground, was forced into administration (bankruptcy) by unexpected cost overruns. Metronet was subsequently bailed out by the UK government, costing the taxpayer around £2 billion, exposing just how little financial risk had actually been transferred to the private sector. In order for the PFI consortia to borrow private finance to carry out the capital works promised in the contract, the public sector had to agree to guarantee 95 per cent of the consortia's debt finance. Metronet was subsequently brought into public ownership, while Tube Lines was bought out for £312 million in 2010, bringing the 30-year Underground PPP to an end after just seven years.

Source: R. Jupe, 'New Labour, public–private partnerships and rail transport policy', *Economic Affairs*, 29:1 (2009), 24.

gain for the SPVs, compared with just £27.3 million for the public sector.[25] The only real risks for the SPVs and their sub-contractors arise from not meeting their contractual standards and targets, making them liable to financial penalties. However, as I will argue in chapter 5, the chances that non-compliance is discovered are radically minimised in the context of construction industry self-regulation, poorly written contracts and the PFI system of self-monitoring. Even when these risks are realised, PFI investors are shielded in that any financial penalties are passed on to the sub-contractors, and by the legal protections afforded by setting up an SPV, which is a 'bankruptcy-remote entity' that allows its owners to protect their assets in the event of their parent companies going bankrupt, or the SPV itself being exposed to losses from a failing project.[26] In other words, SPVs are effectively finance companies, not set up to deliver works and services, but risk-securitised vehicles for money to flow from public to private bodies. In procurement, risk is amplified and exaggerated to exact the most favourable contract terms from the public sector, but once the contract is operational, the risk is then minimised; it is the difference between the two that represents a major source of financial extraction and value creation that is not recaptured by the public sector.

The scale of profiteering

As I will show in chapter 6 in relation to housing regeneration, PFI has enabled commercial lenders, investors, contractors and consultants to profiteer on the back of the taxpayer, what Nick Hildyard calls 'licensed larceny'.[27] The scale of this profiteering is revealed by the lucrative PFI secondary market and the exit rates of return being earned by the original investors when selling on their shareholdings in SPVs or being taken over by other investors. These equity stakes are usually bought by specialist infrastructure funds – investment vehicles that provide their owners, whether banks, private equity firms, pension funds, insurance companies and even the odd government, with handsome dividend payments. Since 2003 a new phenomenon has taken off in the secondary market for PFI equity, with the creation of major secondary market infrastructure funds that specialise in buying and selling on other infrastructure funds. PFI expert Dexter Whitfield found that between 1998 and 2016, there were 462 transactions involving the direct sale of equity in 1,003 UK PPP/PFI projects worth £10.3 billion, which gave an average annual rate of return of 28.7 per cent. In addition, from 2003 to 2016, 33 secondary market infra-structure funds were either fully or partly sold, involving equity in 1,151 PFI/PPP project companies worth £7.4 billion.[28]

The size of these profits and the trading of equity are in-extricably linked to systematic corporate tax avoidance. Many PFI schemes are owned by companies registered 'offshore', in countries or territories like Jersey, Guernsey, Luxembourg and the Caribbean islands – tax havens as they are more commonly known – where they are normally exempt from paying taxes on income, profit and capital gains.[29] The main investor in the disastrous Barts Health NHS Trust PFI project is Innisfree – a fund management company in the City of London that is majority-owned by Jersey-based Coutts & Co., which in turn is part of RBS Group. Innisfree is now the largest private investor in PFI schemes in the NHS, education and defence accommodation, owning dozens of hospitals and hundreds of schools. It aims to achieve an 8–10 per cent return for its investors – mainly UK pension funds; in 2014/15 its seven directors shared salaries totalling £5.3 million, and its chief executive, David Metter, appeared in the *Sunday Times* Rich List in 2013, with a personal fortune of £82 million.[30] These sales of equity and the takeover of parent companies have generated enormous concentration and power across the PPP sector in the hands of offshore infrastructure funds. As of 2017, offshore funds owned stakes in 546 PFI schemes, amounting to 51.3 per cent of total equity in the PFI programme.[31] The five largest offshore funds – HICL (Guernsey), John Laing Infrastructure Fund (Guernsey), 3i Infrastructure PLC (Jersey), International Public Partnerships Limited (Guernsey) and Bilfinger Berger Global Infrastructure (Luxembourg) – made a total profit of £2.9 billion between 2011 and 2017, on which they paid just 0.47 per cent corporation tax. This represents a potential loss of over £600 million in UK tax revenues had these companies been registered in the UK.[32] When we look at who is investing in and profiting from these offshore infrastructure funds and the PFI schemes they own, we see a small group of private equity firms like Blackrock, commercial banks like Lloyds, RBS, HSBC and HBOS, investment banks like Schroders, and, perversely, even public sector pension funds like that of Transport for London.[33]

Although proponents of PFI accept it is a more expensive way of paying for up-front investment in public services than traditional public borrowing, they maintain that the resulting infrastructure and services still offer better value for money to the taxpayer. However, as this book will show with respect to public housing regeneration, such claims contrast with residents' appalling lived experiences of PFI.

The council housing PFI programme[34]

As outlined in chapter 1, in 2000 the New Labour government launched its Decent Homes programme to bring all public and social rented housing up to a minimum standard by 2010. Instead of allowing local authorities the financial freedoms to meet this target, New Labour made access to the necessary investment conditional on 'choosing' one or more of three demunicipalisation 'options': stock transfer, ALMOs and – the focus of this book – PFI. Between 1998 and 2008, New Labour launched six rounds of competitive bidding for English local authorities to be selected on to its housing PFI programme. Local authorities were asked to send 'expressions of interest' for public housing regeneration schemes that combined meeting the Decent Homes target with a more ambitious regeneration project. In March 1999, the first eight 'Pathfinder' PFI regeneration projects were announced; these were to share a £300 million funding pot. They had been chosen by government as an experimental test-bed to see where PFI could work best in housing, as they represented a diverse range of housing estates and stock types, and of regeneration projects. Later rounds would generate a total of 33 public housing regeneration schemes across England, but geographically concentrated in London, Greater Manchester and West Yorkshire.[35] However, as I will discuss later in this chapter, nationally, only 20 PFI regeneration projects have (eventually) gone ahead (see table 2.1) – the final contract being signed in March 2014 – with the rest either abandoned or culled as part of the Coalition government's decision in 2010 to withdraw promised funding as part of its austerity drive. In total, these 20 schemes represent £1.59 billion capital investment in over 20,000 homes owned by local councils, with contractual payments totalling £5.58 billion over the period 2003 to 2044.

The need for regeneration in Islington, Camden and Lambeth

This book presents evidence from three London local authority case studies of PFI housing regeneration: Islington, Camden and

Table 2.1 Overview of the 20 council housing PFI schemes

Scheme	Date signed	Duration (years)	Capital value (£m)	Total contract value (£m)	Summary	SPV and original main companies involved
Islington street properties PFI-1	1/3/03	30	89.00	356.98	Refurbishes 2,345 homes in Georgian and Victorian street properties across the borough	Partners for Improvement in Islington 1 Ltd (United House, Hyde Housing Association, Bank of Scotland) with Rydon Group
Manchester, Plymouth Grove	1/3/03	30	35.16	162.67	Refurbishes 545 homes and demolishes 436; wider estate remodelling; over 600 new homes for market sale outside of PFI contract	Grove Village Ltd (MJ Gleeson, Manchester and District Housing Association, and Nationwide) with Powerminster Ltd
Reading, North Whitley	31/3/04	30	30.70	211.00	Refurbishes 1,370 homes	Affinity (Reading) Ltd (Southern Housing Group and Windsor & District Housing Association Ltd), with Wates and Nationwide
Leeds, Swarcliffe	31/3/05	30	105.00	271.80	Refurbishes 1,659 homes and demolishes 949 including nine tower blocks in east Leeds; 460 new homes for market sale built on cleared sites outside of PFI contract	Yorkshire Transformations Ltd (Yorkshire Community Housing Ltd, Carillion, Bank of Scotland)
Newham, Canning Town	3/6/05	31	19.40	188.43	Refurbishes 1,237 homes; 108 new social rented homes and 149 for market sale outside of PFI contract	Regenter LCEP Ltd (John Laing and Pinnacle) with Royal Bank of Scotland, Rydon Group, Equion
Sandwell, Hawthorns Fields	1/3/06	26	61.00	211.39	Refurbishes 870 homes, demolishes and re-provides 168; 204 new homes for market sale outside of PFI contract	Riverside Housing Association Ltd with Sumitomo Mitsui Banking Corporation (SMBC) Mansell, Haden
Camden, Chalcots Estate	2/5/06	15	66.18	147.14	Refurbishes and maintains 712 flats in five high-rise blocks built in the late 1960s	Partners for Improvement in Camden Ltd (United House, Bank of Scotland) with Rydon Group

Scheme	Date signed	Duration (years)	Capital value (£m)	Total contract value (£m)	Summary	SPV and original main companies involved
Islington street properties PFI-2	15/9/06	16	153.00	421.32	Refurbishes 4,118 homes in Georgian and Victorian street properties across the borough	Partners for Improvement in Islington 2 Ltd (United House, Hyde Housing Association, Bank of Scotland) with Rydon Group
Oldham, sheltered housing PFI	20/10/06	30	108.00	439.87	Refurbishes 1,354 sheltered housing units, removes 256, builds 99 new homes across Oldham	Oldham Retirement Housing Partnership Ltd (Housing & Care 21) with Allied Irish Bank Group, PRG Bullock Construction Ltd, Calford Seaden
Manchester, Miles Platting	22/3/07	31	84.86	566.83	Refurbishes 1,540 homes, demolishes 660; approximately 1,300 new homes for market sale outside of PFI contract	Renaissance Miles Platting Ltd (Investors in the Community Group, Adactus Housing Association Ltd, Lovell) with Dexia Public Finance Bank
Ashford, Stanhope Estate	14/4/07	30	68.22	129.40	Refurbishes 326 homes, demolishes 302 amid wider estate remodelling, plus 440 new homes outside of PFI contract (a mixture of private and shared ownership, and social rent)	Chrysalis (Stanhope) Limited (Gleeson, Moat Housing Group, Nationwide) with Denne, Powerminster Gleeson Services Ltd
Lewisham, Brockley Housing	4/6/07	20	96.00	297.09	Refurbishes 1,365 council homes and 484 leaseholder dwellings in a mix of multi-storey flats and individual street properties	Regenter B3 Ltd (John Laing and Pinnacle) with SMBC, Higgins Group, Rydon Group
Newham, Forest Gate	2/2/09	21	47.13	174.06	Refurbishes 890 homes (a loss of 17); external works to a further 448 leaseholder homes; new housing for sale and rent outside of PFI contract	Swan Housing Group Ltd with Royal Bank of Scotland, Higgins Group, Axis Europe Ltd
Oldham, Gateways to Oldham	30/11/11	25	77.00	218.53	Refurbishes 322 homes, demolishes 308, builds 320 new council homes; 107 homes for market sale outside of PFI contract	Inspiral Oldham Ltd (John Laing) with Great Places Housing Group, Barclays, Co-operative Bank, Santander, Pinnacle, Wates Group
Kirklees, 'Excellent Homes for Life'	20/12/11	23	74.81	197.44	Demolishes 650 homes, replaces them with 550 new council homes on a number of sites (general needs as well as extra care properties)	JLW Excellent Homes For Life Ltd (John Laing PLC), with Nord/LB, Co-operative Bank / Nationwide, Wates Group, Pinnacle

Scheme	Date signed	Duration (years)	Capital value (£m)	Total contract value (£m)	Summary	SPV and original main companies involved
Lambeth, Myatts Field North	4/5/12	26	80.68	272.38	Demolishes and replaces 305 council homes (including 58 leaseholder), refurbishes 172 homes, estate remodelling, new park and community centre, and a new district heating system	Regenter Myatts Field North Ltd (John Laing and Pinnacle) with Nord/LB / Co-operative Bank / Nationwide, Higgins Group, Rydon Group, E.ON UK PLC
Leeds, Little London/Beeston Holbeck	5/7/13	20	138.00	335.20	Refurbishes 1,222 council homes, demolishes 662 and builds 501 new council homes on two separate Leeds inner-city council estates	Sustainable Communities for Leeds Ltd (Keepmoat, Equitix, Uberior Infrastructure) with bond finance
Salford, "Creating a New Pendleton'	17/9/13	30	80.70	427.33	Refurbishes and remodels 1,253 homes, demolishes 860, including four tower blocks; 1,500 new homes, of which 460 will be 'affordable rent', 950 for market sale, and minimum of 25 units for shared ownership outside of PFI contract	Pendleton Together Operating Ltd (Chevin Housing Association) with Keepmoat and bond finance
Manchester, Brunswick	17/12/13	25	82.57	273.34	Refurbishes 654 existing homes (including reversing 124); demolishes 278 homes; and builds 522 new homes, 300 for market sale and the rest for social rent	S4B Ltd (Equitix, Contour Homes, Galliford Try) with Mears and bond finance
North Tyneside, provision for older people	24/3/14	28	87.94	272.68	Modernises 33 sheltered housing schemes: refurbishes 582 homes, 342 new build homes and demolishes 309	Solutions 4 North Tyneside Ltd (Equitix, Galliford Try) with Morgan Sindall and bond finance

Source: HM Treasury, *Private Finance Initiative and Private Finance 2 Projects: Current Projects as at 31 March 2017* (London: HM Treasury, 2018); author's own data compiled from press releases and individual local authority project documents

Lambeth. Historically speaking, these were three of the largest council house builders and municipal landlords in London and across the UK. The financial straitjacket on councils' housing departments described in chapter 1 meant that by the early 2000s they each faced an enormous repair backlog and large numbers of their homes either immediately failed the government's decency standard or were projected to fail by 2010. In Islington, this amounted to 81 per cent of its 40,000 homes; in Camden, the figure was 91.5 per cent of its 33,000 council homes; and in Lambeth, the 'vast majority' of its 41,726 homes were implicated. New Labour's ongoing financial straitjacket meant that each council faced major funding gaps between the investment needs of the housing stock and the resources available – gaps of £266 million, £204 million and £112 million, respectively.[36]

One reason for these funding gaps was the condition and investment needs of specific kinds of housing. In Islington, the municipalisation and repair of thousands of Victorian and Georgian street properties (figure 2.1) – some dating back to the 18th century – during the 1960s and 1970s posed a particular challenge. A significant proportion were listed buildings or located in conservation areas due to their national architectural and historic significance. Islington housing officers told me that the street properties 'in particular had been really under-maintained … we'd not had enough money to do cyclical works on all of our properties over the years, and the money was generally concentrated on the estates because obviously it's a bit more efficient to do that kind of renovation work'.[37] Street properties thus required 'the greatest investment of any council housing in Islington'.[38] I spoke to a number of tenants (whose names I have changed here, to protect their identity), who told me that leaking roofs, poor insulation, crumbling plasterwork and draughts from rotting sash windows were common. 'Harry', a former tenant (now leaseholder) who had left his previous council estate in the belief that a street property would be better, described the conditions in his ground-floor flat when he moved in during the mid-2000s: 'Every surface was in an appalling state of disrepair, with crumbling walls and ripped wallpaper. I hadn't appreciated the extent of structural disrepair. It was dreadful, shocking.'[39] Another tenant, 'Daisy', had

Figure 2.1 Typical Islington council-owned street properties, 2018[40]
Source: 'Edward'

moved into a street property with her two children in the 1990s under a court order after an arsonist set fire to the block of flats she had been living in. The flat was fine with the exception of the windows: 'we kept telling them that one day the whole frame and the two windows it holds will drop out and fall onto somebody in the street and kill them'.[41]

Camden also had Georgian and Victorian street properties in disrepair, but some of the largest investment needs were to be found on the Chalcots Estate in the Swiss Cottage area, in the north of the borough. Built between 1965 and 1968, the Chalcots

Estate was originally a private high-rise development with four identical 23-storey towers, each hosting three large apartments per floor and targeting the then growing luxury end of the market. It had been initiated by Eton College Estates, the major landowner and developer in the area since 1449, and the towers were named after villages or areas near Eton College – Taplow, Burnham, Bray and Dorney. However, the 1968 Ronan Point disaster badly hit demand for the flats as construction was nearing completion. In the context of severe housing shortages, Camden council decided to buy and convert the four blocks into public rented housing and build a fifth block, of 20 storeys, called Blashford, resulting in 711 council flats. 'Michael', a resident since 1993 who lives on the top floor of one block, remembers how sought-after the flats were when he moved in: 'They were great blocks in one of the most mixed areas of London, just a few minutes from Primrose Hill park, where famous millionaire actors lived alongside ordinary people. It's how urban planning should be: no vast sprawling estates for miles that can become no-go areas, but a total mixed community of townhouses and council blocks'.[42]

However, over the years, residents in the five towers (figure 2.2) increasingly suffered from the poor thermal protection and ventilation provided by the concrete structure and the growing disrepair from decades of minimal maintenance. Apart from the familiar array of leaks and communal services out of order, residents lived with condensation and black fungal mould that was growing behind the paint and plaster inside the concrete; they were freezing cold in the winter months but suffered from overheating in the summer, while subject to constant noise pollution and draughts from the flimsy windows. Michael recalls the conditions:

The Chalcots Estate is on one of the highest points in London and a gust of wind would blow the heat out of the flat in a couple of minutes. The windows all had towels on the ledges and in winter they would be coated with condensation. Rainwater would also get under the old aluminium single-glazed sash window that over time had lost their rubber blades. I had to silicon around the window frames every few years to help keep the rain out. The door entry-phone system had stopped working and I remember an elderly neighbour who lived on the 22nd floor going out in the

Figure 2.2 A view of the Chalcots Estate, 1988
Source: Prof. Miles Glendinning, http://www.towerblock.eca.ed.ac.uk/

middle of a winter's night to wait for the doctor coming to see her
very ill husband because people would often wedge the doors open,
leading to the lifts being routinely vandalised and left out of order.[43]

Lambeth also faced major disrepair and structural problems on
some of its post-war estates. One of these was the MFN estate
(figure 2.3). Located one mile north of Brixton town centre, the
estate was built in phases over the mid-1970s and early 1980s
as part of a slum clearance and redevelopment programme.
In contrast to the fashion for high-rise blocks that produced
the Chalcots Estate, Lambeth's chief architect 1962–81, Ted
Hollamby, who was a passionate believer in council housing, had
designed a low-rise urban village that catered for all ages, household sizes and disabled people. The result was a mixture of tightly

Figure 2.3 Myatts Field North estate in May 2012, just before the PFI scheme
Source: Author

packed houses, bungalows and two- to four-storey apartment blocks with underneath lock-up garages, set out in cul-de-sacs to prevent through-traffic, with accompanying shops, a nursery, a pub and a health centre. Each home enjoyed heating and hot water from the estate's district heating system. The layout allowed the maximum number of rooms to look out on to the resulting 11 acres of landscaped and child-friendly open amenity space.[44] The estate quickly became home to an ethnically diverse working-class community strongly rooted in the African Caribbean culture of Brixton's post-war migrants. 'Gillian', who moved to the estate in the early 1980s, fondly remembered the early years of this innovative and green estate, very different from the Rachmanite conditions previously evident in Brixton: 'It was structurally sound and home to a good community. We all knew our neighbours, especially where I was, because we'd all been there a long time, and all of our kids grew up together. We used to look after each other and go on day trips.'[45]

Decades of lack of investment, however, turned manageable structural defects and design flaws into chronic dampness from water leaking through the internal guttering and pipes that were difficult to locate. The interleaving of homes had led to poor sound insulation, the district heating system was dogged by poor reliability and an absence of individual controls, the underground garages had been taken out of use soon after construction due to safety concerns, and the various play areas and green amenity spaces had been allowed to deteriorate, becoming unpopular and under-used. The estate's physical decline went hand in hand with growing social problems that saw it increasingly stigmatised in the press due to gang violence, which gave the estate the name 'Baghdad' and nearly cost Gillian her life: 'It was difficult at times: we had violence, guns, gangs, drugs. One day a stray bullet from a shootout came through my front door, just missing us.'[46] In 1993, Lambeth won an £11 million government grant to remodel the estate's three spine blocks but rising construction costs pushed the bill to £17 million. In the end, only the smallest block was improved and over 300 homes were left untouched, apart from being disconnected from the failing district heating system in favour of individual gas boilers.

Consultation without choice – PFI as 'the only game in town'

Islington, Camden and Lambeth pursued similar strategies to meet the Decent Homes investment gap. They each decided to set up an ALMO to unlock a greater permitted amount of borrowing needed to repair and modernise the majority of their council homes, knowing that wholesale stock transfer would likely be rejected in a ballot. In the end, Camden's ALMO never got off the ground, due to tenant opposition. This was supplemented by the stock transfer of some estates to housing associations: in Lambeth, six estates were subject to stock transfer, although two were defeated by tenant 'no' votes.[47] Finally, they earmarked the aforementioned housing stocks – Islington's street properties, Camden's Chalcots Estate and Lambeth's MFN estate – for PFI, which required a much larger amount of investment than the ALMO route could provide and would be deemed too risky for a housing association to take on – PFI was 'the only game in town'. One Islington housing officer told me that while the council did not 'necessarily buy into PFI as a concept' it was being 'realistic and pragmatic'.[48]

Inevitably, the controversial use of PFI in public services and the NHS outlined earlier in this chapter filtered down to some of the estates where councils opted for PFI to improve homes. A number of proposed schemes – including those featured here – were met by anti-PFI campaigns by councillors, residents' groups and trade unions, who viewed PFI as backdoor privatisation that would casualise housing workers, raise rents to pay for the profits of banks and investors, while draining councils' repair and main-tenance budgets. Many residents did not want their homes and communities to be a testing ground for commercial exploitation, and were alarmed at the scale of demolition and private develop-ment involved. However, with no statutory right to a ballot, campaigners found it hard to mobilise opposition, as councils stuck to the disingenuous line that PFI was 'the only game in town' for repairing homes, was not privatisation *per se* (as the council remained the legal landlord) and rents would not rise even when their PFI financial models depended on it. When campaigners looked like they were starting to gain support, councils resorted to using the magic mantra of PFI – that the public sector would be able to force the private contractors to deliver high-quality work and services through the threat of fines for poor performance.

On the rare occasion when campaigns did manage to secure a voluntary ballot, councils did everything possible to secure a 'yes' vote, warning tenants that if they voted 'no' there would be no other source of investment and stock transfer would be the only alternative, as the Labour government had made very clear. When a majority of tenants still voted 'no', their views were effectively disregarded, as happened on the Little London estate in Leeds in 2002. A senior Labour councillor who had been serving at the time told me that despite promising to respect the result, the council could not afford to lose such a massive amount of money, and so removed from the scheme a portion of the homes that had voted 'no' and re-ran the ballot, getting a 'yes':

> We just wouldn't have been able to do anything down there without that money – and there should never have been a ballot, there was no requirement for one – and so it was clear that we had to try again.... I took the view that we had to get the money in and look after the long-term future for that estate ... and face down the opponents. It might be a bit paternalistic but that's essentially the job we've got to do.[49]

In Islington, although the incumbent Liberal Democrat council was officially opposed to PFI, it resisted the campaign by the now defunct Federation of Islington Tenants Associations (FITA) for residents to have a binding ballot on PFI on the grounds that there was simply no alternative. Council leader at the time, Steve Hitchens, told the local press: 'I have asked FITA what they would like us to put on a ballot paper. Perhaps it could be stay as we are, rotting in hell, or go for PFI and see homes improved'.[50] FITA's former chair, Dr Brian Potter, recalls the undemocratic consultation process:

> The consultation meetings were designed not to be attended. One meeting was in a tiny little office. I said to them, 'How can you expect people to come here? There's no transport, there's no lighting, it's dangerous and you are starting it at 6 p.m. in the evening.' They picked the places where people couldn't or wouldn't go to, times that they couldn't or wouldn't attend. It was all very deliberate.[51]

Once the decision to go ahead had been made, government expected councils to involve elected residents' representatives in every stage of the PFI process, with as much access as possible to the project documentation. However, meaningful consultation was near impossible as councils were under no legal obligation to listen. Government provided funding for residents to be supported through the process by so-called 'independent tenant advisors' (ITAs), but their neutrality was highly dubious and in some places they were clearly contracted by the council to deliver residents' acquiescence to the council's preferred option. Residents' access to key contractual information was routinely blocked on 'commercial confidentiality' grounds. There were numerous examples of residents being told that unless they signed a confidentiality agreement, they would be not be permitted to join the councils' 'steering groups' that would develop the eventual regeneration scheme. Danny Moriati, a tenant representative from Kirklees, recalls the chilling effect on residents' democratic structures:

> we were told, whatever you hear, whatever you see, in here now, is confidential. The officers couldn't even tell the councillors what was going on: it was really secretive. In the tenants' organisation we all report back on everything, everything we do; even if I went down to the local church for a meeting, I'd send a report in about it. But I never spoke about the PFI meetings. I was representing at that time 25,000 tenants but none of them knew, and it was so annoying to people – they couldn't understand why I wouldn't say anything. You end up in a situation with the burden of making the decisions because you can't ask anyone else what they think, and it opens up the danger that you could end up with somebody being a 'yes' person, a tool in the hands of the contractors.[52]

Regeneration or gentrification?

The second point of controversy has been the nature of regeneration itself under PFI. New Labour's overarching policy approach, unveiled in 1999 by the Urban Task Force, was branded *Towards an Urban Renaissance*. Influenced by the high-density, mixed-income urban communities of continental Europe, Labour's vision was most notable for its unabashed gentrification ambition of 'bringing the middle classes back to the city'.[53] Although New Labour never formally defined what it meant by 'regeneration', in policy and practical terms its agenda was unambiguously clear: top-down gentrification projects aimed at replacing spatial concentrations of so-called 'mono-tenure' social housing with 'mixed and balanced communities' by increasing the proportion of middle-class owner-occupiers and the amount of private housing for sale. The discourse of decline and regeneration implicitly and in some cases explicitly stigmatised the residents and architecture of public housing estates, most notably post-war inner-urban estates characterised by brutalist design, targeting them for demolition, remodelling and redevelopment.[54]

After the first schemes had seen contracts signed from the PFI Pathfinder round, which was mainly focused on refurbishment-only schemes, New Labour told local authorities that successful bids for PFI funding would now have to bring about 'mixed developments' and 'tenure diversification'.[55] Local authorities were financially incentivised to engage in this gentrification approach by the complex financial model devised to pay for their housing PFI scheme. While government provided an annual subsidy ('PFI credits') to cover the capital costs of the scheme, the remainder of the contract had to be financed from the local authority's own resources. However, as the government's subsidy was normally fixed prior to the procurement of a PFI contractor, local authorities had to guarantee to plug any financial holes should the cost of the contract increase during procurement. They also had to design regeneration schemes that would actively *reduce* the risks to be transferred to the private sector, so as to increase both commercial attractiveness and public sector affordability. This difficult balancing act was heightened by the fluctuating forecasts during the procurement process of future interest, retail and wage inflation rates, swap deals, and construction costs that often increased the cost of the PFI scheme before it had even started.

Remodelling council estates as part of tenure diversification strategies thus came with the incentive of generating a local funding stream additional to the council's HRA. This incentivised councils to design schemes that released the most developer-attractive and financially valuable land parcels for private housing while simultaneously demolishing housing associated with the greatest long-term risks of physical 'viability' (higher maintenance costs) and social 'attractiveness' (i.e. so-called 'undesirable tenants' who might put a dampener on property prices). Out of the 15 housing PFI regeneration schemes that involved demolition, nine involved a net loss of public or social housing amounting to 3,676 fewer secure, affordable and decent homes. These demolitions in turn created space for over 4,500 new homes for market sale, and in four council estates turned public housing into a minority tenure.[56] Evidence from several PFI regeneration schemes suggests the main outcome has been support for buy-to-let investors rather than for low-income first-time buyers.

Affordability gaps and delays

According to government guidelines, PFI schemes should have taken three years to start from being selected onto the PFI programme.[57] However, as table 2.2 shows, all housing PFI schemes took far longer than expected to start, and have cost far more than originally budgeted for. The average delay was over three and half years from the original target start date, reaching up to nine years late in the Little London scheme in Leeds. The delays in housing PFI procurement in turn engendered enormous capital cost increases to approved business plans, ranging from 55 per cent (Stanhope Estate, Ashford) to 338 per cent (Swarcliffe, Leeds), mainly because of high construction cost inflation between 2002 and 2007.[58] All the time, the councils and the winning SPV were paying private sector consultants to advise them, racking up the overall bill even further. With the PFI companies' and banks' profit margins protected, the higher costs were either met by increased public spending, or by reducing costs. Eleven out of the 20 PFI housing regeneration projects saw their planned 30-year contracts reduced in length, including the Islington, Camden and Lambeth schemes. Local authorities were forced to 're-scope' the output specification to reduce the overall costs. Cost-cutting involved removing key parts of the contract or engaging in so-called 'value engineering', which is an industry euphemism for using cheaper materials and systems than originally specified. As we saw in chapter 1, it was 'value engineering' that turned Grenfell's cladding from fire-safe to flammable. In housing PFI schemes, any higher costs that could not be cut usually became the responsibility of the local authority to finance, placing it under constant pressure to 'transfer resources from other parts of the housing budget to pay for its PFI obligations'.[59] For example, the cost of Oldham's sheltered housing PFI scheme contributed to a

Table 2.2 Comparison of pre-contract delays and cost inflation in the 20 council housing PFI schemes

Scheme	Date signed	Contract value (nominal £m)	Delay (months)	Cost increase (%)
Islington street properties PFI-1	1/3/03	356.98	12	275
Manchester, Plymouth Grove	1/3/03	162.67	25	131
Reading, North Whitley	31/3/04	211.00	28	79
Leeds, Swarcliffe	31/3/05	271.80	41	338
Newham, Canning Town	3/6/05	188.43	47	100
Sandwell, Hawthorns Fields	1/3/06	211.39	53	97
Camden, Chalcots Estate	2/5/06	147.14	52	117
Islington street properties PFI-2	15/9/06	421.32	33	200
Oldham, sheltered housing PFI	20/10/06	439.87	36	160
Manchester, Miles Platting	22/3/07	566.83	48	195
Ashford, Stanhope Estate	14/4/07	129.40	36	55
Lewisham, Brockley Housing	4/6/07	297.09	44	164
Newham, Forest Gate	2/2/09	174.06	61	150
Oldham, Gateways to Oldham	30/11/11	218.53	31	n/a
Kirklees, 'Excellent Homes for Life'	20/12/11	197.44	57	n/a
Lambeth, Myatts Field North	4/5/12	272.38	49	100
Leeds, Little London/Beeston Holbeck	5/7/13	335.20	108/42	n/a
Salford, 'Creating a New Pendleton'	17/9/13	427.33	30	n/a
Manchester, Brunswick	17/12/13	273.34	45	n/a
North Tyneside, provision for older people	24/3/14	272.68	45	n/a

Source: National Audit Office, *PFI in Housing* (London: The Stationery Office, 2010); author's own data collected from local authority reports; HM Treasury, *Private Finance Initiative and Private Finance 2 Projects: Current Projects as at 31 March 2017* (London: HM Treasury, 2018)

£4 million cut in annual expenditure in 2006/07, leading to 40 staff being made redundant and a number of area offices closing.[60] The other outcome, as we will see with respect to the MFN estate in chapter 4, has been increasing the amount of private residential development to help plug growing affordability gaps.

The particular complexities of housing regeneration under PFI were spectacularly exposed by the 2008 global financial crisis, which had a crippling effect on both affordability and the availability of private finance. The collapse in the housing market in turn rendered any business plans depending on land sales and private development unviable. All unsigned PFI schemes suffered major delays because they had to be re-scoped, and had their financial models de-coupled from planned private developments that in most cases were postponed 'until the market returns'. Some projects were then hit again by the post-2010 austerity project that saw the Coalition government conduct a 'value for money' review of unsigned PFI projects, resulting in eight projects being cancelled and others having to find savings in government subsidy costs of between 10 and 16 per cent. In some places private housing was dramatically increased to plug financial holes, while in other places it was dramatically decreased or removed altogether due to the housing market collapse. In other words, residents paid either by getting less of what they had been promised, or by getting more of what they did not want, namely higher numbers of buy-to-let housing on their estates.

Conclusion

This chapter has set out the origins of the PFI public housing regeneration programme under New Labour. It has shown that the PFI model of outsourced regeneration involves an unnecessarily expensive method of private financing, justified by a dubious discourse of 'value for money'. While PFI advocates vociferously deny that PFI is privatisation of public services because the frontline services remain free at the point of use and the teachers, doctors, librarians and so on remain public sector workers, PFI in housing regeneration is privatisation in all but name. The

residents concerned must now deal on a day-to-day basis with
for-profit private companies operating in what is effectively a
private monopoly, providing most if not all the frontline housing
services in return for their rents and service charges. While PFI
does not involve a change of landlord or owner, it clearly represents a profound qualitative shift in the provision, governance
and accountability of council housing services, and arguably
erodes residents' statutory rights. And while these companies
might have to meet performance targets each month, they are
driven by one objective only – to minimise their costs in doing so
in order to maximise their profits from the contract. As we shall
see, this commercial imperative can have terrible consequences for
people's lives.

Notes

1 H. Champ, 'At least 60 firms involved in Grenfell Tower refurb',
   Building, 29 June 2017, at https://www.building.co.uk/news/at-least-
   60-firms-involved-in-grenfell-tower-refurb/5088495.article (accessed 13
   October 2018); L. Barratt, 'Police investigation reveals 383 companies
   were involved in Grenfell refurbishment', *Inside Housing*, 11 December
   2017, at https://www.insidehousing.co.uk/news/news/police-investigation-
   reveals-383-companies-were-involved-in-grenfell-refurbishment-53557
   (accessed 13 October 2018).
2 Interview with civil servant involved in the housing PFI programme, 19
   March 2010.
3 D. Whitfield, *Public Services or Corporate Welfare: Rethinking the Nation
   State in the Global Economy* (London: Pluto Press, 2001), p. 196.
4 D. Kerr, 'The Private Finance Initiative and the changing governance of the
   built environment', *Urban Studies*, 35:12 (1998), 2277–2301.
5 M. Harrison, 'Shake-up for the Private Finance Initiative', *Independent*,
   23 June 1997, at https://www.independent.co.uk/news/business/shake-up-
   for-private-finance-initiative-1257604.html (accessed 13 October 2018);
   A. Murdoch, 'Invaluable perspectives – Chris Elliott', Project Finance
   International website (no date), at http://www.pfie.com/invaluable-
   perspectives-chris-elliott/21071331.fullarticle (accessed 13 October 2018).
6 P. Foot, 'P. F. Eye. "An idiot's guide to the Private Finance Initiative"',
   Private Eye (no date), at http://www.private-eye.co.uk/pictures/special_
   reports/pf-eye.pdf (accessed 13 October 2018).
7 HM Treasury, Memorandum to Select Committee on Treasury, Uncorrected
   evidence (2000), at https://publications.parliament.uk/pa/cm199900/cm
   select/cmtreasy/uc147/uc14702.htm (accessed 13 October 2018).

8   BBC Radio 4, Transcript of *File on 4*, Current Affairs Group, Programme n. 04VY3027LHO, 6 July 2004, at http://news.bbc.co.uk/nol/shared/bsp/hi/pdfs/fileon4_20040706_pfi.pdf (accessed 13 October 2018).

9   J. Benjamin, 'PFI is a failed Treasury policy', Bella Caledonia website, 19 May 2016, at https://bellacaledonia.org.uk/2016/05/19/pfi-is-a-failed-treasury-policy (accessed 13 October 2018). In 2009, PUK took joint ownership of 4Ps and it was rebranded Local Partnerships; in 2011, Local Partnerships was disbanded.

10 UK HM Treasury, 'Private Finance Initiative and Private Finance 2 projects: current projects as at 31 March 2017, UK government website, 2018, at https://www.gov.uk/government/publications/private-finance-initiative-and-private-finance-2-projects-2017-summary-data (accessed 13 October 2018); this figure excludes the dozens of expired PFI projects, the 31 schemes that have been subject to public sector buy-outs and early terminations, and the Scottish government's variant model of PFI misleadingly called the Non-Profit Distribution scheme, which merely caps the profits made by the private financiers behind a contract.

11 Most PFI debt is recorded as 'off balance sheet' under the European system of accounts (ESA), which determines the official levels of public sector net borrowing and net debt. In contrast, the International Financial Reporting Standards (IFRS) classify most PFI debt as 'on balance sheet'.

12 For an excellent explanation of the PFI financing scam, see the booklet by Helen Mercer, *The Private Finance Initiative (PFI): How Come We're Still Paying For This?* (London: People versus PFI, 2017), at http://peoplevspfi.org.uk/exhibition-how-come-were-still-paying-for-this (accessed 13 October 2018).

13 A. Pettifor, *The Production of Money: How to Break the Power of the Banks* (London: Verso, 2017).

14 Senior debt is usually secured against the assets of the borrower and takes priority over unsecured or more junior debt owed by the borrower should it go bankrupt or enter liquidation.

15 L. Booth and V. Starodubtseva, 'PFI costs and benefits', House of Commons Library Briefing Paper No. 6007, 13 May 2015, at http://researchbriefings.files.parliament.uk/documents/SN06007/SN06007.pdf (accessed 13 October 2018).

16 National Audit Office, *The Choice of Finance for Capital Investment* (London: National Audit Office, March 2015), p. 36, at https://www.nao.org.uk/wp-content/uploads/2015/03/The-choice-of-finance-for-capital-investment.pdf (accessed 13 October 2018).

17 M. Cuthbert and J. Cuthbert, 'The effect of PFI commitments on local authority finances', *Fraser of Allander Economic Commentary*, 34:3 (2011), 53–62.

18 Mott MacDonald, *Review of Large Public Procurement in the UK* (Croydon: Mott MacDonald, July 2002).

19 For the best analysis of how the VFM analysis works, see the work of Jean Shaoul, in particular: J. Shaoul, 'A critical financial analysis of the Private Finance Initiative: selecting a financing method or allocating economic wealth?', *Critical Perspectives on Accounting*, 16:4 (2005), 441–471.

20 J. Owen, 'Exclusive: £8k for a blind, £2 for a tap; the true cost of PFI', *TES News*, 21 April 2017, at https://www.tes.com/news/exclusive-ps8k-blind-ps2k-tap-true-cost-pfi (accessed 13 October 2018).

21 National Audit Office, *PF1 and PFI2*, HC 718 Session 2017–2019 (London: National Audit Office, 2018), at https://www.nao.org.uk/wp-content/uploads/2018/01/PFI-and-PF2.pdf (accessed 13 October 2018); National Audit Office, *Review of the VFM Assessment Process for PFI* (London: National Audit Office, October 2013), at https://www.nao.org.uk/wp-content/uploads/2014/01/Review-of-VFM-assessment-process-for-PFI1.pdf (accessed 13 October 2018).

22 Interview with PFI advisor 1 (major global law firm), 18 March 2010.

23 A. Pollock, J. Shaoul and N. Vickers, 'Private finance and value for money in NHS hospitals: a policy in search of a rationale?', *British Medical Journal*, 324 (2002), 1205–1209.

24 J. Lister, 'Bart's: a flagship hits the rocks of PFI', Open Democracy website, 18 March 2015, at https://www.opendemocracy.net/ournhs/john-lister/bart per centE2 per cent80 per cent99s-flagship-hits-rocks-of-pfi (accessed 14 October 2018).

25 D. Whitfield, *Financing Infrastructure in the 21st Century: The Long Term Impacts of Public Private Partnerships in Britain and Australia*, Dunstan Paper 2 (Newcastle upon Tyne: Sustainable Cities Research Institute, Northumbria University, 2007), p. 8, at https://european-services-strategy.org.uk.archived.website/outsourcing-ppp-library/pfi-ppp/financing-infrastructure-21st-century/finance-infrastructure.pdf (accessed 14 October 2018).

26 Blossom Wealth Management, 'Understanding the complexities of the special purpose vehicle', Blossom Wealth Management website, 3 April 2015, at http://www.blossomwm.com/understanding-the-complexities-of-the-special-purpose-vehicle/ (accessed 14 October 2018); H. Mercer and D. Whitfield, *Nationalising Special Purpose Vehicles to End PFI: A Discussion of the Costs and Benefits* (London: Public Services International Research Unit (PSIRU), April 2018), at http://gala.gre.ac.uk/20016/1/20016%20_MERCER_Nationalising_Special_Purpose_Vehicles_to_End_PFI%20_2018.pdf (accessed 14 October 2018).

27 N. Hildyard, *Licensed Larceny: Infrastructure, Financial Extraction and the Global South* (Manchester: Manchester University Press, 2016).

28 D. Whitfield, *The Financial Commodification of Public Infrastructure*, Research Report No. 8 (Tralee: European Services Strategy Unit, October 2016), at https://www.european-services-strategy.org.uk/wp-content/uploads/2017/01/financial-commodification-public-infrastructure.pdf (accessed 14 October 2018).

29 *Ibid.*

30 J. Dickens, 'PFI Firms: the low-key investment firm that owns 260 UK schools', *Schools Week*, 4 March 2016, at https://schoolsweek.co.uk/the-low-key-investment-firm-that-owns-260-uk-schools (accessed 14 October 2018).

31 Mercer and Whitfield, *Nationalising Special Purpose Vehicles to End PFI*.

32 D. Whitfield, 'New evidence of the scale of UK PFI/PPP equity offshoring and tax avoidance', European Services Strategy Unit website, 27 October 2017, at https://www.european-services-strategy.org.uk/news/2017/new-evidence-of-the-scale-of-uk-pfippp-equity-offshoring-and-tax-avoidance (accessed 14 October 2018).

33 Whitfield, *The Financial Commodification of Public Infrastructure*.

34 This discussion extends and updates research originally published in 2011: S. Hodkinson, 'The Private Finance Initiative in English council housing regeneration: a privatisation too far?', *Housing Studies*, 26:6 (2011), 911–932.

35 These are schemes for public housing owned by local authorities and funded within their housing revenue account (HRA). A further 20 housing PFI schemes were selected for non-HRA projects that involved social housing owned and managed by housing associations – three of these were also cancelled. I focus only on HRA schemes in this book.

36 London Borough of Islington, *Housing Strategy: 2004–07* (London: London Borough of Islington, 2002), at https://democracy.islington.gov.uk/Data/Council/200207231930/Agenda/$Report%20Appendix%201%20-%20Housing%20Strategy%20Statement%20and%20Business%20Plan%202003-2004.doc.pdf (accessed 12 December 2018); London Borough of Camden, *Housing Strategy: 2005–2010* (London: London Borough of Camden), cached version at https://webcache.googleusercontent.com/search?q=cache:ev4_NjYYqOUJ:https://www.camden.gov.uk/ccm/cms-service/stream/asset/Housing%2520Strategy.pdf%3Fasset_id%3D363143+&cd=2&hl=en&ct=clnk&gl=uk (accessed 12 December 2018); Lambeth Housing, *Lambeth Housing Revenue Account Business Plan 2003/04* (London: London Borough of Lambeth, 2002), at https://moderngov.lambeth.gov.uk/Data/Executive%20(replaced%20by%20the%20Cabinet%20on%2024-05-06)/20020930/Agenda/Report%20-%20Housing%20Investment%20Programme%20-%20HIP2%20-%2030-09-2002.pdf (accessed 14 October 2018).

37 Interview with Islington council housing officers, 11 June 2013.

38 London Borough of Islington, *Islington PFI 2 Housing Scheme: Invitation to Negotiate. Instructions and Guidance to Bidders* (London: London Borough of Islington, May 2004), at https://www.whatdotheyknow.com/request/182187/response/455653/attach/2/INVITATION%20TO%20NEGOTIATE%20PFI%20R2%20REDACTED%202013.pdf (accessed 16 October 2018).

39 Interview with 'Harry', Islington leaseholder, 10 June 2013.

40 This photograph was taken by 'Edward', an Islington tenant featured in chapter 3. It is reproduced here with his permission, along with figures 3.1 and 5.1.

41 Interview with 'Daisy', Islington tenant, 3 June 2013.

42 Interview with 'Michael', Camden leaseholder, 1 August 2018.

43 *Ibid.*

44 London Borough of Lambeth, *Myatts Field North Development: Phases 2, 3, 4 and 6* (London: London Borough of Lambeth, 1974).

45 Interview with 'Gillian', Lambeth tenant, 9 March 2015.

46 *Ibid.*
47 P. Watt, 'Housing stock transfers, regeneration and state-led gentrification in London', *Urban Policy and Research*, 27:3 (2009), 229–242.
48 Interview with Islington housing officers, 11 June 2013.
49 Interview with Leeds city council senior councillor, 11 December 2008; see also S. Hodkinson 'Housing regeneration and the Private Finance Initiative in England: unstitching the neoliberal urban straitjacket', *Antipode*, 43:2 (2011), 358–383.
50 Staff reporter 'Islington picks PFI after transfer opposition', *Inside Housing*, 9 July 2001.
51 Interview with Dr Brian Potter, Chair of Islington Leaseholders Association, 3 June 2013.
52 Interview with Danny Moriati, Kirklees Federation of Tenants and Residents Associations, 3 August 2012.
53 M. Davidson, 'Spoiled mixture: where does state-led "positive" gentrification end?', *Urban Studies*, 45:12 (2008), 2387–2405.
54 L. Lees, 'The urban injustices of New Labour's "new urban renewal": the case of the Aylesbury Estate in London', *Antipode*, 46:4 (2013), 921–947; P. Watt, 'Social housing and regeneration in London', in R. Imrie, L. Lees and M. Raco (eds), *Regenerating London* (London: Routledge, 2009).
55 Office of the Deputy Prime Minister, *Private Finance Initiative Schemes for HRA/Non-HRA Housing: Guidance for Authorities Making Proposals* (London: The Stationery Office, 2005), pp. 11–12.
56 Author's calculations from analysing individual local authority project documents.
57 Office of the Deputy Prime Minister and 4Ps, *Housing PFI Procurement Pack* (London: The Stationery Office, 2004).
58 National Audit Office, *PFI in Housing* (London: The Stationery Office, 2010).
59 R. Hodges and S. Grubnic, 'Public policy transfer: the case of PFI in housing', *International Journal of Public Policy*, 1:1–2 (2005), 63.
60 M. Hilditch, 'Leading ALMOs forced to make cuts', *Inside Housing*, 8 December 2006.

3   Partners for improvement?
Corporate vandalism in Islington
and Camden

Having seen how the PFI public housing regeneration programme emerged under New Labour after 1997, this chapter tells the story of residents' experiences of PFI schemes in the neighbouring north London boroughs of Islington and Camden. In Islington, PFI was selected as the regeneration vehicle for the thousands of street properties in the borough municipalised during the 1960s and 1970s, with the works divided into two separate contracts: PFI-1, which started in 2003; and PFI-2, which began in 2006. Meanwhile, Camden chose PFI for its five tower blocks on the Chalcots Estate, which had been municipalised in 1968 following the Ronan Point disaster. Although very different in nature, the Islington street properties and Camden Chalcots Estate were both victims of the destructive impact of Thatcherism, which had turned often manageable problems into a cycle of decline and despair. The eventual PFI contracts for these schemes had another important feature in common – they were awarded to the same PFI contractor, Partners for Improvement, led by United House and the Bank of Scotland. The chapter takes each scheme in turn, beginning with Islington, and discusses the refurbishment projects outsourced to the PFI consortium, before recounting residents' terrible experiences at the hands of both the private companies involved and the local authorities they had been contracted by.

Islington PFI: vandalising heritage while devastating lives

In March 2003, Islington signed the first of its two housing PFI schemes: a 30-year contract worth £350 million with the SPV,

Partners for Improvement in Islington Ltd (henceforth 'Partners'). PFI-1 had taken four years from being selected onto the government's Pathfinder programme, but was officially the first PFI council housing regeneration scheme in England to begin. Partners was owned by a consortium of three investors: United House, which would undertake the major refurbishment works; Hyde Housing Association, which would manage the lettings and rent collection; and the Bank of Scotland, which provided the senior debt finance. Partners also sub-contracted Rydon to provide responsive repairs and cyclical maintenance. The PFI-1 contract would inject some £50 million of investment into 2,348 homes (including 445 leaseholders in RTB properties) in Georgian and Victorian buildings peppered across the borough. For tenants, the main works comprised the installation of new heating, kitchens, bathrooms and electrics, some internal redecoration, together with refurbishment of the building fabric through damp proofing, major structural repairs, external roof works, wall repairs and decoration, and any other works necessary to meet the Decent Homes standard. As leaseholders were responsible for maintaining the inside of their homes, leasehold properties would only receive external works, with major repair bills capped at £10,000 every five years.

Problems from inception

Within just months of Partners taking over the housing from Islington, the post bags of local councillors, Islington's Labour MPs Jeremy Corbyn and Emily Thornberry, and the influential *Islington Tribune* newspaper began filling up with terrifying refurbishment tales from residents. 'Daisy', whose home was one of the first to have PFI refurbishment works, in 2004, was one of them:

> It was horrible. The contractors hired a load of people that didn't speak English – somebody told me they were only getting £30 a day. They put a nail through a water pipe and brought the ceiling down from the bathroom to the living room, smashing a cabinet along the way, which they refused to compensate. They linked all the lights together so when you come in all the downstairs lights turn

on – they never came back to fix that. They put the wrong sealant around the bath, so it became mouldy and the guy who was mixing the cement was throwing it down the toilet, meaning it got blocked. It was clear that they had bought up a load of bankrupt stock and just dumped it on us. They put in smaller radiators that don't heat the house up any more and the kitchen lino scars and looks really bad with streaks and skid marks on it. I didn't have the lime scale problems in my old bath that I have with the one they fitted. The kitchen cupboard doors were blowing after less than 12 months but Partners would not replace them saying 'that's down to you', but the stock doesn't exist any more. They left behind so many repair and maintenance problems that became my responsibility under the terms of my tenancy agreement.[1]

The staggering level of complaints so early in the PFI-1 scheme led the council to employ its own inspector, Consul Chartered Surveyors, in November 2004 to independently investigate. Consul visited 24 homes formally signed off by United House and then by the so-called 'independent certifier', Faithorn Farrell Timms (FFT), as meeting the Decent Homes standard and for which Partners was now receiving the full payments for meeting the 'availability standards' (see chapter 2). As we will see in chapter 6, FFT was in fact employed by Partners, and a former Partners' employee I interviewed alleged that FFT was signing off homes as meeting the required contract specification without conducting proper inspections.[2] Consul was shocked at the poor quality of finished works, standards of health and safety on site, and the lack of care and protection of residents' property. There was 'no consistency of quality design in the kitchen layouts', with kitchen drawer fronts and doors 'misaligned', sink tops so badly fitted they could be 'pushed up from below', and electrical fittings such as thermostat controls and sockets 'very loose'. The wrong screws had been used to fix the toilets in place and were 'rusting or had not been screwed down correctly'. In many cases electrical cables connected to boilers were not chased into plasterwork and were in contact with hot pipes, 'giving rise to obvious safety concerns'. United House's sub-contractors 'caused excessive damage to floor boards, walls, ceilings, skirting boards etc. as well as personal items and furniture' and 'much of the redecoration compensation was used to make good this damage'. The vast majority of homes took at least three months – not the promised 30 days – to finish. All of the residents Consul spoke to said 'that if they had realised what they would have to go through during the course of work inside their homes, they would never have allowed the contractor to commence work'.[3]

Partners accepted most of the findings, placed a moratorium on any further work and forced United House to introduce an action plan to put things right. New measures included return site inspections when complaints about sub-standard works were raised, compensation to tenants when work was delayed, and a new, stricter code of conduct, which its workers had to follow. The managing director of Partners and other directors from United House abruptly left amid allegations of fraud. 'Frank', an Islington leaseholder, remembers that the scheme 'was in horrendous trouble … they paid off all that original contracting crew in December and then hired a new team'.[4] The council leader at the time, Steve Hitchins, sought to reassure residents that all would turn out well, telling them in March 2005:

> We've been aware there were problems and the council is monitoring the contract closely. We've put procedures in place to make sure tenants and leaseholders get value for money. I'm convinced that at the end there will be a high-quality improvement to people's homes.[5]

Unfortunately for some residents, the work done by Partners and United House did not get better – it got far, far worse. 'Edward' and his family moved into their early 1800s grade II listed Georgian terraced street property sited in the Barnsbury Conservation Area of Islington at the beginning of the 1990s: 'It was beautiful on the outside but inside it had been neglected over the years by Islington and needed a lot of TLC to make it homely'.[6] As a self-employed builder and carpenter, Edward undertook a significant amount of repair and improvement work and regarded it as largely free of disrepair. He personally restored many of the home's historic features and replaced the dilapidated kitchen units with a bespoke kitchen.

By the summer of 2005, 15 years after Edward and family moved in, Partners and United House began conducting surveys of all council-owned houses in his street ahead of refurbishment under PFI. In this close-knit neighbourhood, word quickly spread of resident disquiet with how these surveys and the works that followed were being undertaken. 'So I carried out my own survey of nearby tenants who had scaffolding outside their homes and horrific stories emerged.' Edward's neighbours complained of 'children's beds falling through floorboards during the works, front doors left open, incompetent workers, damage to possessions, severe distress, and people going to the doctors to be treated for anxiety'. These experiences mirrored the high-profile problems affecting the scheme and regularly appearing in the local press. Edward took his survey findings to the Partners PFI Residents Forum, which met every few months in Islington town hall. He raised concerns about the potential impact of the planned works on his severely mentally disabled son and sought specific assurances about health and safety. In total, more than a dozen pre-work talks and meetings were held with Partners to agree an efficient and safe schedule and conduct of work. However, just two days after work finally started, in September 2005, Edward was shocked to find that workers had left several two-inch rusty nails sticking out near the bath, and had left more of these nails protruding from the old floor after they had removed the covering. This rendered the bathroom dangerous. Believing that health and safety laws and residents' welfare were being recklessly flouted, Edward photographed the hazards and uploaded them to a website to ensure that other residents were informed. He also told Partners that the workers who had violated his family's safety would not be allowed to re-enter his home. When other workers just a few days later failed to use dust sheets and covered family belongings with dust likely to contain asbestos he demanded a meeting with a senior Partners manager. In response, Partners informed Edward 'out of the blue' that the family would no longer be allowed to stay in the house during the works, claiming that structural surveys had revealed the need for more intrusive inspections and works to the floors. However, Edward believed this was a cover story to get him out of the way:

> They realised that with me living there, I was going to watch and
> document every single act of vandalism and sub-standard work.
> I was going to make them do a proper job. And that's not how
> PFI works, it's not how these unmonitored sub-contracting chains
> work, and they were determined to get me out.[7]

Fearful of what they would do to his home and the emotional
toll that moving into temporary accommodation would have on
his son, Edward refused to leave until he was provided with a
schedule of proposed works and a clear statement about the time
they would take. Partners claimed this was impossible due to the
impracticality of surveying the home while the family was living
there, and instructed Islington council to serve a 'notice seeking
possession', threatening the family with permanently losing their
home if they did not move to temporary accommodation. By now,
Edward's health and family situation were rapidly deteriorating:
'due to the stress and anxiety imposed on me, I found it ever
more difficult to care and support my son as his mental health
got gradually much worse'. After an 11-month battle to agree a
'decanting' agreement, a removal firm packed up their belongings
and moved them to a temporary home in October 2006, which
they were advised would be for four months. Yet despite the
urgency with which they wanted Edward and family to leave,
Partners and United House nailed corrugated iron on all doors and
windows and left the home empty for nearly three months. In fact,
building works only started after a small demonstration organised
by Edward and local residents outside the town hall.

In February 2007, Partners informed Edward that all building
works were 'complete' and the family could now move back
home. Before taking them at their word, Edward made a request
to inspect the refurbished home, which was granted. He vividly
remembers the 'carnage' awaiting him:

> Rather than repair and improve the property, the building works
> were incomplete, shabby and in some places dangerous. Every-
> where was covered in dust and debris. Previously nicely decorated
> walls had massive holes and beautifully varnished Georgian floor-
> boards had been scratched and damaged with nails sticking out
> where floorboards had been lifted. As I inspected the basement a

piece of plasterboard actually fell on my head and arm. There were clear signs that a major flood had occurred in the room above the kitchen, causing them to rip out my beautiful high-quality timber suite and replace it with cheap ill-fitting units which literally fell apart as soon as you opened drawers. The new kitchen layout had left the wall cupboards virtually inaccessible as you now had to stand on chairs to reach inside them. The paint on the walls rubbed off on cloths and clothes as they had used unsuitable emulsion unfit for kitchens given the condensation. They'd placed power sockets in such a way that normal kitchen appliances couldn't be readily plugged in and used, creating an increased health and safety risk. In several rooms floors were giving under pressure; it felt like being on a bouncy castle. The springiness of the kitchen floor was so bad that you could overturn a pan of boiling water just by gently walking up and down. The new boiler flue hadn't been cemented in, while boiling-hot water came out of the garden water tap. I was heartbroken.[8]

From Edward's knowledge of building regulations, and gas, electrical and water safety, he believed that the works were dangerously defective (figure 3.1), and broke the law in multiple ways. He submitted photos and a complaint to Islington but was told that

Figure 3.1 Structural damage to floor joists (left) and fire safety failings of ceiling repair (right) in Edward's Islington home
Source: 'Edward'

the work had been signed off and was ignored. Partners threatened Edward with costs and court action if the family did not 'ready themselves to be transported' home. Despite the property clearly now failing the Decent Homes standard and knowing that moving their possessions back in would make it more difficult to rectify, Edward was so afraid of losing his family's home that he agreed, under duress, to return in early March 2007. He then set about proving that the works were dangerous and needed to be put right. He immediately called in Corgi gas safety inspectors, who found the works carried out to be seriously defective and a 'risk to life and property'. They disconnected the gas supply in order to prevent explosion and issued an enforcement notice against United House. Edward then called in Islington council's own listed-building officer, who compiled a long list of breaches of listed-building regulations and laws. An inspection carried out on behalf of the water safety regulator identified 33 breaches of water safety legislation, prompting an enforcement notice against Islington council. An electrical safety inspector jointly appointed by Islington and Edward found 26 breaches of electrical regulations, causing category 1 hazards under the HHSRS system (see chapter 1). After input from several pro-bono architects and various friends in the building trade, Edward submitted a document that itemised 180 defects and omissions from the works. The most serious of these was the massive structural damage caused by United House's contractors cutting through and undermining a third of the house's joists when installing the new central heating radiators and pipes. After conducting an inspection, the council's own conservation officer informed Edward that much of the work done had been undertaken 'without listed-building consent' and was therefore potentially a 'criminal offence', adding that some of it was 'downright dangerous' and should be 'attended to as a matter of extreme urgency'.[9]

But Partners did not act urgently. Several months went by before Partners would even agree to inspect the work, and it took the company nearly a year to accept that something had gone wrong and agree to rectify *some* of it. In the meantime, the danger-ous kitchen and bathroom floors were temporarily stabilised with acrow props while Edward waited for the structural damage to be corrected. His disabled son's ground-floor bedroom had been made uninhabitable as the first-floor bathroom was above it. As a result, mental health services had formally notified Edward that the home 'was no longer suitable to provide care' for his son, who was shortly afterwards sectioned and detained in hospital under the Mental Health Act. As we will see in chapter 5, a protracted legal dispute then took hold that lasted nearly seven years. An eminent surveyor, Stephen Boniface, was appointed as the court's single joint expert to investigate the alleged breaches. Boniface's subsequent report, in 2009, upheld almost every single one of Edward's schedule of 180 defects and omissions, and concluded:

> The work does not meet the requirements of the building regulations and by implication this therefore means that they do not meet British Standards or the requirements set out by various regulatory bodies. [It has] been carried out to an unacceptable sub-standard and extensive work is required to deal with the defects and problems identified.[10]

However, it would take until 2014 for the main repairs to Edward's home to be completed. What had begun as a Decent Homes improvement plan to simply rewire the electrics, install a new boiler, repair a couple of roof slates and renew the bathtub, originally estimated to take two months, ended up taking nine years. Partners had been paid £31,000 by Islington for wrecking this grade II listed building. Edward never received a penny of compensation or even an apology for what he and his family had been put through. As he told me a few years later, 'while I am grateful that my health just about held out, the same regrettably cannot be said for my son and that is really unforgivable'.

PFI-2 – treating residents as human sewage

The fallout from the Islington street properties PFI-1 was a factor behind Ashford council in Kent dropping a Partners consortium as the preferred bidder for its £200 million Stanhope Estate scheme in June 2005.[11] But rather than follow suit, Islington rewarded Partners with a much larger and financially more lucrative street properties PFI contract – known as 'PFI 2' – for another 4,118 homes, including those of 1,164 leaseholders. While residents found this baffling, by holding the first housing contract Partners had virtually guaranteed itself the second one, due to both its enormous knowledge advantage over any rival bidders and the council's understandable reluctance to have two different PFI consortia managing the stock of street properties. Consequently, Partners had acquired considerable negotiating power and was able to increase the contract price significantly, with the capital investment valued over 300 per cent more than in the first scheme. This created a major affordability gap for the council and by the time the £421 million 'PFI-2' deal was signed, in September 2006, the contract length had been cut from 30 to 16 years and nearly 900 homes had been removed from the project, to cut costs.

While the sums of money involved might have changed, the problems of poor refurbishment and the appalling treatment of residents did not. Following unsuccessful attempts to get redress as individuals, in October 2010 the residents of seven homes in the Highbury area of Islington made a collective complaint against Partners and its sub-contractors. One of the residents was 'Harry', whom we met in chapter 2. He recalled the first meeting they had in his flat:

> In one home United House repaired the roof leak but left behind a new one. In another, they refurbished the kitchen so badly the fridge no longer fitted and the new kitchen windows let rain in. Instead of removing the plaster and tanking the bathroom walls to prevent damp from coming through, they painted stain block directly onto the crumbling surfaces. Another home had a faulty new ventilation system in the bathroom that would never switch off, and works to the rear door fire escape had made it difficult to open and shut. But the one that shocked us most was the working single mum with two kids who had left the contractor her keys and one afternoon her daughter came home from school to find him in a hi-vis jacket and hard hat asleep in her bed.[12]

Harry himself had moved into his flat in the summer of 2009, supposedly after the Decent Homes work was finished, to find a large amount of work had never been done, and several structural defects that Islington subsequently declared to contravene building regulations. It took another year for the contractors to come back, yet they failed to rectify the structural problems and left behind more shoddy work, including painting the windows and doors shut. A freedom of information request revealed that despite all of the problems identified by the residents, four of the homes had been certified by United House and FFT as meeting the 'full availability standard' in 2010.[13] Partners in fact withdrew the full availability certificate for Harry's home in 2012, claiming it had been mistakenly issued, and reimbursed the council for two years of unwarranted payments, but the problems in Harry's home continued for another three years.

As I will discuss in chapter 5, this was not an isolated incident, but one of many examples of work being signed off as complete when the homes were clearly not fit for purpose. This points to a systemic failure of building control made worse by PFI. Indeed, such was the level of complaints about United House and Rydon's work to listed buildings that, in 2011, Partners commissioned Montagu Evans (planning consultants) to investigate. Islington, however, dismissed its report and council conservation officers undertook their own inspections in 2014 and 2015 of works to 50 grade II or grade II* listed street properties originally carried out between 2006 and 2009. The council initially tried to keep the findings secret but was forced to disclose them following a freedom of information request by a PFI leaseholder.[14] The council's report found that 50 homes required remedial work and there was widespread non-compliance with listed-building regulations and the contractual specification, as well as missing documentation about the nature of works and materials originally used. The most serious digression was the poor quality of repointing works, with evidence of unskilled workers using a completely inappropriate mortar mix that posed long-term damage to the buildings if not corrected. Almost 10 years after the original Consul report that declared Partners and United House's work not fit for purpose, the listed-building revelations were a damning indictment of the continuing failure and social cost of the Islington PFI contracts.

But they were nothing compared with the shocking depths of negligence and indifference to which the PFI contractors would stoop in their pursuit of profit in our next story. 'Jenny' and her son 'Ethan' moved into a street property in the summer of 2011, after many painful years of escalating physical and verbal abuse from neighbours in their previous council flat. Things had become so bad that Ethan would rarely step outside the front door apart from going to and from school, and the pair were 'sleeping with hammers under our pillows in the same room'.[15] Only after Jenny had got the police and local MP involved did Islington's housing department agree to offer her a direct 'management transfer' to a street property, and she was put in contact with Partners. But despite the family's urgent safety needs and her own poor physical health, Jenny was offered only a few viewings and was never given first refusal. After a year of getting nowhere, she was able to prove that tenants accorded fewer points on the council's priority need assessment system were being given preferential treatment and she was convinced as to why:

> Management transfers are often associated with 'problem tenants', you know, anti-social behaviour, and problem tenants cause land-lords a lot of problems, like damage to property, even being evicted, and that costs money, doesn't it? What happened to us was obviously confidential, so they wouldn't have known why we were being given this transfer; they just assumed we were dodgy and were clearly trying to fob us off.[16]

Jenny's instincts were probably correct, as, under the PFI contract, Partners would bear the financial cost of anti-social behaviour and had performance targets for rent collection and arrears reduction – Jenny would have been seen as a 'financial risk'. After she went to a solicitor with her evidence, she quickly found herself top of the list for a street property maisonette that had been refurbished under PFI-2. She recalled her feelings of relief and excitement when she first saw it:

> I nearly wet myself. I mean I was like, 'Oh my god, we're going to be happy, we're going to have a normal home, we're going to have peace at last'.... The only thing I remember at the time was that the lounge floor had dirty fibreboard on it that I asked them to replace, and there was a strange smell in the basement downstairs where the bedrooms would be. The woman who was showing me the property pretended she couldn't smell anything but said they would have a

look and fix whatever needed to be fixed. And I wasn't worried at
the time, but then I had rose-coloured glasses on. I must have done.

Jenny accepted the street property on the spot and they moved in a
few months later. When she handed in the keys to her old flat and
signed for the new ones, Partners told her that the rent had risen
from the £135 a week when she viewed the property to £166 a
week. Although she was worried it would be unaffordable if her
housing benefit was ever reduced, she had no choice but to accept
it: 'What could I do? Make ourselves homeless?' With the shock of
the higher rent still sinking in, Jenny and her son opened the door
to their new home and were immediately hit by a terrible stench:

> You could smell the basement straightaway. I went downstairs and
> discovered that they hadn't fixed the basement at all and it was
> rank. The delivery man helping us with our belongings was also
> a builder, and was kicking the floor and fibres were just coming
> up. There were insects crawling in from outside through big holes
> in the walls. He pleaded with me, 'You can't stay in here. This is
> disgusting. This is health and safety.' But we had nowhere to go and
> we weren't going back where we came from.

Jenny phoned the Partners helpline and she was put through to the
same housing officer who had originally shown her the flat: 'She
told me there was nothing wrong with the floor'. Jenny was then
put through to Rydon's call centre, which stuck to the same script,
telling her 'We've been over to that property. There's nothing
wrong with it at all; it's all been sorted.' The delivery man took
the phone from her and insisted that Rydon come immediately to
put a protective covering on the floor but this was refused, so he
advised Jenny to paint the floor as the next best thing.

> It took me 22 coats of paint because the staining kept coming
> through. I got stain blocker paint [but] it came through that and
> I thought, 'Bloody hell, this is a bit weird', so then I put on, I
> don't know, 10 more layers of stain removal. And then eventually
> that worked.

After four months of sleeping in the lounge with all their belongings Jenny and Ethan laid laminate flooring on top of the painted
basement floors, repaired and redecorated the walls and were

finally ready to move into their bedrooms. Unfortunately, as they began shifting their belongings from the lounge down into their new bedrooms in the basement, a new and even more appalling problem was discovered in the lounge:

> I had boxes and boxes of books that were pushed against that wall. When I moved them away, the stench of urine and poo hit me in the face. You could see it running down the walls; it had come right out and it was disgusting. The boxes had hidden all of this – that's why I didn't know that there was a problem. Honestly, it killed us.

Jenny immediately cleaned the walls with bleach and again rang Partners, which put her through to Rydon, which then took the 25-day standard non-emergency responsive repair time frame to come out. But Rydon told Jenny that there was no leak and that she was just 'imagining it'. Over the next eight months, Rydon very slowly went from outright denial of the problem to finally accepting that human sewage was leaking from the upstairs flat. In the meantime, Jenny had found out from her neighbours that the previous tenants had complained about the same leak and Partners had already investigated: 'I suspect they knew all along there was a leaking stack pipe but didn't want find it because they would be liable for the costs of fixing it'. Just when Jenny thought the nightmare was going to finally end, disaster struck once again in the basement:

> The damp smell in the basement started to come back, so one day I picked up the mattress in Ethan's bedroom and saw this huge stain from damp that had come through the fibre, the 22 coats of paint, the underlay and the laminate flooring. I just cried. I cried for two days, for the pain that we'd been through. I just thought 'How the hell am I going to fix it?'

When I asked Jenny what Islington council had said to her about these problems, her reply was as shocking as it was predictable:

> The council is not involved. They made it quite clear to me when I met one of the housing officers at a residents' forum that 'This has got nothing to do with us – it's all down to Partners'. He said 'They are paid a lot of money to manage these properties; that's why we've paid them, so we don't have to do this.'

To make matters worse, while Jenny was trying to get Partners to take the disrepair seriously, she found that her housing benefit was going to be cut by £34 a week because of the Coalition government's 'bedroom tax', introduced in April 2013. At first she thought it was an administrative error, because she and her son were living in a two-bed flat and were not deemed to be 'under-occupying' according to the new law. So she contacted Islington's housing benefit department, which told her that Partners had put a note on the system saying 'yes, they agree it's a two-bedroom but they're going to charge for a three-bedroom because the property reflects a three-bedroom rent'. The housing benefit team told Jenny they had no power to change this because the landlord sets the rent. Jenny went to see her MP and after a phone call to Partners the £34 bedroom tax was withdrawn immediately, but she wondered to me 'how many other tenants has Partners done this to?'

It would take until December 2015 for Rydon and Partners to complete the repair works needed to stop the damp in the basement – nearly four and half years after Jenny and Ethan had moved in and reported it. When I spoke to Jenny again in 2018, she told me that her legal disrepair case was still ongoing and Partners and Islington were still standing in the way of justice:

> My son had a whole chunk of his teenage years without a bedroom and I had to fight for every single thing they did. They protested about doing anything the whole way through, insisting right to the end that the works didn't need doing despite the evidence. They are still refusing to pay for the extensive damage to my home, instead offering a paltry sum that does not even begin to cover any of the stress, harm and torture we have been through.[17]

As we will see next, Islington residents have not been the only ones suffering under Partners, Rydon and PFI.

The Chalcots Estate in Camden: lives endangered behind the façade of improvement

Despite being selected onto the government's PFI Pathfinder programme in 1999 at the same time as PFI-1 in Islington, it

would take until May 2006 for the refurbishment of the Chalcots
Estate in Camden to finally begin under Partners for Improvement
in Camden. Beyond the new bathrooms and kitchens, which were
standard for Decent Homes work, the Chalcots scheme was in
many ways a carbon copy of the Grenfell Tower refurbishment
project (see introduction). There would be a new central heating
and hot water system for tenants; the towers would have new
insulated and waterproof roofs, insulated rain screen cladding,
double-glazed self-cleaning aluminium windows, a video door
entry system, and new emergency fire protection systems such as
automatic opening vents to control smoke ventilation, signage,
smoke alarms, lighting to stairwells, dry risers (vertical water
mains fitted into staircase or lift enclosures for the fire brigade to
use in the event of a fire) and repairs to communal fire doors.[18]
Moreover, just as at Grenfell, Rydon was appointed as the principal refurbishment contractor, with the installation of the new
cladding outsourced to Harley Facades.

A disastrous procurement

The reason why the Chalcots scheme had taken more than three
years longer to set up than the neighbouring Islington PFI-1 was
down to a disastrous procurement process. It was hit first by the
sudden withdrawal in mid-2002 of the other shortlisted consortia,
which left Camden with just the Partners consortium, far earlier in
the process than would normally be permitted.[19] Six months were
lost waiting for the government to confirm that the procurement
could carry on. Negotiations with Partners resumed in late 2002
but were hit by new delays caused by legal wrangling over which
party would take the financial risks posed by the Chalcots' 110
leaseholders.[20] These particular residents had statutory rights to be
consulted about the appointment of contractors and the projected
costs of any major works for which they would be liable. They
would also have any major repair bills capped at £10,000 every
five years, and had the right to legally challenge these costs at a
leasehold valuation tribunal. All the time, the tower blocks were
left to rot, with Camden refusing to replace the door entry systems

or fix the lifts for eight years, each time saying the 'PFI scheme is imminent; you'll be getting everything replaced in about a year'. The accountability vacuum residents confronted was captured powerfully in the 2005 film *Tower Blocked*.[21] The filmmaker, Paul Perkins, a Chalcots resident and youth worker, was featured making desperate appeals for information to the council, local MPs and the government, only for calls and emails to go unanswered and requests for interviews to be routinely denied.

These delays had combined with Partner's monopoly power as the single bidder to push up the capital cost by nearly 600 per cent, to £117 million, from the estimated £21 million needed back in 1999. As a result, in February 2005, the Treasury pulled the plug on the scheme, saying it no longer represented value for money.[22] Following huge political pressure on the Labour government to change its mind, led by local Labour MP, Glenda Jackson, Camden and Partners were eventually given a second chance: if they could re-scope the project to save over £50 million, then the government would provide a £65 million grant. The need for such massive savings led to the length of the contract being halved, to 15 years, and the planned five-year works programme trimmed to just three and a half, to save on labour and borrowing costs. But this was not enough, and so 'an extensive value-engineering exercise' took place, which meant using cheaper and inevitably lower-quality materials. In an ominous portent to the Grenfell disaster, the council agreed to use 'cheaper techniques for cladding the blocks'.[23] Certain works were abandoned – such as internal painting of communal stairwells, external landscaping works, external lighting, improvement to basement car parking areas and plastering in tenants' homes. Some of the new affordable housing units planned for the basement were also removed. Camden also removed other works from the PFI contract to carry out itself at a lower cost, including replacing the communal lifts and renewing the water, gas and electrical mains. Unlike the PFI works, there would be no £10,000 cap on leaseholder bills for these non-PFI works, meaning that the full cost could be recovered, again saving Camden money. With sufficient savings made, in May 2006 a 15-year contract worth £153 million was signed between Camden and Partners, and the works began.

The Chalcots' PFI makeover

Compared with thousands of very old street properties of different types, ages and conditions in Islington, the Chalcots scheme was a relatively straightforward project involving essentially identical blocks. Nevertheless, things did not go smoothly and by the end of 2008 resident unhappiness had led to hundreds of complaints, covering a wide range of problems extensively documented on a website by Chalcots leaseholder and resident representative Nigel Rumble. There were the familiar allegations that flats were being signed off by the independent certifier – Faithful and Gould – as meeting the Decent Homes standard, despite 'leaking radiators, faulty windows and poorly regulated central heating controls'.[24] United House's claims in a newspaper article that flats were being refurbished in just 12 days contrasted with stories of residents waiting nearly two months and in some cases over one year for works to end. The routing of the new heating and water pipework had to be redesigned and redone to hundreds of flats after six copper pipes were left 'exposed all round the properties'.[25] Cuts to the original contract had led to the absence of external lighting in the entrance ways and underground parking, leaving residents afraid for their safety. Over the Christmas service shut-down period in 2007, an emergency contact number circulated to residents was out of service, advising callers 'This line does not receive in-coming calls'.[26] There were also a number of serious health and safety incidents involving the scaffolding, with workers smoking in plain sight of residents while fitting the new cladding,[27] and a number of objects falling from height, including a protective metal plate and wooden planks, fortunately with no injuries.[28]

But the most disconcerting problems concerned the new windows and cladding. Residents began to notice black mould on the new window frames after a few months. This was apparently the result of cost-cutting measures that had slashed to the absolute minimum the quality of silicon sealant and metallic windows, causing condensation, which in turned fed the health-endangering fungal spores.[29] Worse, on three of the tower blocks, the new cladding had begun to de-laminate after only weeks of being erected. It took over a year for the cladding to be removed and replaced with a different product, because of a contractual dispute over liability, with some residents left with limited light, views and restricted ability to open their windows all this time. The scale of complaints led councillors on Camden's Housing and Adult Social Care Scrutiny Committee to investigate the PFI scheme. During their inquiry, Camden's director of housing confirmed that all of these problems were real, but he believed things were going well overall: 'Improvements have been delivered on time, to budget and to a high standard. Where there have been challenges and issues, they have been addressed in partnership and working with residents'.[30]

At the same time, the non-PFI works to the communal lifts and gas, water and electricity mains being undertaken directly by Camden council were in total disarray. Camden had contracted Lift Engineering Services and Powerminster Gleeson to carry out the improvements, and NIFES to design and project manage these works on its behalf. In other words, there were two different sets of contractors working on the Chalcots Estate inside the tower blocks to very different contractual arrangements at the same time. Under the PFI contract, Partners (and thus United House and Rydon) was responsible for the electrical wiring and gas and water pipes inside each flat from the front door, while NIFES (and thus Powerminster Gleeson) was responsible for the same services in the communal areas up to the front door of each flat. To complicate matters further, in his capacity as one of the leaseholder representatives, Nigel Rumble had learned that the 'gas pipes in the communal areas had to be moved before some of the work could start inside the flats but Rydon had dictated that it would not work on site with Powerminster Gleeson at the same time'. As a result, Rydon was given an additional contract to undertake some of the communal pipework to two of the blocks as part of the non-PFI works.

Predictably, where the PFI and non-PFI works overlapped, works were badly botched: all the brand new electrical risers installed up 23 floors had to be ripped out and replaced due to the poor quality of the work; likewise, all the new electricals in the false ceilings to individual flats and communal areas posed a fire hazard so they were removed and reinstalled; and internal water pipes installed by Rydon under the PFI contract were the wrong diameter and had to be replaced, this time by Powerminster.[31] Instead of NIFES, Powerminster or Rydon bearing all the financial risk for these mistakes, much of the cost fell on the council, with the electrical part of the tender alone rising from £2.35 million to around £3 million. A self-employed contractor working for NIFES came forward as a whistle-blower, sending a damning account of what had gone wrong to Camden councillors and senior officers. He revealed that NIFES' original electrical design was substantially flawed and had had to be completely redesigned, meaning NIFES had in effect charged Camden twice for the same design. Due to the original design flaws, Powerminster Gleeson had also charged Camden for additional work. To top it off, the whistle-blower alleged that NIFES would earn a fee of 4.3 per cent of the final contract value – not the original estimated value – meaning it had a vested interest in ensuring that the final bill was as high as possible through cost and time overruns.[32] 'Michael' told me that this arrangement had been confirmed by the council at a public meeting, and that he had been subsequently told that 'Camden's own project manager was also a contractor and for each week the project overran he earned another £1,000'.[33] The NIFES whistle-blower claims he was sacked in August 2008 for providing evidence to the police that his manager was demanding that contractors like him pay a bribe at the end of week to keep their jobs.[34]

It was not just Camden that bore the financial burden of this outsourcing racket. Camden's 111 leaseholders had originally been promised that the PFI works would be capped at £10,000 and many tenants bought flats ahead of the regeneration on the basis of this promise. According to Michael, however, once the PFI contract was signed, 'they changed the wording to "every five years"'. As a result, Chalcots leaseholders ended up with PFI works bills of £30,000, paid in £2,000 annual instalments, on top of the £20,000 many were charged for the non-PFI works, taking the overall bill to £50,000 each. These huge leaseholder bills were even more difficult to accept given the problems that later surfaced. A recurring problem was the new windows. Some residents complained that their flats suffered from more road noise than before the double-glazing was fitted. There were at least seven instances where the hinges failed in strong winds and parts of the window fell to the ground.[35] But instead of accepting that the windows were not fit for purpose, Partners and Camden insinuated that residents were to blame, because they had overridden the restrictors to the windows.[36] Yet, after the insulated cladding and double-glazing had been fitted during the refurbishment, some residents in the upper floors of the blocks had no choice other than to open their windows in summer because internal temperatures would reach over 40 degrees. Residents also regularly complained about the communal fire doors being stuck open and broken, and raised the issue of missing emergency fire signage for four years until Rydon finally took action. However, the signage was inappropriate for the tower blocks and different parts of the buildings.[37] It transpired that Rydon had 'bought a lot of generic fire signs designed for offices, not residential buildings', and refused to install the correct signage despite further representations by residents.[38]

Post-Grenfell: the evacuation of the Chalcots Estate

During urgent checks following the Grenfell Tower fire, residents were alarmed to discover a strong connection between the Grenfell cladding and that used on the Chalcots Estate. Not only was it a similar aluminium composite material (ACM) but it had also been installed by the same two companies – Rydon and Harley Facades. On 21 June 2017, samples of the cladding panels were sent for fire tests. Camden initially believed the cladding system was safe, as it included non-combustible rock wool insulation underneath the outer ACM tile. Later that day, however, the mood music changed as Camden was informed that the Chalcots cladding had 'no flame-retardant properties' and would have to be removed as soon as possible.[39] Camden told residents this would be 'in weeks, not months', and issued a public statement that laid the blame firmly at Rydon's door: 'the panels that were fitted were not to the standard that we had commissioned ... we will be taking urgent legal advice'.[40]

The accused companies immediately hit back. Harley Facades claimed that the 'works were as described in the contractual specification and approved in the usual process for construction and building control by the London Borough of Camden'.[41] Rydon reportedly threatened to sue Camden for damaging its reputation unless it publicly retracted its 'inflammatory statements'.[42] Two days after the failed cladding tests, however, an inspection by the London Fire Brigade found serious fire safety breaches inside the tower blocks that made continued residency of the estate too great a risk in the event of a fire. There was a systematic failure of fire stopping throughout every part of the buildings. Front doors to most flats did not provide the legal minimum 30-minute fire protection, lacking functioning self-closers, strips and seals, with fire proofing compromised by holes drilled into doors and panels to enable cables to enter flats from outside. There was inadequate fire stopping in the electrical and water risers on most floors and 'combustible storage in some cupboards'. The Fire Brigade could not be confident that a fire would be contained, making the existing 'stay put' advice inappropriate. Yet with both firefighters and such large numbers of residents dependent on the same single fire escape route – as at Grenfell – evacuating any block on fire would not be 'a safe or practical proposition'.[43] The Fire Brigade told Camden it had no choice but to start evacuating the tower blocks or it would issue a formal prohibition notice, shutting the estate down immediately. On the evening of Friday 23 June 2017, the council began what a later official investigation called 'probably the largest evacuation in the country since World War II', affecting over 2,000 people.[44] Many were placed in hotels and other temporary accommodation for weeks, at a cost of nearly £15 million.[45]

Danger behind the cladding

Camden council temporarily took back control of the estate from Partners using its 'step-in' rights under the PFI contract. It employed five new contractors – Wates, Kier, Mulalley and Company Ltd, Openview Security Solutions Ltd and GEM – to start priority remedial works to the cladding and internal compartmentation. In total, 1,000 new fire doors with 60-minute protection were ordered to replace all 708 front doors and fire doors to communal areas. Removal of the cladding commenced in October 2017, but far from taking weeks, as first promised, it took until late January 2018 – seven months after the cladding was declared unlawful and dangerous – to be fully removed. Engineers were then able to inspect the blocks' curtain wall – the metal structure attached to the concrete towers containing the windows and insulation panels – and found further safety threats to residents from the poor standards of PFI works. There were 'structural fixing irregularities, sill heights that do not meet the regulatory minimum guidance, failed hardware to window systems and the presence of non-regulatory material behind fixing brackets and spandrel panels'.[46] This 'non-regulatory material' turned out to be flammable sealant foam, which was also found to have been used on Grenfell Tower. The council followed its engineering consultants' advice and decided that as well as replacing the cladding with a non-combustible product, it would completely replace the curtain wall and windows originally fitted by Rydon.

At the time of writing this book, the total cost of making the Chalcots Estate safe after Grenfell had reached a staggering £92.9 million.[47] In November 2017, Camden stopped all PFI contract payments to Partners, to 'protect the public purse and recoup any costs'.[48] As a result, in May 2018 Partners filed for insolvency, with debts of just £12 million, and the company was wound up, putting Camden back in permanent control of its own housing estate exactly 12 years after the PFI contract started. Rydon was replaced as the maintenance contractor on 11 July 2018, and in November 2018 Camden officially terminated the PFI contract and initiated legal action against Partners and its sub-contractors to recover its losses. It did secure £80 million in funding from central government for recladding and new curtain walling.[49] But in a sign of just how financially insulated PFI companies and investors are, Camden has to date managed to claw back only £36.6 million of the £92.9 million it spent on the post-Grenfell safety bill, having already paid Partners £121.4 million out of the £157 million contract. As we will see in chapter 6, Partners' investors – RBS, United House and Rydon – have all made large profits from this botched regeneration scheme, while the public sector has been left £56.3 million out of pocket.

However, not all the blame should be placed at the door of the PFI companies. Camden had known all along that, as a result of the so-called 'value-engineering' exercise in 2006 to save £55 million from the bloated PFI contract, 'cheaper cladding techniques' and the lowest-quality windows would be used, to save costs. The decision made in 2006 to take the renewal of buildings services out of the PFI contract to save money also played a major role in rendering the communal areas of the tower blocks unsafe. While Rydon should have done annual checks on the fire doors and other fire safety, it was revealed that the council knew back in 2012 that the fire doors did not meet fire safety regulations, and despite residents making representations about these doors for the next five years, nothing was done.[50] Camden was as indifferent to the safety of its residents as were Partners and the other PFI contractors. That indifference appeared to continue after the PFI contract was terminated. Residents reported frequent breakdowns of the lifts under Camden's management of the estate and, as this book went to press, residents were told by the council that the recladding of the towers would be delayed by at least another year because of problems sourcing tiles with the right colour.[51]

Conclusion

In this chapter we have seen how what should have been a 'partnership for improvement' in Islington and Camden became a living nightmare for thousands of residents. But pinning all the blame on Partners, Rydon and its sub-contractors does not capture the apparent political negligence on display. Both Islington and Camden had been given a very stark warning about both the incompetence and indifference of the PFI contractors, and the problems with PFI more generally, from the complaints that engulfed the first Islington street properties scheme after 2003. Yet both councils hid behind the convenient 'only show in town' rhetoric to force PFI on to their tenants and leaseholders in, respectively, the second street properties contract and the Chalcots Estate scheme. In both Islington and Camden, the failure to have in place sufficient arrangements to monitor the performance standards in these particular PFI schemes raises justifiable questions about authority-wide monitoring arrangements in relation to PFI. We will turn to this issue in chapter 5, once we have looked at another regeneration horror story under PFI across the Thames River in Lambeth.

Notes

1 Interview with 'Daisy', Islington tenant, 3 June 2013.
2 Interview with former employee of Partners for Improvement in Islington Ltd, 19 April 2018.
3 Consul, 'Partners for Islington PFI – United House Refurbishment and Maintenance of Local Authority Dwellings' (1 January 2005), pp. 37–38. Unpublished, obtained through a freedom of information request, also quoted in 'File reveals PFI homes repairs fury', *Islington Tribune*, 25 March 2015, available via at http://www.defendcouncilhousing.org.uk/ dch/resources/IslingtonPFIDisaster.doc (accessed 15 October 2018).
4 Interview with 'Frank', Islington leaseholder, 4 June 2013.
5 'File reveals PFI homes repairs fury', *Islington Tribune*.
6 From a series of interviews with 'Edward', Islington tenant, recorded during visits to his home between 2011 and 2015.
7 *Ibid.*
8 *Ibid.*
9 Email from conservation officer at the London Borough of Islington to 'Edward', 3 March 2007.
10 London Borough of Islington – v – Mr [redacted], 'Single joint expert report of Stephen L. Boniface', January 2009 (privately held court document).
11 'Disunity leads consortium astray' *Inside Housing*, 8 June 2005.
12 Interview with 'Harry', Islington leaseholder, 10 June 2013.
13 What do they know, 'Response by LB Islington to FOI request by Oriel Hutchinson, 18 October 2010' (15 November 2010), available via https://www.whatdotheyknow.com/request/major_pfi_social_housing_buildin#incoming-126709 (accessed 16 October 2018).
14 London Borough of Islington, 'PFI Historic Buildings Project: Pilot Study Buildings 1 to 50 Final Report', January 2015, available at https://www.whatdotheyknow.com/request/231070/response/604702/ attach/3/Partners%20listed%20buildings%20reportjan.pdf?cookie_ passthrough=1 (accessed 15 October 2018).
15 Interview with 'Jenny', Islington tenant, 13 June 2013.
16 *Ibid.* 'Management transfers' mean the council has taken the tenant out of its choice-based letting system. Following quotes are from the same interview.
17 Follow-up interview with 'Jenny', Islington tenant, 17 July 2018.
18 London Borough of Camden, *Interim Project Review of the Refurbishment and Major Repair Works to the Chalcots Estate*, Report of Director of

Housing to the Housing and Adult Care Scrutiny Committee (London: London Borough of Camden, 20 July 2009), para. 3.5.

19 'Camden PFI pullout puts plans in doubt', *Inside Housing*, 27 June 2002.

20 K. Cooper, 'Spiralling costs loom large for beleaguered Chalcot PFI', *Inside Housing*, 13 January 2006.

21 P. Perkins *Tower Blocked* (2005), available at https://www.youtube.com/watch?v=yBp7C8kynnA (accessed 15 October 2018).

22 'Camden PFI pullout puts plans in doubt', *Inside Housing*, 27 June 2002; 'Camden hit by new blow', *Inside Housing*, 25 February 2005; 'Camden fall-out threat to private finance', *Inside Housing*, 1 March 2005; N. Rumble, 'The PFI debacle in Camden social housing', Belsize Activist blogsite, 20 January 2009, at http://thebelsizeactivist.blogspot.com/2009/01/pfi-debacle-in-camden-social-housing.html (accessed 16 October 2018).

23 B. Willis, 'Bid to revive homes improvement plan', *Guardian*, 15 April 2005, at https://www.theguardian.com/society/2005/apr/15/privatefinance.uknews (accessed 16 October 2018).

24 N. Rumble 'Camden PFI Chalcots', Nigel for Belsize blogsite, 3 December 2008, at https://nigel4belsize.blogspot.com/2008/12/camden-pfi-chalcots-december-2008.html (accessed 126 October 2018).

25 N. Rumble 'Health and safety on the Chalcots', Nigel for Belsize blogsite, 6 December 2008, at https://nigel4belsize.blogspot.com/2008/12/health-and-safety-on-chalcots.html (accessed 12 October 2018).

26 N. Rumble (2008), 'Chalcots PFI enters the Christmas shutdown', Belsize activist blogsite, 16 December 2008, at https://belsize-activist.blogspot.com/2008/12/chalcots-pfi-enters-christmas-shutdown.html (accessed 12 October 2018).

27 Interview with 'Michael', Camden leaseholder, 1 August 2018.

28 London Borough of Camden, *Interim Project Review of the Refurbishment and Major Repairs Works to the Chalcots Estate*, para. 7.5.

29 Rumble, 'The PFI debacle in Camden social housing'; N. Rumble, 'Black mould (fungus) hits the Chalcots PFI £150m project', Belsize Activist blogsite, 29 December 2008, at https://nigel4belsize.blogspot.com/2008/12/black-mould-fungus-hits-chalcots-pfi.html (accessed 16 October 2018).

30 London Borough of Camden, *Interim Project Review of the Refurbishment and Major Repair Works to the Chalcots Estate*, para. 9.2.

31 Interview with Nigel Rumble, Camden leaseholder, 7 July 2017.

32 Email from NIFES whistle-blower to Camden council, 19 August 2008, disclosed to me by a Camden resident.

33 Interview with 'Michael', Camden leaseholder, 1 August 2018.

34 Email correspondence from NIFES whistle-blower.

35 London Borough of Camden, *Replacement of the Curtain Wall System on the Chalcots Estate*, Report of Leader of the Council (London: London Borough of Camden, 9 March 2008), available at http://democracy.camden.gov.uk/documents/s67900/Replacement%20of%20the%20curtain%20wall%20system%20at%20the%20Chalcots%20Estate%20FINAL.pdf (accessed 16 October 2018).

36 Interview with 'Michael'.

37 Interview with Nigel Rumble.

38 *Ibid.*

39 London Borough of Camden, Freedom of information requests: information regarding tower blocks' (no date), at https://camden.gov.uk/ccm/navigation/housing/council-tenants-and-leaseholders/housing-repairs-/major-repair-work/chalcots-estate/freedom-of-information-requests (accessed 16 October 2018).

40 London Borough of Camden, 'Camden set to remove cladding from Chalcots Estate tower blocks', 22 June 2017, at https://news.camden.gov.uk/camden-set-to-remove-cladding-from-chalcots-estate-tower-blocks/ (accessed 16 October 2018).

41 N. Stinson 'Grenfell Tower building firm accused of "using sub-standard cladding on more blocks"', *Express*, 23 June 2017, at https://www.express.co.uk/news/uk/820342/london-fire-grenfell-tower-combustible-cladding-camden-building-firm-rydon-harley-facades (accessed 16 October 2018).

42 R. Booth, 'Firm that refurbished Grenfell Tower threatens legal action against council', *Guardian*, 30 June 2017, at https://www.theguardian.com/uk-news/2017/jun/30/firm-that-refurbished-grenfell-tower-takes-legal-action-against-council (accessed 16 October 2018).

43 M. Harrington, *The Evacuation of the Chalcots Estate: An Independent Review* (London: London Borough of Camden, 2018), pp. 8–9, at https://www.camden.gov.uk/ccm/cms-service/stream/asset/?asset_id=3720723& (accessed 16 October 2018).

44 *Ibid.*

45 *Ibid.*

46 London Borough of Camden, 'Replacement of the curtain wall system on the Chalcots Estate' (9 March 2018), available at https://democracy.camden.gov.uk/documents/s67900/Replacement%20of%20the%20curtain%20wall%20system%20at%20the%20Chalcots%20Estate%20FINAL.pdf (accessed 16 October 2018).

47 London Borough of Camden, 'Response to independent review of the evacuation of the Chalcots Estate (SC/2018/45)' (23 July 2018), available at https://democracy.camden.gov.uk/documents/s70106/Response%20to%20the%20Independent%20Review%20of%20the%20Evacuation%20of%20the%20Chalcots%20Estate%20July%202018.pdf (accessed 16 October 2018).

48 W. McLennan, 'Chalcots Estate: Camden council stop payments to PFI firm behind flammable cladding', *Camden New Journal*, 25 January 2018, at http://camdennewjournal.com/article/chalcots-estate-camden-council-stop-payments-to-pfi-firm-behind-flammable-cladding (accessed 17 October 2018).

49 M. Smulian, 'Council ends PFI deal, takes legal action over tower block cladding', Local Government Lawyer website, 30 October 2018, at http://www.localgovernmentlawyer.co.uk/index.php?option=com_content&view=article&id=37149:council-ends-pfi-deal-takes-legal-action-over-tower-block-cladding&catid=1:latest-stories (accessed 11 December 2018).

50 R. Booth, 'London council that evacuated building knew of fire door problem five years ago', *Guardian*, 28 June 2017, at https://www. theguardian.com/uk-news/2017/jun/28/london-council-that-evacuated-building-knew-of-fire-door-problem-five-years-ago (accessed 17 October 2018).

51 Personal communication with 'Jane', Camden tenant and Chalcots resident, 12 December 2018.

4 Not fit for purpose: the Myatts Field North PFI horror show

In contrast to the refurbishment-only PFI schemes in Islington and Camden described in the previous chapter, this chapter tells the story of a far more radical type of housing regeneration under PFI. Located between Brixton and Oval in the London Borough of Lambeth, the 480 homes on the MFN estate were built by the local authority in the mid-1970s as part of a slum clearance and area improvement plan. The estate's subsequent decline from decades of lack of investment led to Lambeth requesting £72 million in PFI funding in 2003 to refurbish 172 homes, support the demolition and replacement of approximately 305 homes – including those of 58 homeowners who had bought under the RTB – and create new community facilities and green spaces. It would take almost nine years for the regeneration scheme to begin, which it did in May 2012 when Lambeth signed a £272.4 million contract with Regenter, a joint venture between Pinnacle Regeneration Group and John Laing Investments Ltd, a global infrastructure and PPP giant. Once again, Rydon would play a key role in this scheme. The chapter begins by discussing the specific origins of the MFN regeneration scheme, contrasting the original promises made to residents with the harsher realities of what was agreed in the PFI contract. The second section documents the extraordinary number of defective works and services that plagued the refurbishment and new housing. The third focuses on residents' appalling experiences under a district heating system run by energy giant E.ON, which broke down 48 times in four years, and yet some residents could not afford to use it. The fourth section then discusses the betrayal of some of the homeowners who had been originally guaranteed a new home on the estate but were forced out. Before the conclusion, the chapter explains the safety defects discovered after the Grenfell fire.

Promises, promises, promises

As outlined in chapter 2, previous efforts by Lambeth to remodel and refurbish the MFN estate had run out of money by the early 2000s, leaving nearly two-thirds of the homes in need of repair and modernisation. The local authority had initially looked to develop a 'cross-subsidy' solution to complete the work, by generating the necessary finance from allowing private residential development on the estate. But this was abandoned in 2002 following a change in local authority policy to protect public space from development.[1] Residents then vocally opposed an alternative plan involving high-rise buildings that would have physically overshadowed the estate. However, after New Labour relaxed its strict opposition to allowing PFI schemes to build new replacement council housing, in December 2003 Lambeth expressed its interest in the third round of the housing PFI programme. Lambeth saw in PFI the solution to a number of previously intractable problems. The subsidy on offer would help avoid the need for unpopular high-density private residential development, and mean all demolished council homes could be replaced on a like-for-like basis to ensure no overall loss of social housing.[2] The estimated £14 million cost of acquiring and compensating the estate's 58 homeowners – not recoverable from PFI credits – could be financed through permitting a modest 187 new private homes for market sale. This mixed-tenure approach also satisfied a government condition of PFI credits, and would provide more 'affordable' homeownership options in a borough with the highest house price rises in inner London in the early 2000s.

However, although the government approved the scheme in May 2004, the decision to bid for PFI met strong resistance from a vocal anti-privatisation campaign led by some of the estate's residents. This was a factor in the government rejecting Lambeth's first outline business case, in April 2005, and requiring the council to consult residents more thoroughly. Lambeth agreed to give tenants and leaseholders a non-binding 'test of opinion' ballot and provided written guarantees to the 58 homeowners that no one would be forced off the estate. It also addressed concerns that PFI would lead to worse services by using the magic mantra of 'payment by results':

> PFI contracts have many safeguards so that residents are protected.... Residents will have a big say in the standard of services provided by the PFI contractor. If the contractor doesn't meet these standards they are paid much less.[3]

In July 2005, residents voted 'yes' to the PFI scheme on a high turnout of 61 per cent, with tenants 55 per cent in favour, and leaseholders a more resounding 64 per cent. Lambeth submitted a revised outline business case in March 2006, but, in common with other housing PFI schemes, the MFN scheme was then hit by a new succession of delays. In 2007, the Greater London Authority, under then Mayor of London Ken Livingstone, objected to Lambeth's outline planning application, insisting the scheme include a new district heating system instead of individual gas boilers, to lower the development's carbon footprint;[4] this was followed by the onset of the 2008 global financial crisis, which saw private finance dry up and the economics of residential development become less favourable, with the consequence that regeneration schemes across the country were stalled or abandoned. This hit the MFN estate particularly hard, due to the need to unravel the PFI's incredibly complex financial model, which had previously relied on the council generating local project finance from selling land and sharing in profits from private residential development.

Eventually, in December 2009, Lambeth announced that Regenter – a joint venture between John Laing and Pinnacle Regeneration Group (see box 4.1) – had beaten Partners for Improvement and Create Homes (an SPV representing Sanctuary Housing and Mansell) to become the scheme's preferred bidder. Pinnacle's housing management arm, Pinnacle PSG, would run the homes and estate services, Rydon Maintenance Ltd would undertake the refurbishment and provide long-term repair and maintenance, and Higgins Construction PLC would build new housing and facilities and remodel the estate. Pinnacle and

Box 4.1 What is Regenter?

Regenter was launched in 2002 as an equal joint venture between John Laing Investments Ltd – a subsidiary of John Laing PLC – and Pinnacle Regeneration Group to bid for social housing PFI contracts. John Laing began as a small family house-building firm in 1848 in the north-west England; after floating on the London Stock Exchange in the 1950s, it grew to become a UK construction giant by the 1980s, building power stations, roads, stadia and railways as well as housing. Following significant losses on certain construction contracts, in the early 2000s John Laing PLC sold off its construction, property and house-building divisions to concentrate on growing its PFI and PPP business. In December 2006 it was acquired by the Jersey-based private equity arm of PPP infrastructure giant Henderson Group and taken into private ownership. Under Henderson, John Laing Group set up a number of separate listed global infrastructure funds that it provided management services to: John Laing Infrastructure Fund in 2010 and John Laing Environmental Assets in 2014. The company was once again listed on the London Stock Exchange in February 2015, and as of October 2018 its shares were controlled by Standard Life Aberdeen (10.52 per cent), Schroder Investment Management (9.61 per cent), Fidelity Investment Management (8.66 per cent), Blackrock Inc. (7.42 per cent), Morgan Stanley Investment Management (5.00 per cent) and Janus Henderson Investors (4.42 per cent).

The other partner in Regenter – Pinnacle – was born in 1994 when it won a housing management contract with Westminster council and has since grown to manage 27,500 homes in the UK on behalf of councils, housing associations and private developers. In June 2011 Cheng Yu-tung – one of Hong Kong's biggest property developers and a billionaire, who died in 2016 – and two fellow Hong Kong investors, developer Sammy Lee and businessman Peter Fung, paid £30 million for 61 per cent of Pinnacle Regeneration Group Ltd through companies incorporated in the British Virgin Islands: Greenmark Enterprises Ltd and New Hampshire Enterprises Ltd. The deal was facilitated by global property agents Savills, which itself took a 3 per cent stake in Pinnacle. In November 2013 Knight Dragon Ltd, also linked to Cheng Yu-Tung, acquired a 100 per cent interest in the 177-acre Greenwich Peninsula development, a partnership with Pinnacle to build mid-price market housing and the affordable housing component of a 10,000-home regeneration project. In January 2014, Greenmark Enterprises acquired a further 46 per cent of Pinnacle's ordinary shares, giving it an 87.8 per cent controlling stake. The Hong Kong investors were motivated by the desire to shift some of their investments out of a soaring property market in Hong Kong and access less risky but rising returns from the post-recession London property market, and the guaranteed government subsidies on offer for social housing. Bloomberg records that Pinnacle's chief executive stated at the time that the company was 'a key into a door – this is the price of the key and gives the option for further investment'. In July 2017, Pinnacle's Hong Kong owners sold the company to US investment firm Starwood Capital and Anglo-Chinese firm Tunstall Real Estate Asset Management for an estimated £50–£60 million.

Sources: John Laing Group PLC, 'Company history' (no date), at https://www. laing.com/who-we-are/john_laing/company_history.html (accessed 16 October 2018); Pinnacle Group, 'About us' (no date), at https://www.pinnaclegroup. co.uk/about-us/ (accessed 16 October 2018); T. Barwell, 'Hong Kong billionaire helps fund gap in U.K. social housing', Bloomberg, 20 July 2011, at https://www.bloomberg.com/news/articles/2011-07-19/hong-kong-billionaire-fills-funding-gap-in-u-k-s-low-cost-housing-market (accessed 14 October 2018); R. Curry, 'Regeneration firm Pinnacle sold to Starwood and new asset manager', Telegraph, 16 June 2017), at https://www.telegraph.co.uk/business/2017/06/15/ regeneration-firm-pinnacle-sold-starwood-new-asset-manager (accessed 17 October 2017).

Higgins Homes PLC would undertake the private residential development through a separate joint venture company outside of the PFI contract. Regenter contracted PRP architects to design the overarching regeneration masterplan. Finally, energy giant E.ON UK PLC would develop and run a new district heating system from a gas-powered combined heat and power (CHP) plant that would generate and sell electricity to the national grid from steam-driven generators, while supplying the resulting heat and hot water to residents.

Regenter's winning bid was the only one deemed to be both affordable to Lambeth and giving value for money, mainly because it offered an additional 105 new social rented homes – part-financed with a government social housing grant – and 41 shared-ownership homes outside of the PFI contract, through the Notting Hill Housing Association.[5] Regenter's development partner also promised an £8 million 'guaranteed minimum contribution' from Regenter in return for 125-year leases on the private development sites; Lambeth would use this sum to fund additional estate improvements, as well as to reimburse the council's procurement and future contract monitoring costs. However, when Savills (global property agents and then a shareholder in Pinnacle – see box 4.1) submitted an outline planning application on behalf of Regenter in April 2010, eagle-eyed residents noticed the regeneration masterplan bore little resemblance to the one they had voted on. The originally promised 187 new private flats for sale had more than doubled to 439 (including the shared-ownership units). Both Lambeth and the GLA had also waived Regenter's requirement under local planning rules to provide up to 50 per cent affordable rooms in any net additional housing provided, arguing that the estate had enough social rented housing already. This was despite the fact that Lambeth had a crisis of social housing availability, with 23,000 households on the waiting list. Local residents' objections on these grounds were rejected, and planning permission was granted in August 2010.

Austerity bites

The protracted consultation and procurement served to drive up the costs of the PFI contract enormously. By January 2011, when Lambeth submitted its interim full business case (FBC), the government's expected contribution had risen by 59.17 per cent, from £72 million to £114.6 million, while Lambeth's expected contribution had increased by 252.33 per cent, from £279,000 (2006 prices) to £983,000 per year (2011 prices). The regeneration scheme was then put on hold again following the May 2010 election of the UK Coalition government and the onset of its austerity policies. The Coalition's subsequent abolition of social housing grants saw £12.4 million removed that had been earmarked for Regenter's promised 105 social rented homes. After conducting a 'value for money' review of PFI schemes, in 2011 the Coalition then cut £15.8 million in PFI credits to £98.8 million.

This £28.2 million funding gap in the overall regeneration scheme forced Lambeth and Regenter to make major changes to the project; these changes were designed to cut costs while protecting the private companies' profit margins. The contract length was cut from 30 to 25 years and the five-year construction period reduced to four – meaning up to 69 households would now have to move into temporary accommodation during the works, despite having originally been told that no one would have to move home more than once. More savings resulted from 'value engineering' the specification, that is, cutting the standards of design and materials to be used. For example, the community centre would be made smaller and would no longer have air conditioning, the frequency of 'bulk refuse' collection would be reduced, as too would the opening hours of Pinnacle's housing office, as well as the budget for tree maintenance; further, the 'handback standard' that the housing and estate would be in when returned to the local authority after 25 years would be lowered.[6] More controversially, in return for more upfront investment to replace the government's funding cut, E.ON's 25-year contract to exclusively supply all residents with heat and hot water was extended to 40 years.[7] The loss of the social housing grant meant that Regenter was also allowed another increase in the number of private homes to be developed, from 398 to 503, turning the promised 105 social rented homes into shared-ownership homes.

But the savings from these changes were still not enough, and so Lambeth was forced to increase its annual financial contribution by a further 102.03 per cent, to £1.986 million in net present value (2011 prices) or by 611.83 per cent since 2004. In nominal terms, this would take its overall contribution to £79 million over the course of 25 years. This increased financial burden on the local authority was in turn passed down to council tenants and leaseholders: £9 million would be raised by increasing rents and service charges above the government's guideline rent levels – to the extent that the average service charge would be increased by 54.71 per cent in just two years (2013/14 to 2014/15)[8] – while £34.9 million would be siphoned out of the repairs budget for the remainder of the council's 21,000 tenants. Lambeth was also forced to give up the £8 million guaranteed minimum contribution originally promised from Regenter's private development partner for the land. This would instead be retained by Regenter and injected into the up-front financing for the PFI works, saving £2.7 million in commercial borrowing costs over the 25-year period.[9] In other words, Lambeth paid £8 million to get £2.7 million back, which is hardly good value for money. In summary, austerity had combined with this heavily financialised form of regeneration to generate huge cuts to Lambeth's housing budget, 105 fewer social homes, reduced quality of design and materials, lower service standards and a huge increase in private development on land that had been effectively gifted to private developers. Nevertheless, Lambeth used those magical discount rates explained in chapter 2 to declare in July 2011 that the PFI scheme represented better value for money than a traditional public-led procurement, by a margin of 3.2 per cent – or £4.9 million in net present value. Eventually, in May 2012, the MFN PFI contract was signed, with a total nominal value of £272.4 million over its 25 years. As we will now see, for many residents the effects of these changes would be disastrous.

'This ain't Chelsea': living inside a regeneration nightmare [10]

The MFN PFI regeneration scheme finally began during the late spring of 2012, five years later than originally planned, nine years after first mooted and close to two decades after earlier improvement work had been left unfinished. The long wait for homes to be repaired and modernised had blighted many lives. While most residents were happy that investment was coming, a small group of tenants and leaseholders had become worried about the controversy surrounding PFI and the growing horror stories of regeneration displacing low-income communities from inner London, so in early 2012 they formed an action group to ensure the council's promises were honoured. It did not take long for familiar problems of poor workmanship and resident treatment to surface.

Health and safety gone missing

During the late summer of 2012, just a few weeks after Rydon began refurbishment work on the first council homes being spared demolition, residents in one part of the estate were so appalled at what they had experienced that they decided – just as residents at Grenfell Tower had done – to collectively refuse Rydon any further access to their homes until their grievances were addressed. As part of my research, I agreed to work with the residents' action group to conduct a survey of the refurbishment works, based on what the contract said should be happening, and to present the findings to the local authority. The survey questions largely reflected the key undertakings made by Rydon about how residents would be consulted and treated during the works.

We piloted the survey in late October and early November 2012 with two residents whom I am calling 'Winston' and 'Dec' to protect their identities. They showed us around all of the appalling work signed off by the independent certifier, Sweett Group, as supposedly meeting both the Decent Homes standard and all other required contractual and legal obligations. Winston's shiny new bathroom looked nice but was no longer fit for purpose. As figure 4.1 shows, the previously functioning toilet had been replaced by one so close to the bathroom wall and door he could no longer sit down on it properly. The new electrical extractor fan was positioned directly next to the shower head, making it a shock hazard. In the hall, wall tiles were missing and hanging off around new radiator pipework, and on the lounge floor lay smashed glass from the frame for a large photograph of his late mother (for which Rydon had left no note of explanation or apology). The kitchen sink by the window had been refitted half a foot above the level of the window pane such that splashed water now pooled on the window sill, making a longer-term damp and rot hazard, and his microwave had disappeared. With his individual combi-boiler now removed in preparation for E.ON to connect his flat to the new district heating system, Winston was temporarily reliant on his immersion heater. However, Rydon had forgotten to turn the water back on, and so the tank did not refill and the heating element eventually burnt out, leaving him without hot water for

Figure 4.1 Shoddy refurbishment works on Myatts Field North, October 2012. Clockwise from top left: Winston's new toilet that he could not sit down on; a smashed glass picture frame is left behind; how new pipework and wall tiles were left; and shower room electrical ventilation is positioned directly next to water.
Source: author

two weeks. When he visited the Pinnacle-run housing office to complain, the housing officer made no notes during the conversation and when he went back to follow up he was told they had no record of his original complaint.[11]

Dec's story was equally appalling. At the start of the work, Rydon had refused to supply dust sheets and gave him just four flat-packed boxes to protect his possessions that were so flimsy everything fell through the bottom when picked up. His new radiators were all different sizes from the old ones, and unsightly holes and marks on the wall from the removal of the latter had not been made good; some of the new radiators had dents and scratches on them, and one was already rusting. The new kitchen cupboards were missing doors, and the new kitchen fire door contravened building safety regulations as there were huge air gaps above and below it. He recounted what he had found after returning home at midnight one Friday after Rydon's electricians had been rewiring the flat all day:

> The cooker had been removed without being replaced, my fridge was not plugged in and no wall sockets were working so I had to run an extension lead from the living room to the kitchen. The toilet had no water in the tank and was not flushing. I had not been given any emergency phone numbers to ring so I had no cooker or toilet for the whole weekend and had to wait until the Monday to visit Rydon's office to report this. A site manager inspected and found that both the kitchen fuse switch and bathroom water valve had not been switched back on. I had no cooker for the next two weeks, only a portable hob but no kitchen work surface to put it on, so I had to put it on the washing machine, which incidentally had been left unplumbed with a broken hose and non-return valve.[12]

Dec went to see Rydon's project manager about these problems, the person officially responsible for 'ensuring compliance with quality standards'. But in a clear parallel to what residents experienced at Grenfell, far from being interested in quality, Rydon's manager told Dec bluntly: 'Look mate, it ain't Chelsea round here'. In other words, the working-class residents of a council estate should not expect anything better: it is all they deserve.

We eventually surveyed 14 homes supposedly refurbished by Rydon and attracting full contract payments. This produced a shocking picture of unsafe work that was strikingly similar to residents' travails in Islington and Camden. Residents reported faulty electrical sockets and wiring, sparking sockets, fuse boxes which kept tripping, electrical sockets positioned in ways that could create hazards, overheating panels on the new induction cookers and high-voltage electricity cables hanging loose. One home experienced frequent electricity outages and so the residents called the electricity firm, EDF: 'They were shocked. They asked if any recent work had been done. They called it an emergency. They had to redo the work Rydon had done.' A diabetic resident was left without power from Friday to the following Monday due to a faulty main fuse box missing a cable. In some homes, re-wiring work was so bad that switches to lights or the cooker sockets would turn on other electrical components or even sound the front door bell. Half of the surveyed homes had experienced leaks, and five had significant flood damage, even extending into neighbours' homes. Tenants reported their front doors being left open all day so that anyone would be able to wander in unchallenged. Workers rarely wore identification badges or signed in and out as required. Some workers used electricity paid for by residents without compensation (a pitiful £5 was later offered after resident pressure). Damage was done to homes and personal property – broken lighting, hanging ceiling pendants, torn new carpets, chipped baths and ripped wallpaper.

Goodbye Myatts Field North ... hello 'Oval Quarter'

As residents grappled with the various problems affecting the refurbished homes, to their surprise and disquiet new advertising hoardings began going up around the perimeter of the new development sites in 2013 announcing 'Oval Quarter: This is where it's at'. Their surprise turned to shock when they visited the www.ovalquarter.com sales website (no longer online) to find that Oval Quarter had completely displaced the MFN estate off the map. No such estate now existed: Oval Quarter was instead presented as *the* regeneration masterplan. The attempt to hide the council housing was taken to extremes, for instance being labelled 'affordable homes' on a map of the area. The Oval Quarter website also featured a promotional film and materials which emphasised easy access to the cultural and retail highlights of central London, hid the connection with Brixton, eviscerated black culture and African Caribbean heritage by foregrounding fictional characters who were predominantly white, and loaded the brand with every cliché of a gentrified lifestyle:

> Oval Quarter is London's most dynamic and desirable new community, offering an unparalleled range of cutting-edge, innovative

apartments in a parkland setting. It's where you'll find all the key ingredients for living in one of the world's greatest cities – right on your doorstep. Wide public boulevards, outstanding modern architecture and seven hectares of verdant parkland, in one of London's most central and convenient inner-city neighbourhoods.... Just 10 minutes by tube to the very heart of the capital and sitting on the edge of London's magnificent cultural belt.... To this remarkably central, yet leafy, spot – hidden between Oval, Kennington, Camberwell and Stockwell – Oval Quarter brings more than 800 homes among a series of new and beautifully crafted large public spaces.[13]

While information about new private housing was included in the planning documentation, at no point was there any mention of the estate itself being *geographically rebranded* in part or whole in Regenter's 2010 planning application. The developer's right to decide on a 'destination name' for the private new build – although not the MFN estate – was buried in a single sentence in the PFI contract. The rebranding exercise stemmed in large part from the desire to attract international investors to buy new homes in the regeneration scheme. Pinnacle Regeneration Group, one half of the development company behind the private new build, had been taken over in 2011 by Hong Kong billionaire, Cheng Yu-tung, and associates Sammy Lee and Peter Fung (see box 4.1). They employed consultancy BradleyDyer to create a marketing strategy for the new homes that directly targeted the Asian investor market, which accounted for 48 per cent of London investment in 2013, so as to generate the finance for construction through off-plan sales. With investors initially put off by the development's association with Brixton – given its stigmatised reputation for race riots and gang crime – the consultants came up with the name 'Oval Quarter'.[14] The new private owners buying into the development would also get the prime location overlooking the new park and green space at the centre of the community, whereas the vast majority of council tenants and leaseholders forced to move to new homes were to be placed behind these private blocks. The overall effect was to transform an overwhelmingly public housing community, with three in every four homes for council tenants, into a predominantly private one, with 62 per cent of all housing for owner occupation (figure 4.2).

Figure 4.2 Two views of Oval Quarter flats on the redeveloped Myatts Field North, January 2018

Source: Paul Waley

It really isn't Chelsea

But beneath the glossy PR, problems much the same as those experienced during the Rydon-led refurbishment phase began to emerge in the new council and private homes being built by Higgins. Ironically, given that a major reason for demolishing existing homes was the irreparable damp caused by leaking flat roofs, residents soon reported leaks from the new roof gardens. I spoke to a homeowner whose family had lived on the estate for over 30 years; a few months after moving into their new replacement home, they reported water leaking through their roof, causing damage to paintwork and the gradual development of dampness. Months went by, emails were sent, complaints made, but nothing was done, forcing them to live with buckets on the stairs. Then the flat suffered a major internal flood due to a poorly fitted pipe in the utility room, prompting more unanswered emails and complaints:

> We discovered that our complaint was not initially logged or tracked – there was nothing on the system. When they finally came to inspect in the summer of 2014, the pipework was not insulated as per the contract, and the leaks were actually caused by a condensation build-up inside the soil vent pipe and duct from the bathrooms that had a faulty air valve system.[15]

In the end, the family received just £1,000 in compensation, when rectifying the physical damage to their property had cost them £5,000. They were so fed up that a few months later they decided to sell up and leave the estate. Some of the leaks were caused by water pooling on the flat roofs, which Higgins initially pretended was supposed to happen, only eventually to admit it required a new design solution. The new roofs also struggled to cope with high winds. One stormy evening in October 2013 five sections of pressed metal coping fell off from the roof pods of one new apartment block into the rear gardens, causing damage to residents' properties and boundary fences, but miraculously no injuries. It took exactly one month for this health and safety near-miss to be properly investigated; the investigation revealed a design fault that had led to a botched installation. As more residents moved into the

Oval Quarter, there were growing complaints of unbearable noise coming from upstairs flats. As one resident wrote in an official complaint to Higgins:

> I spoke at length to my neighbour who lives below me last night. She says that when we are in our kitchen she can hear every footstep we make like a 'herd of elephants' in her bedroom.[16]

Higgins carried out acoustic tests that showed no breaches of building regulations and claimed it was just 'people moving into new accommodation and getting used to the new properties and different background noises'.[17] Further investigation by Higgins, however, showed that corners had been cut in the construction of the properties, as acoustic foam and sealant were missing in parts of the flat. Higgins claimed this had all been rectified subsequently and did not affect the acoustic noise tests, but this was because the tests were for high-frequency sounds of music and voices, whereas residents were reporting low-frequency thuds of impact noise. Eventually, once again, it was revealed that the source of the problem was the poor design of the building's non-traditional steel-frame structure.

These problems were part of a wider concern voiced consistently by residents about health and safety negligence. One woman had to rush out of her house waving her hands frantically to stop it being demolished, while another in her eighties fell and broke her arm after workers left materials in her home. Residents repeatedly complained that when they rang the out-of-hours emergency service, the call centre was unable to find their homes listed on the computer database, and so the repair requests were refused. For a few months even emergency services were not able to locate some people when they called 999. There were also problems caused by the physical obstacles to emergency vehicle access caused by the construction works and contractor parking: on one occasion this meant that a second, smaller fire truck had to be called out to deal with a house fire after the first fire truck could not get down the street. At one point, approximately half of the 36 CCTV cameras were not working due to development works and cable damage by construction workers, and the whole network was down for two lengthy periods totalling five months, meaning crimes committed during this time were not recorded – yet tenants and leaseholders were still paying for the CCTV through their service charges. The building works also led to an increase in the number of rats and mice, but this was nothing compared with the annual summer and autumn fly infestations inside and outside of homes, which residents blamed on the new pod bins leaking, and the fact that refuse remained uncollected for weeks – one of the cost-saving measures made to the contract in 2011. Regenter initially tried to blame residents for not properly bagging rubbish and parking in front of the pods, preventing collection, only for it to be revealed that the pod bins had a known design fault that affected four other local authorities.

PFI's failing energy monopoly

As the increasingly acrimonious regeneration progressed, a new problem gradually came to dominate all residents' lives under PFI – the systematic service failures and eye-watering bills from E.ON's 40-year energy monopoly in the shape of its district heating system.[18] Before the first homes had even been connected to the gas-powered combined heat and power plant located under the estate, the PFI's district heating deal was proving controversial. Residents claimed that they found out they were losing their individual gas boilers and instead being forcibly connected to E.ON for 40 years only when Rydon began stripping out their boilers during the refurbishment. Some tenants resisted the disconnection of their gas supply, including 'Janet', a disabled council tenant whom Lambeth's occupational health team said benefited from having a gas cooker. Janet was told by Pinnacle that if she did not allow E.ON access, she would face eviction.[19] Eventually Pinnacle backed down in Janet's case and allowed her to retain her gas supply for cooking, but continued to threaten legal proceedings until she signed the E.ON heat agreement and stopped obstructing E.ON's remaining conversion works. The legal basis for E.ON's right to assert its partial energy monopoly over residents for 40 years was extremely dubious. Consumer law entitles tenants and leaseholders on estates to connect to any energy supplier they prefer, unless the estate's supply infrastructure is unable to support it or doing so would lead to a severe economic impact on the landlord. As the PFI contract was denying the MFN residents this right, by law the landlord should have consulted tenants and leaseholders, yet residents were adamant that no such consultation had ever taken place and no paperwork had been provided to substantiate Regenter's claims that it had. It seems that the district heating became a *fait accompli* during the largely secret PFI contract negotiations.

Residents would not have minded one bit about being married to E.ON for 40 years if their heating and hot water were affordable and reliable, as promised, but the PFI energy monopoly lurched from one disaster to another, although in fact every company in the PFI consortium was responsible in some way for the mess. The warning signs started flashing in early 2013, when the first homes connected were left without heating and hot water one weekend due to 'dirt getting into the new system'. This happened again in April 2013, leaving some elderly and vulnerable residents without hot water and heating over the weekend, only to discover that the E.ON emergency phone numbers were incorrectly advertised. As more homes were connected, the problem of sudden outages was compounded by inconsistent water temperatures, which forced some households to use kettles to heat water or to top up baths. Individual homes also suffered from faulty parts or workmanship, and the repeated failure of E.ON and other PFI contractors to respond to repair requests or fix the problems for days, weeks, months and even more than a year. Some delays were caused by E.ON, Rydon and Higgins trying to pass responsibility for the problems on to each other, citing the PFI contract. The impact for some was scandalous: a pensioner couple forced to shower at the local gym at £4.40 per day for 21 days; a household with three young children, including a 17-month-old baby, left without heating for almost a year. 'Jane' moved into her new flat in April 2014 and had no hot water or heating until January 2015, but no compensation was offered. She was forced to boil the kettle to have a wash, but due to arthritis in her hands had 'great difficulty gripping the kettle which makes it unsafe'.[20] This was not what

Regenter and E.ON had promised in their final tender documents to Lambeth in 2011:

> The district heating network has been designed to avoid traditional energy supply interruptions stemming from leaks of the pipework ... should the centralised plant fail, E.ON will be able to respond and rectify faults before they create a problem with the residents.[21]

Matters came to a head on Christmas day in 2014 when the majority of homes had no hot water from early morning until late afternoon. Soon after, 260 residents signed a petition calling on Lambeth to end the E.ON contract. Lambeth and Regenter wrote to residents to 'acknowledge and apologise [for the] ... intermittent service to the estate for several months', but claimed that measures were being put in place to improve the service and there was no opt-out from the E.ON system. Things did not improve, however: between February 2013 and April 2017, the hot water and heating supply experienced an unscheduled outage for part or all of 48 separate days – one day a month on average – and there have been more unscheduled outages since. Each time the system went down, some new cause would be blamed – an electrical failure, a programming error, an over-performing safety system, damage to cables from builders, a water outage, a London-wide energy grid failure, and so on.

What made these abysmal service failures harder to stomach were the large monthly bills many residents were receiving. Again, the PFI contract had in fact promised the opposite, that E.ON tariff charges – the unit price and service charge combined – would always be 'equivalent to or less than ... using a traditional, gas-fired condensing boiler solution'.[22] To ensure that residents were billed for 'actual energy used', as required by the PFI contract, E.ON promised smart, remote metering that recorded all heat consumption, avoiding the inconvenience of meter readers, and guaranteeing 'accurate up-to-date readings rather than estimates so residents pay for heat units used'.[23] But residents' bills bore no relationship to actual usage or E.ON's price cap guarantee.[24] E.ON sent one household a demand for £1,000 for a single month, another was billed £113 for a month during which they had been on holiday and not consumed any heat or hot water. Some households were affected by back-billing after E.ON took several months to set them up on the customer database. A disabled resident who had no hot water or heating for around 15 months, and had to sleep in her day clothes to keep warm, was then billed for £468. There was also significant variation in regular household bills, from £14 to over £100, which could not be explained by different property types or consumption patterns. Harrowing stories of fuel poverty were presented to the residents' association (more on which later) of residents' rationing heating to six or seven hours a week, cutting down on food, no longer washing dishes in hot water, or using electric or oil heaters, or of simply turning off the heating and hot water altogether while paying to be connected. Households reported living in fear of their next E.ON bill, having to challenge their erroneous bills on a monthly basis with the threat of disconnection constantly present, or being intimidated into paying by the threat of £10 late-payment penalties. Councillor Jacqui Dyer MBE, local ward member and vice-chair of NHS England's Mental Health Taskforce, told me how this had a particularly bad impact on vulnerable residents:

> My neighbour would be regularly ... knocking at my door with anxiety about his E.ON heating bills that were in the first instance estimated at £100 a month for heating and hot water that he literally wasn't using. And then he received an overall bill of a £1,000 with a formal demand for immediate payment. I contacted E.ON to resolve the issue, took photos of the meter and they were telling me that it wasn't his reading. I told them, 'I'm in his house!' Finally, they accepted what I was saying and calculated that in fact E.ON *owed him* money. So if I am having to negotiate to that degree to get a right outcome, imagine how it would feel to someone more vulnerable – it will put you in crisis.[25]

When residents looked at the small print in E.ON's PFI energy contract, they discovered that the promise to cap heating bills at average gas prices was not quite as it had been sold to them. E.ON was in fact promising to go no higher than a unit tariff that excluded all standing charges plus discounts for direct debit, online billing or dual fuel supply, and that was based on an average of the so-called 'big six' energy companies' basic standard variable tariffs – which have been widely condemned by politicians, the consumer energy regulator Ofgem and the media as 'ripping off' customers, who are urged to switch suppliers to get a better deal.[26] The tariff structure also paid no attention to vastly unequal energy needs of the less energy-efficient existing homes and the new-build flats, meaning residents in refurbished homes were paying more than double those in the new-build. Homeowners were particularly cheated, initially paying an annual service charge of £376.18 (at March 2013 prices and excluding VAT) just to be connected to the district heating system. When comparing the combined heat tariff and service charge for MFN homeowners with those in equivalent district heating schemes in London, residents found they were at the top end of the market, second only to energy company SSE's controversial scheme on Orchard Village in Havering.[27] As a result, many were paying more per kWh than if they were able to choose a fixed-price deal from a 'big six' energy supplier.

Uzoamaka Okafor, the chair of Myatts Field North Residents Association and PFI Monitoring Board (MFN RAMB) between 2014 and 2017, explained in interview how no one from Lambeth, Regenter, E.ON and the other PFI contractors would initially listen to what the residents were saying: 'For the first couple of years after the district heating was connected, we were repeatedly made to feel by Regenter and E.ON that we were imagining a problem that did not exist'.[28] When residents challenged the Higgins project director on various problems in June 2013 he stated 'there was nothing wrong with their equipment; the residents could not be bothered to learn how to use it'.[29] Eventually, drip by drip, Regenter and E.ON admitted a series of design and construction defects: technical flaws were compounded by a seven-month delay in Higgins' construction phase that meant vital pipework was not installed on time; a lack of insulation was identified as the main cause of the overheating corridors; the huge bills were caused by E.ON's automated smart meter readers failing to send and receive signals, made worse by the steel structure of the new buildings. Despite nearly a year of works to fix this problem, in December 2015 E.ON reported to Lambeth that it was 'unable to guarantee' that it could provide even 'one accurate bill a month'.[30] By December 2016, E.ON claimed that 75 per cent of residents' meters were now being read accurately by remote access. But this improvement came too late for one resident. Edward Connell, an elderly man thought to have been suffering with a form of dementia who had repeatedly told MFN RAMB he was struggling with high E.ON bills, died of heart failure in October 2016. Residents were told there was no food in his flat when he died. As Uzoamaka Okafor told me:

> He was in his 70s and had lived on the estate for more than 25 years. He repeatedly went into the housing office to raise concerns about E.ON and his bills…. He wasn't eating, he couldn't work the heat controls, he didn't understand why his bills were as high as he wasn't actually using the heating. The last time … I saw him on 25 July 2016, he was talking about the bills…. He had chosen to pay his heating bills instead of buy[ing] food and this was a factor that contributed to his death.

Uzoamaka and other MFN RAMB members were devastated by his death, unable to stop feeling guilty and responsible, even though they knew the fault lay elsewhere. Sadly, as we will see, Mr Connell was not the only MFN resident whose death would be in part attributed to the toll of the regeneration scheme.

The betrayal of the homeowners

One of the key promises made by Lambeth prior to regeneration was that the 58 households facing demolition would be supported to stay in new homes on the redeveloped estate. These were nearly all former tenants who had bought their council houses under the RTB over the course of the 1990s and early 2000s, and remained on the estate despite all of its reputed problems. Compulsory purchase regulations required the council to pay these home-owners the market value for their homes plus an additional 10 per cent in compensation, and develop options to support those faced with buying a more expensive home or one they could not afford. Lambeth made cast-iron guarantees that retaining the home-owners would be integral to the estate's successful regeneration.[31] In a public newsletter in 2005 with the heading 'Please don't leave us!', the council acknowledged them as 'an important part of the strong community that exists on the estate' and promised to enable everyone to stay on the improved estate through 'a range of affordable options to cover any gap between the value of your old home and the value of your new home'.[32] This explains why this particular group of residents who potentially had the most to lose from regeneration delivered the highest 'yes' vote for PFI in July 2005, with 67 per cent in favour. By September 2007, the council's options for support to stay had been formally clarified as a shared-equity arrangement with the council, joining a shared-ownership scheme or, in special circumstances, reverting to a council tenancy.[33]

At no point over the next five years of delays to the PFI scheme did Lambeth indicate to the homeowners that anything had changed with respect to these promises. Yet when Pinnacle took over the management of homeowner rehousing in May 2012, homeowners were pleasantly surprised to be told that instead of having to sell up and then buy a new home on the estate, they would instead be offered a simple 'like for like' property and lease swap, with no money changing hands, avoiding a lot of legal fees and uncertainty. This offer had arisen as a means of reducing costs after the government's funding cuts to the PFI scheme.[34] On paper, it looked like a great deal, as residents would be swapping older homes with structural problems for brand new properties with values on the open market of between £560,000 and £600,000 in 2014. Pinnacle reassured homeowners with existing mortgages that they would be able to 'port' (move) them to their new property and explicitly promised that should anyone encounter obstacles to this 'we will liaise with your lender, explore shared ownership options, [and] pay for costs relating to changing/ transfer of your mortgage'.[35]

However, one distressed homeowner after another came forward with a very different story to the one Pinnacle was spinning; eventually 19 homeowners – a third of those facing demolition – revealed that their mortgage lender had rejected a request to port their mortgage, because their policies either did not permit it or because of legal risks from the proposed lease swap in terms of title to land. The banks told them that in order to move house they would have to redeem their existing mortgage and apply for a new loan. But when they did, homeowners were refused outright or were offered just a portion of what they needed on grounds of poor credit rating, their age or low or unreliable income, even though most had never missed a mortgage payment. A major factor here was that in 2014, UK mortgage lending rules changed, to stop banks making loans to those deemed too risky. The homeowners were in effect being treated as new customers (for a new mortgage they did not need), and in the post-financial crisis era, their personal and financial circumstances no longer met the risk-averse lending criteria of the banking sector.

Each homeowner in this situation I interviewed talked about the extreme stress and the sleepless nights of being 'left in limbo'. One of those affected was the chair of the residents association, Uzoamaka Okafor, who had been living on the MFN estate since 1982 and for whom her three-bed council maisonette meant everything: 'I had an unsettled childhood and I was one of the first to move into the new flats. My daughter was born here and I felt really safe and grounded in a permanent place.'[36] Having built a career as a training consultant from her previous experience in social work and as a local government investigator, she saved enough money to exercise her RTB in 2004 on a standard 25-year repayment mortgage. In 2009 her mum had a stroke and Uzoamaka used her savings to stop work and take care of her. Although she did not want to move, she accepted the inevitable. With her mother's health deteriorating she contacted her bank to arrange for the mortgage to be ported, but was told no.

> My lender said it was not possible to move my existing mortgage to my new home under the bank's rules and it wouldn't give me a new mortgage because of my recent low income, even though I'd never ever had a problem with paying my mortgage. The only option they gave me was a buy-to-let mortgage that would have increased my interest payments, but this meant I would have had to move out of my own house, so I could not accept it.

As Uzoamaka went from bank to broker in vain, her mother passed away and she found life had become almost unbearable: 'I became very depressed and unwell, not least because I was overwhelmed with helping other residents deal with all of these different problems.'

In a further cruel twist, some homeowners' applications were being refused partly because of their poor credit rating, which was linked to the decades of disrepair on the estate. 'Kate' and her three teenage children were one such family. She had moved onto the MFN estate in the early 1990s and bought her home at the same time as Uzoamaka. Soon afterwards the house suffered major damage and chronic damp from an ongoing roof leak. But Lambeth council, which was responsible for repairing it as the freeholder, disputed the works. Kate explained that the dispute 'dragged on for three years until Lambeth finally sent someone to fix the roof and paint the rooms affected by the leak, but the problems were never properly sorted'. During this time, Kate lost her job due to her deteriorating health, and so was forced to borrow money to complete the rest of the repair works that Lambeth left behind, and she refused to pay the annual service charge in protest. Her severance pay and incapacity benefit helped her keep up with mortgage payments until July 2012, shortly after the PFI contract began, when the Department for Work and Pensions mistakenly stopped her benefits and she went into mortgage arrears; within a few months, that triggered repossession proceedings by the bank.

Believing she would now be unable to take up the property-swap offer, Kate told Pinnacle she was interested in selling up. An independent valuer suggested a sale price of £275,000 in December 2012, but Kate quickly changed her mind when Pinnacle offered her just £175,000: 'If I had sold at that price we would have almost certainly faced having to leave London or splitting up the family given the impossible cost of housing.' Worried about the impact on her daughter, who was sitting GCSEs, Kate borrowed more money from a friend to pay the bank and court costs. With her benefits reinstated and the threat of repossession lifted, in January 2013 she informed Pinnacle that the family had chosen to remain on the estate, only to discover that her bank would not agree to port her mortgage. Repossession proceedings started again after the Department for Work and Pensions' controversial work capability assessments – another outsourcing disaster – found Kate fit to work and stopped her benefits right at the time she was applying for a new mortgage. Kate eventually tried six different mortgage lenders to no avail, all blaming her low income, unemployed status and poor credit rating from the service charge and mortgage arrears on her record.

'Port or sell'

So it came as a huge shock to Kate and other homeowners that when they approached Pinnacle for the help previously promised, they found a brick wall. The best Pinnacle would do was hand them the phone number of a single mortgage broker whose details had originally been provided to Pinnacle by one of the affected homeowners. Repeated requests for template letters for banks, meetings and explanations of Pinnacle's low valuations were all met with prevarication for months on end – the only useful information was provided by the MFN RAMB. When residents reminded the Pinnacle manager about the council's promise to help the homeowners stay on the regenerated estate dating back to 2005, he told them that when 'the contract was signed a lot of the nice things were basically taken away'.[37] Struggling homeowners were instead given an ultimatum: 'port or sell'.

With such low valuations being offered by Pinnacle, some homeowners took desperate actions to cling onto their homes. One informally borrowed £100,000 at a 9 per cent interest rate to pay off the outstanding mortgage and move into a like-for-like property. Another took a loan from her employer, two home-owners were forced to accept new mortgages with higher monthly payments from their existing lenders, and one homeowner re-luctantly put their adult child on the mortgage. But this hard-line approach had a particularly devastating effect on Kate. Pinnacle told her that if she sold up quickly she would be able to buy into one of Notting Hill Housing's shared-ownership homes in the new Oval Quarter development. Notting Hill told her she needed to be in a position to put down a 40 per cent deposit by mid-September 2013, and so Kate reluctantly accepted Pinnacle's revised offer of £228,000 in July 2013. Notting Hill then ruled her ineligible for the Oval Quarter shared-ownership scheme because her annual household income was below the £61,000 qualification limit, something Pinnacle should have been aware of. Kate was trapped:

> I became very stressed, I did not know what to do, but what choice did I have? I could not move my mortgage or take out a new one. Pinnacle told me that Lambeth would not help and so there was only one option – sell.

Believing she had no choice, she completed the sale of her house in October 2013 but 'immediately realised it had been a terrible mistake'. After paying off her outstanding mortgage and the overpayment penalty, plus all of the debts she had incurred to repair her house and prevent repossession, Kate was in complete limbo: she did not have enough money even to buy a garage in London, but now had too much to qualify for welfare benefits. The only option was to rent in the private rented sector, where the family faced paying £2,400 a month – compared with her monthly mortgage repayments of just over £600 – that would eat away at the money left over from the forced sale of her home and eventually become impossible to afford without an income and with her children in full-time education. Realising that before long they would be made homeless, the family made the difficult decision to occupy their former home and negotiate with the local authority to help them remain on their estate.

Official minutes of contract monitoring meetings show clearly that residents were raising problems like Kate's with Lambeth and Regenter as early as July 2013. Yet it took until November 2013 for Lambeth officers to take the matter seriously. They told residents they had put together a flowchart of people's mortgage journeys and were working up a proposal to enable the local authority to step in as 'a kind of lender of last resort' and to 'make absolutely sure that nobody lost their home as a result of the regeneration project':

> just be assured nobody is going to lose their home as a result of this process ... we would obviously try and take every step to support homeowners to secure the future of their home independently but the council is there as a last resort should that be necessary ... Lambeth will not let anyone fall through the cracks. We are considering becoming mortgage lenders in our own right.[38]

Having raised hopes, Lambeth then cruelly dashed them at a follow-up meeting in February 2014, informing homeowners there would be no lender of last resort and denying that officers had ever made such a public commitment. Instead, Lambeth now promised that possession proceedings would begin only after all the options – now excluding the lender of last resort – had been explored to help them stay on the redeveloped estate. By now, the homeowners' mortgage porting crisis was holding up the demolition and construction programme, contractual deadlines were being missed and financial penalties of £10,000 per week were rumoured to be accruing on whoever was deemed responsible.

To try to unblock the impasse, Pinnacle offered several homeowners a temporary 'licence to occupy' what would be their new home for three to six months to enable demolition to proceed and give them more time to find a solution. In the absence of any other support, Kate refused, believing it would hand all the power to Lambeth and Regenter to wash their hands of the problem. Those who did take up the offer found she was right. One homeowner, pressured into signing an agreement to surrender her lease and move into her new home under a temporary licence, stalled when it came to the move over uncertainty about what would happen to her family if the mortgage offer fell through. Pinnacle also realised this could happen, and refused to pay her the £6,000 in disturbance costs she needed to move home in case the mortgage offer was withdrawn. A few weeks later, Pinnacle sent bailiffs to evict her illegally from her own home, falsely telling them that she was a tenant and was illegally sub-letting, a deceit that somehow managed to get circulated around the wider community. The bailiffs kicked down her bedroom door and emptied her belongings into the garden. After being treated for severe stress and anxiety, and receiving mortgage confirmation, she finally moved into a new home in May 2014. Other homeowners like Uzoamaka were also coming under forms of intimidation from the increasingly brutalising environment of the regeneration:

> At one stage it was just me and a vulnerable, elderly lady left on our part of the estate and things were going downhill fast. People were going round breaking in and vandalising the empty blocks,

graffitiing the surrounding walls; they even put a hangman on the door next to her and wrote 'alone'. I witnessed two guys attack one of the wardens with a screwdriver right outside my house. Communal areas were not being cleaned, rubbish was being left piled up, and sometimes we would come home to find a walkway blocked without any notification. We felt we were being trapped in. The more people that left, the colder it got on the estate; we had foxes and mice, and it was awful. And on the eighth of July 2014 they turned off the lights and CCTV cameras. They never even informed the police that we were living there. I had to notify them. One night in May 2015 my window was smashed. It was becoming really dangerous, and I thought, 'No, you're not putting me at risk on the estate, I can't stay here any more'.[39]

Desperate to get out, Uzoamaka pleaded to move into her new house but because she did not have a mortgage even in principle, her request was refused. Instead, she was encouraged by Pinnacle to reduce her mortgage debt as fast as possible by making over-payments, as this would supposedly make it more likely she would find a new mortgage, and Pinnacle even offered to wipe off the remaining balance if she got it low enough. Believing them, she 'ate up the rest of my savings, turned off the heating, cut down on essentials, and went hungry' and, with a loan from a sympathetic acquaintance, she reduced her mortgage debt by £20,000 in one year. But the banks kept saying no and Pinnacle's offer of wiping off the balance never materialised. Finally, a mortgage offer came through and Uzoamaka moved in to her new home in June 2015. Figure 4.3 captures her final poignant moments outside her home of 30 years.

Sadly, her friend 'Annie' did not make it through the ordeal. Annie had lived on the estate for 20 years and, after much anguish and stress, had eventually managed to get a new interest-only mortgage by putting one of her adult children on it. But the monthly payments were much higher than before and so was her annual council tax bill, up by over £400, after new homes on the estate were moved from council tax band C to E.[40] As a result, Annie was working two jobs every day to make ends meet. Uzoamaka remembered the intolerable toll that the stress of not being able to move the mortgage had placed on her, while seeing

Figure 4.3 Uzoamaka Okafor sitting outside her home of 30 years for the final time, June 2015

Source: Ross Domoney's 2016 film *Uprooted*, at https://vimeo.com/rossdomoney

other homeowners being forced to sell up: 'She was concerned about her E.ON bills; she had been taken to court about council tax even though she'd paid it; she was worried about service charges.' Late one evening, Annie collapsed and died suddenly from an apparent heart attack, leaving behind five children.

Lambeth eventually told Kate that it would not offer her a council tenancy as she did not meet the council's allocation criteria for social rented housing and no exceptions would be made. MFN RAMB and some local councillors pressured Regenter and Lambeth into offering Kate and her family an assured short-hold tenancy for three years in the private rented sector, to which they would contribute 20 per cent of the monthly rent – later upped to four years and 50 per cent – and a financial incentive to the landlord. But there was a catch – eviction proceedings would be stopped only if she accepted the offer in principle. Without an alternative, Kate began viewing private rented properties around the beginning of April 2014, the same time as Pinnacle, on behalf of Lambeth, was granted a possession order. Despite this pressure, Kate and her family were unable to accept the properties on offer as they were either too small or unsuitable for Kate's significant health needs. The offer of a four-year tenancy in the private rented sector was later withdrawn, and Lambeth informed Kate and her family of its intention to evict them, which eventually took place on 27 August 2014 by bailiffs and police. Uzoamaka recalls seeing 'Pinnacle and Rydon officers openly laughing amongst themselves as we moved the family's belongings'. The family was rendered immediately homeless and ended up in the private rented sector on a six-month tenancy paying £1,800 a month. Kate was still living there as of October 2018 in a property that was completely unsuitable for her health needs as she could not climb the stairs.

Eventually, 14 homeowners 'voluntarily' sold their homes back to Pinnacle between 2012 and 2015, for an average price of just £200,000 in a local property market where in 2012 the average sale price for leasehold flats was £297,792 and three-bed homes on the neighbouring council estate sold for an average of £315,000. To put this figure into further context, documents released under the Freedom of Information Act show that Pinnacle paid homeowners on average less than what Lambeth had expected to pay them in 2008 as part of its original financial model.[41] The local MP, Kate Hoey, declared at a public meeting in March 2014 that the 'undervaluing was quite shocking'.[42] When challenged, Pinnacle dishonestly told homeowners that its hands had been tied by a tribunal in March 2011 that set a valuation precedent of £150,000 for a three-bed property on the estate in response to a homeowner issuing a blight notice on Lambeth because he could not sell his home. Pinnacle repeatedly warned homeowners that if they waited for a compulsory purchase order, they could get less because of that precedent.[43] What made the situation truly unfair was that while several homeowners who moved away were forced to rent from private landlords, other homeowners who were mortgage-free or able to port their mortgages were now sitting on a massive capital gain – new three-bed flats in the Oval Quarter development were selling for £600,000 on the open market.

No one in either Lambeth or Regenter appears to have ever foreseen the mortgage blockage. Yet, given that these 58 home-owners were predominantly of an ethnic minority background, with many being elderly and having disabilities or health problems, this should have been identified by Lambeth's equality impact assessment – a statutory requirement to ensure public bodies do not discriminate against minority groups. However, the equality impact assessment makes no mention of this issue, and Uzoamaka was told by three council officers that these concerns had been raised at early stages but they were told 'not to get involved'.

Follow the money

But this was not just the result of political negligence – as we will see more clearly in chapter 6, what could be seen as vested interests and private greed at the heart of this outsourced regeneration scheme played a decisive factor behind Lambeth, Regenter and Pinnacle refusing to help residents with mortgage problems and instead pressuring them to sell up for such low prices. Under the PFI contract, Pinnacle managed the homeowner rehousing process, but Lambeth financed the costs up to an agreed upper limit, after which Regenter would underwrite any additional expense. So Pinnacle was financially incentivised, through both performance bonuses and penalties, not to allow the cost of buying homes and compensating residents to exceed this limit. At the same time, the PFI contract also stipulated that the private developer of Oval Quarter – part-owned by Higgins and Pinnacle – would be able to buy from Lambeth every 'like-for-like' property not taken up by an existing resident, for approximately £180,000 for one-bed homes and £280,000 for three-bed homes, and then sell them on the open market. Thus Pinnacle also had a vested financial interest in the sale of 'unwanted' like-for-like homes. Perversely, Lambeth also had a financial interest in these sales taking place, as it would receive a financial share of the developer's profits from the sale of new homes on the estate. Both Pinnacle and Lambeth thus had a plausible interest in devaluing the price paid to homeowners, while maximising the number of like-for-like homeowner properties not taken up, so that they could sell them on the open market. As a result, the PFI scheme ended up dispossessing some of the very residents that the original design of the scheme had tried to protect.

After Grenfell: the mask comes off

In 2017, Regenter declared the MFN works complete. To the outside world, the regeneration of this previously stigmatised council estate and the creation of Oval Quarter is a PPP success story. It has won several national awards (Affordable Home Ownership Awards 2012, UK Property Awards 2014, National Housing Awards 2017) and judges at the 2017 Building Awards ceremony commended the project as 'an exemplar for how to deliver genuine regeneration and retain a socially mixed community'.[44] But for some residents of the MFN estate, the nightmare of unsafe housing under a regime of outsourcing and self-regulation continued. Following the Grenfell Tower disaster, residents in one new block (built in 2014) inspected communal fire doors and safety signage and suspected that defects identified in a fire risk assessment (FRA) from 25 April 2014 – over three years previously – had never been attended to. ITV News agreed to investigate, and sent an independent fire safety expert, Stephen McKenzie, who found that not only had Rydon failed to carry out the FRA appropriately, but that none of the issues raised had been addressed. The most serious breaches involved fire doors in the staircases not fitted to British Standards, with air gaps between doors and frames on four out of six floors, emergency escape lighting not fitted to British Standard, fire exit signs missing and the use of non-fire-retardant paint.

What is most shocking about this episode is that a resident had written to Pinnacle twice about this particular FRA in 2014 to ask how the identified problems were being addressed, but never received an answer. ITV News ran its exclusive on 14 July 2017, including an interview with a former Rydon manager who claimed that the work it had carried out on the MFN and other estates had put lives at risk.[45] Before going out on air, residents observed a director of Higgins putting up new signs in the communal areas of the apartment blocks it built. They were clearly trying to clean up their mess before the news story broke. During the post-Grenfell media investigations, Joel Hills, business editor at ITN News, brought the cameras to the MFN estate to find out about residents' experiences of Rydon. As he arrived, he said to me off-camera: 'This is a council estate? It looks magnificent. Looking at this place it's really hard to imagine there is anything wrong. Are you sure?' After seeing with his own eyes the fire safety issues, he was sure. It was a salutary reminder of how easy it is to create the illusion of progress, of improvement, of safety on the surface when underneath lie the foundations of social murder.

Conclusion

By tracing the privatised delivery mode of public housing re-generation under PFI down to the lived places where regeneration happens, we have uncovered: how residents' health and safety have been put at risk through unsafe works and failing services; how residents' consumer rights to the most competitive and reliable energy contracts have been removed through the creation of a corporate energy supply monopoly that failed to work properly yet from which there was no escape for 40 years; how homeowners have lost their homes through discrimination, negli-gence and greed of those in both the private and public sectors; and how even a community's attachment to place has been severed through the estate's rebranding as Oval Quarter. Behind each act of dispossession was a very clear financial imperative running through the PFI model to capture profit from land and services at the expense of residents' well-being. This underlines how the financing underpinning Lambeth's PFI regeneration scheme – and the crucial acquisition and rehousing of homeowners – depended hugely on the commodification, marketisation and gentrification of the estate, unlocking existing open and built space for the purpose of profit-seeking private development. We now turn to the heroic yet frequently frustrated efforts by residents of all three schemes to hold their landlord and PFI consortia to account.

Notes

1 Greater London Authority, *Planning Report PDU/0467/01: Mostyn Gardens, Myatts Field North Estate in the London Borough of Lambeth* (London: GLA, 8 March 2002).

2 London Borough of Lambeth, *Executive Report: Rebuilding Myatts Fields – Pursuing a PFI Option* (London: London Borough of Lambeth, 8 December 2003), at https://moderngov.lambeth.gov.uk/Data/Executive%20(replaced%20by%20the%20Cabinet%20on%2024-05-06)/20031208/Agenda/Report%20-%20Rebuilding%20Myatts%20Fields%20-%20Pursuing%20a%20PFI%20Option%20-%2008-12-2003.pdf (accessed 12 December 2018).

3 London Borough of Lambeth, 'Newsletter to residents' (2005).

4 Greater London Authority, *Planning Report PDU/1492/01: Myatts Field North Estate in the London Borough of Lambeth*, Planning Application No. 07/00157/OUT (London: GLA, 9 May 2007).

5 The following project information and financial data come from analysing documents released after a freedom of information request: London Borough of Lambeth, 'Myatts Field North housing PFI: outline business case', March 2006; and London Borough of Lambeth, 'Myatts Field North housing PFI: full business case, version 14', July 2011. They can be viewed along with other official project documentation at http://peoplevspfi.org.uk/home/myatts-field-north-regeneration (accessed 14 October 2018).

6 London Borough of Lambeth, 'Myatts Field North housing PFI: full business case', p. 53, p. 59 and appendix.

7 K. Cooper, 'The story of the Camberwell submarine', *Inside Housing*, 19 February 2016, at https://www.insidehousing.co.uk/insight/insight/the-story-of-the-camberwell-submarine-46186 (accessed 14 October 2016).

8 H. Smith, 'An investigation into the lived experiences and financial impact of the PFI-led regeneration of Myatts Field North estate in London on the existing homeowners', geography undergraduate dissertation, University of Leeds, 2015.

9 London Borough of Lambeth, 'Myatts Field North housing PFI: full business case', p.53, p. 59 and appendix.

10 The evidence presented in this section has been collated from a number of sources. I was given access to anonymised transcripts of emails and telephone communications from individual residents to the MFN RAMB as well as anonymised copies of formal complaints made by residents and the MFN RAMB to Regenter and Lambeth between May 2012 and October 2018. In conjunction with MFN RAMB, I conducted a survey between November 2012 and June 2013 of 14 households whose homes were refurbished by Rydon on behalf of Regenter, the findings of which can be viewed here: J. Dyer, S. Hodkinson and C. Essen, Resident Experiences of Internal refurbishments under the Myatts Field North PFI contract' (MFN RAMB and University of Leeds, February 2014) (February 2014), https://goo.gl/g3zrCk (accessed 14 October 2018). I also conducted a number of formal interviews with residents between August 2012 and present that

were recorded and transcribed, and visited the estate numerous times from May 2012 to July 2017, taking photographs, attending residents' association meetings, and holding informal conversations with residents. The evidence gathered was compiled into a second report on health and safety concerns and incidents: S. Hodkinson, C. Essen, U. Okafor, J. Cornillon and S. Hack, 'Health and safety concerns on the Myatts Field North estate under the Private Finance Initiative' (MFN RAMB and University of Leeds, June, 2014), at http://peoplevspfi.org.uk/wp-content/uploads/2017/07/HealthSafetyReport_REDACTED.pdf (accessed 14 October 2018).

11   Interview with 'Winston', Lambeth tenant, 1 November 2012.

12   Interview with 'Dec', Lambeth tenant, 31 October 2012.

13   Oval Quarter marketing website, http://www.ovalquarter.com. With all the homes now built and sold, the website is no longer online, but the brand discourse can be found on multiple property websites: see http://realestatecoulisse.com/londons-most-dynamic-and-desirable-new-community-oval-quarter (accessed 16 October 2018).

14   S. Lennon-Smith, 'The Foxton effect: the role of third party agents in the gentrification of Brixton', geography undergraduate dissertation, University of Leeds, 2014.

15   Interview with 'Femi', Lambeth leaseholder, 10 October 2014.

16   Email correspondence from a Lambeth leaseholder to Higgins, 10 July 2014, made available to me by MFN RAMB.

17   Z. Williams, 'The real cost of regeneration', *Guardian*, 21 July 2017, at https://www.theguardian.com/society/2017/jul/21/the-real-cost-of-regeneration-social-housing-private-developers-pfi (accessed 16 October 2018).

18   The evidence presented here captures more than 300 households' experiences since January 2013 and is a summary of findings presented in a report I co-wrote with Ruth London of Fuel Poverty Action: S. Hodkinson and R. London, '*Not fit for Purpose: Residents' Experiences of E.ON's District Heating System on the Myatts Field North Estate and Oval Quarter Development in Lambeth, London* (London: Fuel Poverty Action, 2017), at https://www.fuelpovertyaction.org.uk/wp-content/uploads/2017/04/MFN_OQ_EON_28-4-17_FINAL.pdf (accessed 16 October 2018). In the real-life examples presented in that report and here, all names have been changed to guarantee anonymity, except for the named representatives of the residents' groups. The report was the main background research for, and featured on, a BBC Radio 5 Live *Investigates* broadcast about district heating on 30 April 2017: see https://www.bbc.co.uk/programmes/b08nrhzq (accessed 16 October 2018).

19   Although the PFI contract allows council tenants the right to waive particular works to their homes (so as to retain their own fixtures, fittings or improvements), this did not cover the connection of their homes to the district heating system.

20   Vassall Labour Party branch survey of winter hot water and heating problems, March 2015, shared with author.

21   Eversheds, 'Project agreement in relation to the Myatts Field North
     Housing HRA PFI project', Schedule 2: contractors' proposals, documents
     5.7.2–001, 'Environmental sustainability' Version E and 5.7.2–002 'ESCo
     solution' Rev I (4 May 2012). These documents were disclosed under the
     2000 Freedom of Information Act and are not available online. A heavily
     redacted version of the project agreement is available at https://goo.
     gl/6EIsoZ (accessed 14 October 2018).
22   Eversheds, 'Project agreement', pp. 339–340.
23   Ibid., schedule 2, 5.7.2–002 'ESCo solution', p. 4.
24   Ibid., pp. 339–340.
25   Testimony by Councillor Jacqui Dyer to a meeting between E.ON
     community energy team and MFN and Oval Quarter residents, Fuel
     Poverty Action, Regenter, the Heat Trust, and the author at E.ON's offices
     in the Port of London Authority building, 24 January 2017.
26   T. Helm and J. Tapper, 'Energy companies "ripping off" millions, ministers
     say', Observer, 12 March 2017, at https://www.theguardian.com/
     money/2017/mar/12/millions-overpaying-energy-bills-admits-ministry-
     big-six (accessed 14 October 2018).
27   C. Farand, 'Watchdog opens investigation over shocking energy bills at
     Orchard Village, Rainham', Romford Recorder, 30 September 2016, at
     https://goo.gl/73edSG (accessed 14 October 2018).
28   Interview with Uzoamaka Okafor, Lambeth leaseholder, 10 March 2015.
29   Interview with elected officers of MFN RAMB, 30 June 2013.
30   Emailed letter from Jeremy Bungey, head of E.ON Community Energy
     Business, to London Borough of Lambeth, 14 December 2015, copied to
     MFN RAMB.
31   The evidence in this section comes from a confidential report compiled
     with MFN RAMB: U. Okafor, S. Hodkinson and C. Essen, Homeowners'
     Experiences of Compulsory Purchase, Homeloss and Rehousing Under the
     Myatts Field North PFI Contract (University of Leeds and MFN RAMB,
     July 2014). A public interim version of this report from March 2014
     can be found at http://peoplevspfi.org.uk/wp-content/uploads/2017/07/
     Interim-Homeowners-REDACTED.pdf (accessed 17 October 2018).
     The report was based on surveys and interviews with affected MFN
     homeowners conducted by email, telephone and in person in order to
     track their individual situations. The data were stored and periodically
     updated in a database. Additional data came from attending public and
     private meetings with homeowners, organising workshops and drop-in
     surgeries with homeowners, correspondence with affected residents,
     Lambeth and Regenter, and analysing local authority reports, contractual
     documentation and reports and minutes from the PFI Project Liaison
     Board and MFN RAMB meetings with Lambeth and Regenter. Through
     this approach, I was able to document the experiences of 19 homeowners
     as well as to collect evidence on the overall process.
32   London Borough of Lambeth, 'Rebuilding Myatts', Newsletter, Issue 4,
     March 2005.
33   London Borough of Lambeth, 'Leaseholder information sheet', September
     2007.

34 London Borough of Lambeth, 'Myatts Field North Housing PFI: full business case'.

35 Regenter, 'Myatts Field North home owners meeting', Presentation to homeowners, 4 July 2012.

36 Interview with Uzoamaka Okafor. Uzoamaka' s emotional attachment to her home can be more fully appreciated in the excellent award-winning 2016 film *Uprooted*, by Ross Domoney, which follows the last days of two residents in their homes on MFN estate before they were due to move out into new homes, available at https://vimeo.com/rossdomoney (accessed 14 October 2018).

37 The quote is taken from a transcript of a resident's audio-recording of a homeowners' meeting with the Pinnacle homeowner manager, November 2013.

38 The quotes are taken from a transcript of a resident's audio-recording of a meeting between Regenter, Lambeth and MFN RAMB, 28 November 2013.

39 Interview with Uzoamaka Okafor.

40 Smith, 'An investigation into the lived experiences and financial impact of the PFI-led regeneration'.

41 London Borough of Lambeth, 'Myatts Field North housing PFI: outline business base', March 2006, available at http://peoplevspfi.org.uk/wp-content/uploads/2017/07/MFN_OBC.pdf (accessed 14 October 2018).

42 Transcript of a resident's recording of a 'special homeowner public meeting' chaired by Councillor Jacqui Dyer involving Lambeth, Regenter, Pinnacle, Kate Hoey MP, local councillors and residents.

43 Interview with Uzoamaka Okafor.

44 'Oval Quarter, Myatts Field North receives a highly commended at the Building Awards', Higgins news website, 21 November 2017, at https://www.higginsconstruction.co.uk/news/2017/oval-quarter-myatts-field-north-receives-a-highly-commended-at-the-building-awards (accessed 14 October 2018).

45 J. Hills, 'Grenfell contractor accused of safety failings on other local authority projects', ITV News website, 14 July 2017, at https://www.itv.com/news/2017-07-14/itv-news-rydon-investigation-grenfell-tower/ (accessed 14 October 2018).

5　The accountability vacuum

The previous two chapters showed at close hand the grim reality of outsourced regeneration under PFI in Islington, Camden and Lambeth. Far from isolated cases, botched design, poor construction and unreliable repairs have featured across the PFI programmes.[1] Drawing on interviews with public and private sector professionals, residents involved in PFI schemes and whistle-blowers, in this chapter I will argue that outsourced public housing under PFI has suffered from a systematic 'accountability vacuum' at the heart of its model. Different parties who might be considered to embody or defend the public interest – residents, elected politicians, courts, regulators and safety authorities – are not able to exercise democratic scrutiny over the decisions and actions taken by the public and private sector partners. I will show that accountability has been specifically designed out of outsourced delivery in three main ways: first, through an extreme form of self-regulation in which the public authority has very little oversight over private sector compliance with the required contractual standards and instead relies almost completely on self-certified performance reporting; second, through poorly written contracts that set largely meaningless KPIs, allow general rectification periods and result in minimal financial penalties despite demonstrable failings; and third, through the local authority's prioritisation of protecting long-term partnerships with private companies over genuine resident involvement and empowerment, accompanied by an absence of structures and processes for holding those responsible for poor performance to account, where those who do speak out are routinely ignored and sometimes actively silenced.

Paying the fox to guard the henhouse

As I explained in chapter 2, proponents of PFI argue that the higher cost of capital under PFI compared with public borrowing will eventually result in better value for money through the magic mantra of private sector efficiency, risk transfer and payment by results. Yet the opposite has happened, as the appalling experiences of residents recounted in the previous chapters have made clear. The first question we need to address is: how did work that was clearly never fit for purpose ever get signed off in the first place as meeting the Decent Homes standards or building regulations?

The dubious role of the 'independent certifier'

Part of the answer lies in the wider context of self-regulation and long sub-contracting chains discussed in chapter 1. A large part of building work is now self-certifiable, and those areas still subject to building control approval are governed by very minimal legal requirements for inspection that are policed by public and private firms competing for customers and profit. However, for the PFI banks and investors, and the insurance companies providing indemnities and warranties to the construction firms, this largely self-regulatory environment of outsourced regeneration was deemed a little too light-touch. To provide an extra layer of assurance, many PFI schemes engaged so-called independent certifiers (ICs). These are supposedly third-party inspectors, jointly appointed by the public authority and the SPV, to survey and sign off refurbishments or new-builds as compliant with the PFI contract and ready for occupation. The IC's role is vitally important to the illusion of accountability. Until an 'availability certificate' is issued, the SPV cannot claim the full contractual payment for that property and the various sub-contractors cannot be paid; and until the target number of availability certificates is reached for a specified period, the bank will not release the next tranche of finance for the next phase of works. The public authority and insurers, meanwhile, rely on the IC's certificate as proof of quality assurance.

However, as we have already seen, residents' experiences in several housing PFI schemes suggest the IC plays a far more dubious role in monitoring contractual and legal compliance. This was corroborated by a key finding of an inquiry into construction defects in the Edinburgh schools PFI scheme, which reported in 2017. Contrary to what local authorities had been led to believe, the IC provided a 'quite limited level of detailed scrutiny'.[2] In Edinburgh, IC inspections were focused on the completion stages of PFI projects, meaning they rarely – if ever – checked the schools' 'build quality' to confirm it met the approved design documentation.[3] Instead of 100 per cent inspections, it was more common for samples to be checked, and for the IC to spend considerably less time than required to conduct on-site inspections due to 'ongoing pressure to reduce the level of fees paid for this service' from competition.[4] The inquiry also questioned the 'independence' of these inspectors, finding that in contrast to the 'joint appointment' rhetoric, it had been the norm for the PFI contractors to appoint their preferred IC in closed-door procurements.[5] Given that the IC is also paid by the SPV, not the public authority, it is under huge pressure to inspect and sign off properties quickly and to put unfinished or faulty work that would normally prevent formal certification on a 'snagging list' – a series of issues for the contractor to deal with after the work is signed off. In other words, the IC is not an independent inspector, but the SPV's contractor, employed to rubber-stamp a piece of paper so that the tap of finance can be turned on and increased over the construction period.

These insights help us to understand why so many homes were signed off in Islington, Camden, Lambeth and elsewhere when they were not clearly fit for purpose. During my research I interviewed the eminent building surveyor Stephen Boniface, who had direct knowledge of the Islington PFI schemes. He told me that such checks should always have taken place where 'listed-building consent' had been granted, yet, in his view, either no inspections had taken place or the person doing them was unqualified. Part of the problem was the extent of the work done under self-certification. He gave an example of a grade II listed building that he had been employed to survey as part of an ongoing court case:

the person who signed off the original works was not qualified and really completely messed up and missed a lot of problems ... certificates for the electrical installation and for the heating installation were incorrectly issued ... that electrician is still going around, for all we know, signing off jobs that should never be signed off, which is potentially life threatening ... this is self-certification.... In terms of building regulations no one is there saying, 'They've done it to the regulation standards'.[6]

Islington council officers I interviewed played down the problem, saying there had been only a 'few issues' of homes being wrongly signed off and 'money ... paid back'.[7] However, a former employee of Partners for Improvement in Islington I interviewed in 2018 told me that, over time, the practice of United House and Partners knowingly signing off works that were not complete and falsifying availability certificates became routine:

For PFI-1, Partners and United House did do a generally thorough job of surveying properties ... the IC who worked in the office ... did visit properties ... and it was taken seriously. By PFI-2, however, it all changed. Condition reports and surveys were at best done by someone driving past the properties if they visited them all. There was no IC, or if there was, they weren't based in our office any more ... the availability certificates were in fact just a photocopied piece of paper with a signature automatically generated by United House that just got filed in the folders ... they meant nothing.[8]

While this affected all residents, it was particularly relevant to leaseholders, as they would be charged for any major works to their home. Under section 20 of the Landlord and Tenant Act 1985 (as amended 2002), leaseholders have to be consulted about any works over £250 and their eventual bill would be capped at the estimated cost set out in the section 20 notice. The only difference under PFI was that ministers had decreed there would be a cap of £10,000 every five years, in common with some other government-assisted regeneration schemes.[9] The Partners whistle-blower explained that some of the estimates produced during PFI-1 had been well under £10,000 when the actual work cost much more than that, which left 'Partners out of pocket'. So for PFI-2, Partners and United House completely changed their approach:

They realised that the minimum they could get away with was to just send everybody an estimate with six to eight lines on it like 'check roof, mend if necessary', then just throw in any figures and the estimate would often come to well over £10,000.

By estimating the cost of the leaseholder works in excess of £10,000, Partners was virtually ensuring that it would always recover £10,000 from the leaseholder, irrespective of whether the works actually cost that much. This is because, should a lease-holder challenge the estimate at a leasehold valuation tribunal, there would be a financial cushion should the tribunal rule to reduce the estimated bill. The former Partners employee initially tried to have clarification meetings with surveyors from United House about the works required, but 'I was eventually told one way or the other "Just send the bill out"'. Not only were the 'estimates a complete load of rubbish' but, according to the whistle-blower, so was the work: 'As far as United House were concerned they were to go in, do the job as cheaply as possible and get out, and the moment we sent the council or the leaseholder the bill, they got paid'. But it was not just poor-quality work – in many cases no work was done at all:

> Some residents had been billed for a complete roof replacement that never took place. We would charge for pointing, but there was no pointing done. We would charge to rebuild a bit of a wall using a very expensive brick to comply with the heritage area but then just use normal bricks.

The former Partners employee believed that the directors at the top of Partners, United House and Rydon took a 'calculated risk' to do an inferior job, safe in the knowledge they would not get caught out, and even if they did, only a tiny fraction of residents would ever go to court, let alone win. A handful of leaseholders did successfully challenge the quality and cost of PFI contractors works at leasehold valuation tribunals, but these were almost always 'very well off, educated people – including the odd *Guardian* journalist – who knew how to work the system'.[10] This behaviour was not isolated to Islington. Lewisham's Brockley PFI scheme was hit by a three-year class action lawsuit brought in 2009 by 23 leaseholders against the council and Regenter (and its main contractor, Higgins). The tribunal upheld all of the residents' claims, including the poor standard of works, some of which was carried out completely unnecessarily and some of which was never carried out all. The case took so long to be heard because Lewisham initially refused to disclose to leaseholders the relevant parts of the PFI contract. When they got hold of the contract, leaseholders discovered that Regenter was entitled to include a huge 36 per cent 'professional' and 'management' fee, which the tribunal reduced to 17 per cent, although on appeal the figure was increased again to 34 per cent.[11]

Marking your own homework: how self-monitoring performance really works

This system of self-regulation does not just feature during the initial construction phase but continues throughout the operational and service delivery life of the contract. The SPV and its main property management and maintenance contractors will run one or more databases to record repair requests and complaints, response times, progress, as well as the availability and delivery of key services such as the customer service telephone, graffiti removal, refuse collection, external lighting and pest control. These databases are set up to automatically record any days of unavailability or where KPIs fall below the required levels, and indicate whether any financial penalties are due, or whether there are any 'excusing events' such as a contractor's inability to gain access to a property to repair it. Yet, residents involved in the various PFI contract monitoring forums in Islington, Camden and Lambeth all noticed a bizarre incongruity between, on the one hand, their own appalling experiences of the PFI contractors and, on the other, the excellent monthly availability and KPI scores broadcast by Partners, Regenter and Rydon, with resident satisfaction always hitting and usually surpassing the contractual target level of 75 per cent. When they asked whether there had been any financial penalties levied against the contractors, they were told that this was 'commercially confidential' and were forced to make freedom of information requests instead. What they discovered shocked them even more: most of the time no financial deductions were made, and when they were, the sums were negligible. In Islington, Partners was fined £48,995 in total within both the PFI-1 and PFI-2 schemes over the period April 2012 to March 2014;[12] in Camden, Partners was fined less than £15,000 between 2007 and 2016; and in Lambeth, Regenter was fined just under £282,000 from May 2012 to March 2017, amounting to less than 0.77 per cent of the £36.85 million unitary charge payments it received over that period.

While such tiny financial deductions could be interpreted as reflecting a successfully delivered contract, in reality the 'payments by results' regime is rigged in favour of the PFI contractor. Once the IC has signed off the homes as meeting the full availability standard, no availability deductions can then be levied unless a resident first reports a disrepair or defect, and only then if the problem is not fixed within the contract's permitted rectification period. First let us consider the amount of deductions that can be levied. The Islington street properties PFI 2 scheme's daily penalty deduction (at 2006 prices) for a rented home being unavailable is £15.57 if the resident remains able to live there, and £18.31 if it is uninhabitable; whereas for the MFN scheme the equivalent deductions (at 2012 prices) are £39.20 and £56.00. Missed KPI targets attract equally low financial penalties. Moreover, all housing PFI contracts have an annual cap on these performance deductions, above which penalties for missing KPI targets are permanently disregarded: in Islington PFI-2, 83 per cent of the unitary charge is protected, while in Lambeth 70 per cent is protected in the MFN scheme. Lambeth's designated PFI contract performance monitoring officer told the MFN RAMB that the financial penalties they could levy on Regenter were so small that it was not cost-effective to go looking for faults:

The penalties are peanuts, to be quite honest ... I could spend a whole month investigating complaints, but would my salary be covered as a result of that? ... I don't care, I get paid anyway but ... how cost-effective is it to invest so much time in one area unless we know something is really, really, really not working and we know we'd be on a winner?[13]

Such tiny penalties offer little incentive to a contractor to do the work properly or on time, compounded by the fact that the contractor usually has a generous amount of time either to fix the problem permanently or to solve it temporarily, before any unavailability deductions can be applied. For example, on the MFN estate, Regenter has 14 calendar days to repair a visible structural defect or rectify fire-stopping defects between the roofs of adjoining properties but can put in place a temporary fix for 20 days, and even longer for roof and window leaks, and dampness. Rydon has a two-week window to offer a repair appointment. But even if the financial penalties and repair time frames were tougher, the way the contract standards are written and interpreted can make them largely meaningless, as they measure very superficial aspects of contract delivery. For example, during the E.ON district heating scandal on the MFN estate (see chapter 4), residents pointed to the contractual requirement for a round-the-clock heat and hot water supply to residents 365 days of the year. However, buried in the contract's small print was a line that financial penalties would kick in only once the outage had lasted 24 hours or longer from the time of it being reported. So E.ON could leave residents without hot water or heating for up to 23 hours, 59 minutes and 59 seconds on each occasion without being fined. Nor could E.ON be financially penalised for supplying hot water at variable temperatures or low water pressure, as these were not referred to or defined in the PFI contract. Similarly, only three out of the 55 KPIs in the MFN PFI contract addressed the actual performance of the repairs service. So there were targets for answering the phone within eight rings during office hours, but no targets for being helpful; there were targets for handling complaints in a timely fashion, but not for properly investigating and responding to them. Exactly the same thing happened with regard to the official performance of KCTMO prior to the Grenfell fire, with KPIs each year matching or exceeding their targets.

The KPIs are not just largely irrelevant but also easy to distort. Compliance is based on what is recorded in the contractor's database, and there is no way of knowing if this is accurate. Residents frequently reported making repair requests that were never properly written down, followed up or dealt with, only to be told by the call centre that, according to the database, the repair had been successful or that no one was home on the day scheduled for the repair. Residents have direct experience of contractors posting 'no access' cards through the door while they were in the house without even trying to gain access, presumably to avoid making the repair. The operator would then issue a new job number, starting the whole cycle again, meaning that properties could almost never be declared unavailable. The potential for fiddling the PFI contractor's performance scores was revealed in May 2013 on the MFN estate when, against the background of growing resident dissatisfaction, Lambeth appointed the surveying firm Gleeds to audit Rydon's self-reported repairs performance of nearly 100 per cent compliance with the repair rectification period. When Gleeds looked at raw data from Rydon's database for March 2013, it found a number of irregularities: 28 repairs had not met the required rectification periods, there were a further 58 instances where Rydon's target date was more generous than specified in the contract, and 113 repair reports were missing from the compliance report. In Gleeds' view, Rydon should have self-declared deductions of £5,118.42, but had declared only £14.45, raising 'a question regarding misreporting of repairs since the start of the contract'.[14] This was not the only time that Rydon's compliance with PFI reporting was questioned. In the same year, a Rydon whistle-blower tipped off Islington council that Rydon 'had manipulated' KPI reporting on both street properties PFI schemes by changing the dates of when repair jobs had taken place so that missed KPI targets would not show. The same employee claimed that Rydon had also falsified safety certificates for its scaffolding sites, pretending it had checked them every seven days, in accordance with regulations, when in fact it had been 'filling in the forms off-site without visiting'. Instead of Islington investigating such serious allegations, Partners did, and found no evidence of wrongdoing.[15] But the former Partners employee I spoke to claimed that the rigging of availability and KPI attainment, as well as the falsification of scaffolding certificates, 'happened all the time'.[16]

The PFI self-monitoring system places the onus on the local authority to create an audit regime that can both incentivise honesty and detect non-compliance. In theory, the local authority does have a monitoring role. In common with all housing PFI schemes, Lambeth assured central government in its 2011 'full business case' that it had devised a 'robust post contract monitoring' strategy for the MFN scheme to 'receive and validate the self-monitoring information provided by the Contractor'.[17] In reality, local authorities' capacity to monitor and financially penalise their PFI partners is heavily constrained by financial, informational and political barriers. The teams are usually made up of just two or three officers, supported periodically by an external consultant. Such an expansive role for so few people means that the council's contract monitoring approach is mainly superficial, with very specific investigations from time to time. As Lambeth's designated PFI contractor performance monitoring officer told MFN residents in June 2013:

> I don't monitor the contract. I don't monitor the KPIs.... The contractor monitors their own performance, they give us their numbers, we look at their numbers and ask 'Do they stack up? Do they add up? Do they make sense? Do we have queries?' ... I will randomly do an audit of something, like complaints, maybe once a year; depends on what the priorities are, the political priorities, and depends on the costs.[18]

Councils do normally have access to the SPV's database, so if there is a complaint or a major query has been raised, they can see what action has been taken. Islington PFI housing officers were keen to assure me that they were 'very quick to challenge if there are divergences with performance information ... they'll have to go away and produce a report. It doesn't just get lost out there.' However, they also conceded that relying on the SPV's reporting data was not ideal: 'We are sort of in the process of enhancing their systems to make sure that nothing slips through any more'.[19] In reality, local authorities normally investigate residents' problems in a PFI contract only if a formal complaint has been made and it has made its way through the normal first two stages of the local complaints procedures without resolution. As the Partners whistle-blower told me, this was very rare in the Islington PFI schemes, because Partners would be very skilled at preventing complaints from going anywhere; and even when a complaint did reach the council, Partners usually got the benefit of the doubt because of the importance of maintaining a strong relationship with the PFI contractor. This partnership approach means that council monitoring teams end up having a close and often cosy relationship with the SPV. Islington's housing officers told me that Partners was 'actually quite a good contractor ... we do find them helpful and willing to try and find solutions with us'.[20] The former Partners employee offered a more critical summary of Islington's monitoring approach: 'It was like, "You've got the contract, you're running it well, off you go and do it"... there was no regular contact with the council'.[21]

This cosy relationship means that local authorities are wary of imposing deductions on housing PFI contractors, for fear of threatening their relationship with, or financially undermining, the SPV; they pursue a flexible approach to sub-standard performance because of the political risks of termination. One PFI advisor told me that councils tend to give the PFI contractors 'the benefit of the doubt.... We don't want to be terminating or giving them too harsh a penalty or they might walk away.'[22] One of the main problems for local authorities looking to penalise their contractor is that liability for unavailability and poor performance can be contested by the contractor if it can show that the local authority or a resident might have prevented it from meeting the contract. Islington's housing officers told me that, given the limited capacity for Islington to monitor the contract, 'We have to risk-assess everything that we do ... it's not about auditing everything to the nth degree, it's about which ones have the biggest impact on the payment mechanism'.[23] The PFI monitoring officer at the MFN estate concurred, telling me that the council had a 'huge list of availability failures that add up to a couple of million pounds', but that they stood little chance of actually deducting this amount.[24] This was because Regenter had made counter-claims against Lambeth for slow management of the tenant rehousing process – a task it had retained under the PFI contract – and its reluctance to sign compulsory purchase orders on some homeowners in mortgage difficulties, preventing Regenter from gaining vacant possession of land for new housing to be built.

Resident involvement: an exercise in PFI window-dressing

Alongside the self-monitoring model of outsourced housing regeneration and management under PFI, government had stipulated
that every housing PFI scheme should have a formal role for
residents to participate in the setting and monitoring of contractor
performance standards.[25] In Islington, Camden and Lambeth, the
PFI contracts set out the requirement for the SPV to create and
resource a residents' 'forum' or 'board' to ensure 'open monitoring
of the Contractor's performance' and provide 'accountability
through reporting on performance to residents'.[26] To this end,
regular monitoring meetings were set up between resident volunteers, the main PFI contractors, the council's monitoring officers
and, on occasion, elected councillors. But in contrast to the warm
rhetoric of accountability, the cold reality of resident involvement
did not take long to set in: the more resident representatives tried
to bring problems and safety concerns to the attention of the PFI
consortium and the local authority, the more they were pushed to
one side.

The reality of 'partnership' with residents in Islington

I interviewed several Islington residents who at various points had
sat on the Partners residents' forum, which met every two months
in Islington town hall. They explained how, on paper, the residents
appeared to be in charge, but in their experience the Forum was 'a
complete sham, deliberately set up to fail by Partners, who would
use a range of tactics to frustrate our residents' ability to monitor
the contract and push for changes'.[27] At the outset, Partners
managed to have a 'friendly tenant' chosen as chair of the forum,
whom other residents called 'the stool pigeon for Partners' because
of the way she managed to shut down criticism of Partners or the
main contractors, and tried to get 'difficult residents' to be either
thrown off or want to leave. Another tactic was to produce inac-
curate minutes and refuse to change the record if it made either
Partners or the council look bad. Direct questions or information requests were routinely evaded with ambiguous responses,

prevarication and evasion, using stock phrases like '"that's all the information that I have", "oh I don't recall that" and "I'll have to get back to you at the next meeting" ... which they never do'.[28] Although council representatives were present at the meetings, they mainly deferred to Partners and residents always felt they were acting in concert, as a united front. 'Daisy' explained that 'as much as Islington council might say they wish the PFI did not exist, they don't help us one iota. They see us as a pain in the butt.' This attitude was corroborated by an Islington housing officer I interviewed, who claimed the PFI contracts had been a success and residents who complained were politically motivated:

> I'm not seeing evidence of poor refurbishment ... we have a lot of people who were very satisfied ... there are some residents who really dislike the concept of PFI and really kind of look for every kind of way to sort of ... expose weaknesses in the contract [to] kind of justify their views on it.[29]

Despite the best efforts of Partners and Islington council to stifle the residents' forum, over time the residents became better organised; they removed the chair through a vote of no confidence and made the forum a magnet for residents to bring individual horror stories of disrepair and poor treatment in order to get issues addressed. Such was the scale of resident dissatisfaction that Partners was pressured into agreeing to a resident-led audit of Rydon's communal repairs. The investigation produced a damning set of findings:

> Rydon's workers – not the big bosses – told us that they work within a fixed repair budget for the year and did not get a penny more to maintain the properties, irrespective of actual need. So it looks like the larger part of the budget is creamed off by the Partners consortium ... we interviewed a roofer who told us he didn't get any support and he was doing jobs all on his own.... We found out that United House and Rydon used poor, inferior materials and that because of this they were coming back again and again to fix and repair. We also found that leaseholders were too afraid to report these problems because they were going to get charged for them.[30]

Inevitably, Partners would not allow the report to be published until it had been toned down: 'They talked about "inaccuracies"…. So we had meetings before we could publish it … [they were] trying to dumb it down a little bit.'[31] The final report, released in January 2013, set out 33 separate areas for service improvement.[32] At the same time, I worked with some of the residents on the forum to help monitor Partners' compliance with cyclical maintenance. It was clear from simply looking at the outside of homes originally refurbished in 2005 that no external repair or decoration was being carried out despite a contractual requirement to do so every seven years from their initial refurbishment date. So in December 2012 a freedom of information request was made to Islington for disclosure of the full postal addresses of all council and leasehold street properties that reached the full availability standard prior to 31 December 2007, and the exact dates on which full unitary charge payments for those homes began.[33] After seven months and several internal reviews of Islington's initial refusal to supply the requested information, it was finally disclosed. Resident volunteers then began to systematically visit and visually survey these properties over the next few years, and collected photographic evidence. The results were once again shocking – properties were in clear disrepair, with flaking paint, rusting iron railings and rotting gutters, windows and front doors. So the residents decided to publish these images in a series of 'PFI street tours' newsletters (figure 5.1) that, through social media, targeted the ruling Labour councillors representing the areas in question. Each newsletter asked a simple but effective question: why was Islington paying nearly £40 million a year to a company that appeared to be leaving the council's homes – many listed buildings – in such visible disrepair?

By 2016, Partners and Islington had clearly had enough of being held to account by elected residents and the increasingly toxic publicity damaging their reputation, and Partners announced that it was arbitrarily changing the forum's terms of reference relating to the election of residents. The proposed rule change would serve to exclude certain individuals who were seen as a thorn in the side of Partners and the council. Residents took their own vote on these changes, and rejected them. So in late 2016, Partners refused to hold elections, stopped calling meetings, and the PFI residents'

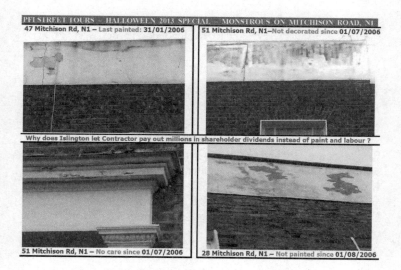

Figure 5.1 An example from a residents' 'PFI street tours' campaign newsletter, October 2013

Source: 'Edward'

forum was 'discontinued'. In January 2017, Partners announced that a new 'open forum' would be held every two months that would be run by Partners with 'no set agenda' and that would be open to all PFI residents to bring questions; individual issues would be followed up separately. Minutes of the meetings were initially put online but this stopped in November 2017.[34] The problems, though, did not go away and in September 2018 Islington's executive member for housing told a council housing scrutiny committee that Partners' official performance scores effectively masked a 'tsunami of cases that fester':

> ... it's very easy to get a satisfaction rating in the 90s if the vast majority of your work is routine jobs. The figure I give importance to is the 11 per cent of cases which go on for more than three months.... Certainly when the Partners contract does come to an

end the default position, and the position that I want and I think most councillors want, right across all political parties, is let's bring it back in-house.[35]

Keeping residents under control on Myatts Field North

Although with a different PFI contractor, Regenter, an almost identical story unfolded on the MFN estate from May 2012. Residents initially had to fight to get the promised residents' board set up and then to prevent Regenter hand-picking its membership. Estate resident Jacqui Dyer MBE, who would later briefly serve as the elected chair of the MFN RAMB before becoming a local Labour councillor, revealed to me in January 2013 some of the underhand tactics being used at the time to try to keep residents' involvement under their control:

> Pinnacle organised a meeting where they announced there would be a selection process to recruit members to a monitoring board. This led to a quite heated debate, as many residents present thought it should be us setting up the monitoring board to ensure it was genuinely independent, especially given our awful experiences of the refurbishment. Neighbours told me that Pinnacle was going around asking residents 'Who were the tenants who were vocal in the meeting? Where do they live?' Lo and behold, after the meeting, nomination forms were sent out to residents, only some of us never got them – the ones who were vocal in the meeting, like me.[36]

After eventually getting hold of those nomination forms, Jacqui was one of 20 residents who began to attend the monthly meetings of the residents' board. She was then tipped off by an insider that 'Pinnacle was running tenancy and benefit checks on some of us, you know, trying to get some dirt as a deliberate tactic to keep out people who they realised were going to hold them to account'.[37] Just as in Islington, a resident clearly sympathetic to the contractor was initially put forward as chair and, according to Jacqui, the initial meetings were tightly controlled by Regenter. Uzoamaka Okafor, MFN RAMB chair from 2014 to 2017, remembers the early meetings as 'a tick-box exercise' with residents given the run-around: 'If you had complaints, they tried to fragment your concerns, sweep them under the carpet. Things weren't followed through from meeting to meeting; key issues that we raised were not being written down, investigated, or addressed.'[38]

After months of going 'round in circles', residents like Jacqui and Uzoamaka decided to work together to ensure the residents' board had real teeth. The first step was to have residents elect their own representatives, who would draw up a new constitution that combined PFI monitoring with a traditional tenants' and residents' association model. In March 2013, MFN RAMB was officially constituted and immediately started to do the job that the council should have been doing from the outset – monitoring the delivery of the contract, collecting evidence of poor standards of work, performance and engagement, and creating an audit trail to hold the contractors to account. As part of my research, I agreed to work with them to devise a contract monitoring methodology that would compare the contractual undertakings made by Regenter with the day-to-day realities of the residents' experience. Residents were forced to make freedom of information requests to get the contract disclosed, although they were denied access to some of the most relevant sections, namely those detailing how much Regenter and its sub-contractors would be paid and how poor performance would be financially penalised. The reason given was that this was 'commercially confidential', and if disclosed could harm both public and private parties' interests. I then read the disclosed parts of the contract in fine detail for key contractual standards and advised on what kinds of additional information should be requested from Lambeth and Regenter to demonstrate compliance.

MFN RAMB encouraged residents to formally log defects, disrepair and other problems, and to use the complaints procedure when requests were not met, so that Lambeth would be informed and could investigate itself should residents not be satisfied with the outcome of the complaint. To collate and further investigate the mounting number of human stories, we co-designed a series of in-depth surveys of different aspects of the regeneration scheme, which would be based on what the contract said should be happening, in order to hold each main sub-contractor to account while providing an overall picture of Regenter's performance. As we saw in chapter 4, our first survey focused on 14 households' experiences of homes refurbished by Rydon. It had taken almost a year to complete, as some residents were simply too frightened to speak out, fearful of the consequences for their tenures and homes, as Jacqui Dyer recalled:

> the Regenter staff were trying to silence people from speaking to other neighbours about their concerns ... things like, 'Don't tell anybody what it is that we are discussing here – this is just private to you. It's not for you to compare with other neighbours; they've got their own individual issues that really is no business or relevance of yours'.... So, it was quite difficult to get people to talk because they were frightened about the comeback they might receive.[39]

This intimidation continued when the report was sent to Lambeth and the PFI contractors. Uzoamaka Okafor recalls Rydon's aggression at a meeting: 'One of Rydon's directors was there and I remember he came up to me really angrily, waving the report, and said "We were getting on fine, you and me, and then you go do something like this"'.[40] While Lambeth's contract monitoring officer initially seemed to be interested in investigating, even ringing me up to ask for advice on how to proceed, it was clear that the 'institutional indifference' towards residents seen so clearly at Grenfell (see introduction) was also present here. Before the contract monitoring officer would accept the authenticity of the refurbishment survey, she wanted to know who had written the report, because, she claimed, MFN RAMB was run by 'nutters who had pushed their way into some people's homes, whipped them up and really blown up all kinds of things when we [the council] were dealing with them and sorting them out. They've politicised some of these things.'[41] She was also clearly worried about the impact on the council's relationship with Regenter:

> We already have the right to monitor without Regenter's permission: we can go in and inspect and check, and they couldn't do anything about it. But we want to work in partnership and I'm reluctant to go around inspecting without them involved because it can damage the relationship.[42]

In the end, Lambeth did appoint an independent consultant to run a shorter survey based on our questions during the summer of 2014. The eventual report painted a remarkably similar picture to our report, with 67 per cent of residents having problems getting work finished or mistakes put right and 48 per cent describing the works as below a satisfactory standard and stating that part of their home had been damaged during refurbishment. However, Lambeth sought to downplay this appalling level of resident dissatisfaction and treatment by saying that, although it 'fell short of reasonable expectation', the feedback from tenants was 'somewhat more favourable than the Leeds survey'; a whole page was dedicated to a graph that helped to make the findings look good for Rydon.[43] Lambeth's response marked a pattern that would be repeated each time the residents presented clear evidence that the PFI contract was failing them.

Shoot the messenger: the perils of speaking out

Across all of the housing PFI schemes in this book, residents found they were hitting a solid brick wall formed by the private companies and local authority, which meant that, for the most part, their concerns were ignored or evaded. However, there was a more sinister side to this culture of impunity, witnessed in how whistle-blowers and others prepared to speak out were treated. We saw in chapter 3 how a self-employed contractor on the Chalcots Estate regeneration lost his job after speaking to the police about the alleged corrupt practices of one of the companies involved. In this section we focus on what happened when residents, former employees and even academics like myself brought problems to the attention of the local authorities and the PFI companies. We begin by returning to what happened to 'Edward', whom we met in chapter 3, after he spoke out against Partners and then Islington's treatment of him.

Using the law to silence and disarm the residents

Between October 2005 and March 2007, Edward and his family had been put through what he describes as 'living hell' by Partners and United House. Dangerous and unlawful work had left their grade II listed street property structurally unsound, with 180 defects and omissions in the refurbishment works. As a result, Edward's mentally ill son was no longer able to stay in the home and had been forced into care. And yet, instead of investigating Edward's formal complaints about the state of his home and the failures of Partners and the council to act, Islington's chief executive declared Edward to be a 'vexatious complainant' in May 2007 and placed him on the council's 'vexatious register':

> They banned me from attending council buildings and all council officers, including social services and social workers, were instructed to not talk to me or respond to my correspondence. My own Member of Parliament whom I informed about the PFI scandal wrote that she would never again 'open any of your emails ... nor reply to letters'.[44]

Given this experience, Edward was determined to ensure that any remedial works were done properly, to protect himself, his family and his home – and public property. With this in mind he took advice from the Information Commissioner's Office (ICO) – the UK's statutory regulator of information rights and data protection laws – and informed Partners that he would be filming and audio-recording their inspections, as was his statutory right, 'for personal or domestic reasons' such as defending himself in any legal action that might arise. However, both Islington and Partners took exception to this and would not enter the property unless he gave an undertaking not to record. Islington then initiated court action in September 2008, on the premise that because he was filming against Partners' wishes he was denying Partners and its sub-contractors access to his home as per his tenancy agreement. Edward contested the court application and made a counter-claim seeking both personal damages for the three years of 'living hell' he and his family had been put through, and a court order to undertake the necessary remedial works to his home.

The scale of the damage and remedial works required were soon established by the court's single joint expert surveyor, Stephen Boniface, who upheld all of Edward's claims and estimated the cost of repair at around £50,000 (in 2009 prices).[45] The judge granted

Partners access but threw out Islington's application to stop Edward from recording. However, Edward's claim for damages was never heard. The council spent some £40,000 instructing external barristers to contest Edward's claim for compensation and some of Boniface's findings in a number of additional court hearings. This ran down Edward's legal aid funding, but when he applied for more to continue his case, it was denied. Legal aid rules stipulated that the potential compensation awarded to a legally aided tenant had to be four times the court costs incurred. Edward was informed by his solicitor that 'the cost of a two-day hearing alone would far exceed the value of my permitted claim for compensation'.[46] As a result, an agreement was made between Edward's representatives and the council that a limited number of remedial works would be undertaken by Islington's own contractor, Kier, under Boniface's supervision, and the court proceedings were 'stayed' – halted for an undefined period of time. In the meantime, Edward's 'vexatious status' came to a head at a Partners residents' forum in May 2010, when Islington and Partners officers refused to allow the meeting to continue until Edward left.

As the repair works to his home dragged on, in December 2012 Edward made a formal objection to Islington's annual accounts for the financial year 2011–12 after being provided with a copy of an invoice from Kier to Islington for £92,432 for the remedial works to his home. This put the estimated total cost to the local taxpayer of the original works, plus the family's rehousing, legal process, council officers' time and inspectors' surveys in excess of £200,000. Edward made his objection to the council's external auditor, which just so happened to be KPMG LLP – a limited liability partnership and member of the KPMG group. This was the same KPMG group that had advised the Partners consortium during the procurement, and was also providing internal auditing advice to one of Partner's shareholders and housing management contractor, Hyde Housing. The auditor reassured Edward that there was no conflict of interest but quickly tried to shut down the objection by declaring that he could see no evidence of wrong-doing despite not having yet received any evidence from Edward. After sending that evidence – over 140 separate pieces of evidence itemising and costing each line of unnecessary expenditure incurred on his and other homes in Islington from the failure of both Islington and Partners to properly manage the PFI contracts – Edward heard nothing back for months. Upon prompting the auditor, Edward was told in June 2013 that Islington had apparently never received his letter, presumed 'lost in the post'. Documents from Islington that KPMG LLP claimed to have shared with Edward were also never received. Eventually, KPMG LLP threw out the objection in June 2014, restating the previous view that no 'significant (financial) losses have been incurred and, where any failings existed, the council has already acted to remedy the deficiencies', despite clear evidence to the contrary.[47] KPMG LLP then confirmed it had charged Islington council £13,800 for handling Edward's objection.[48]

Finally, in August 2014, seven years after Edward and his family had first been forced by Islington and Partners to return to an unsafe home, the repair works were declared complete. Edward was then told that his home was no longer included in the PFI contract and was back under direct control of Islington council, the result of a secret deal in 2009 between the council and Partners. However, Edward's euphoria over being 'the first tenant transferred out of the PFI hell' was tempered by the devastation it had wreaked on the lives of his family:

> Because I stood up to Islington council and their PFI Partners they declared me vexatious and sought to render me mentally unwell, and even asked the courts to have me examined by a psychiatrist who vindicated me for taking the position I did by declaring that I was reacting in a perfectly normal way given the horrendous circumstances my landlord and their agents had exposed me to. I will never understand why the PFI companies and contract were never taken to task by the council who are currently paying £43 million a year to Partners. To this day it still shocks me when I think about the continual wall of silence I was met with.[49]

The Rydon whistle-blower

Such outright collusion between the public and private partners in a PFI scheme to try to limit their liability for problems and shut down damaging criticism took a different turn in the MFN scheme. Around the time Lambeth was investigating our refurbishment survey report discussed earlier in this chapter, in late March 2014 a former Rydon worker sent the MFN RAMB very specific allegations in an email about contractual and legal breaches of health, safety, building and service standards by all of the main contractors on the MFN PFI scheme.[50] He began by making clear his feelings about Rydon:

> I have never worked for such a bunch of cowboys in my career ... the standard of workmanship that I have come across when repairs have been reported by residents was an embarrassment to follow up.... It will take the RAMB to ensure cowboy builders like Rydon, [Regenter], Higgins are held to account.

His most significant allegation was that Regenter was breaching the Regulatory Reform (Fire Safety) Order 2005, with no FRAs being carried out in relation to the communal areas of either the refurbished homes or the new-build flats. He claimed to have seen emails from Rydon directors to his site manager instructing them to ignore, due to cost, the London Fire Brigade's advice following an inspection to carry out FRAs before properties could be signed off as available for immediate occupancy. He also claimed:

- to have personally raised examples of insufficient fire-stopping and the absence of certificates to prove emergency lighting had been tested prior to occupancy;
- that none of the housing was being risk-assessed in compliance with the HHSRS;
- that some refurbished homes which had failed the availability standards had been fraudulently signed off, with Rydon filling out the IC's availability certificates (he accused Regenter of either knowing this took place or failing to conduct the necessary checks to ensure the veracity of documentation);
- that Lambeth was similarly failing to undertake its own checks during hand-over, and that there had been little sign of building control checks (contracted out to BBS Building Control) during his experience of the works.

The whistle-blower initially raised this list of allegations and his concerns with the City of London's trading standards team, who told him they could not 'see any breaches of Trading Standards legislation'. I contacted the whistle-blower and received specific details of his allegations. Over the next two months I worked with MFN RAMB to collate the main potential health and safety breaches that we had uncovered in our survey of residents. In late May 2014 I informally alerted the Lambeth PFI monitoring officer of the allegations, and our intention to report them imminently. She was initially disbelieving, confidently claiming that the 'fire risk assessment certificates definitely exist' on the online database they shared with Regenter, only to quickly admit 'we haven't looked at them yet, or accessed them, but we know they exist, or we have been told they exist'. At this point the officer told me to pass on the whistle-blower allegations and any other evidence to Lambeth's Orwellian-sounding 'head of corporate resilience'.

We compiled the allegations into a seven-page letter and our own evidence of some 65 incidents and examples into a 33-page report, which concluded that the scale of problems showed 'a systemic problem of performance and compliance monitoring' and called for 'an urgent, high level intervention ... to sort out the management of the regeneration scheme because lives are being put at risk'.[51] Given residents' prior experiences of raising concerns with Lambeth and Regenter only to be fobbed off, we agreed that the report should be sent to the chief executive and leader of the council, the local MP Kate Hoey, the local fire service and the HSE. The report was also sent to the other local authorities whose housing PFI schemes were named by the whistle-blower as having safety issues. The report was sent on 5 June 2014. Although Lambeth's head of corporate resilience replied four days later with platitudes about resident health and safety being 'a prime concern' for the council, that it took 'very seriously the allegations raised', he stated that the council was 'confident that these issues have already been addressed in the past weeks'.[52]

In that now familiar pattern of 'delay, deny, defend' tactics borrowed from the insurance industry to shield institutions from risk, it took more than 50 days (until 22 July 2014) from my first conversation with the council for Lambeth and Regenter to meet to agree the 'key lines of enquiry' into the allegations, which they believed would take another two months. Curiously, this was exactly the same day that, after several reminders, the HSE finally replied to my original letter (of 5 June 2014) to confirm the matter had been assigned to an inspector. All the while, tensions on the estate were running very high over health and safety issues and the general disdain with which residents were being treated. On 25 July 2014, 60 residents decided 'enough was enough' and held a demonstration march to the town hall. The protest was featured live on the local TV station, London Live, which also featured interviews with those affected.[53] The leading industry magazine *Construction News* attended the march, found out about the whistle-blower allegations and our report, and decided to run an exclusive story about the health and safety failings. At this point, Rydon came knocking on my door, or rather my employer's, sending a menacing letter to senior management at the University of Leeds requesting that they disown the report and with an implicit threat of legal consequences:

> We are interested in knowing if the endorsement of the report and letter by your university is actually the case and if you were aware of this representation by Dr Hodkinson on your behalf ... with extracts of Dr Hodkinson's report likely to be published in a leading trade publication, the impact of his report may result in potentially serious commercial consequences to our business.... Our impression is that the intention of both the report and the letter would appear to be politically and/or ideologically motivated and aims to discredit the role of private sector organisations, such as ours, in delivering these services to the public sector ... [it has] the potential to also cause damage [sic] the reputation of your university.... We would hope that, in light of all of the above, you would not continue to allow Dr Hodkinson to use your institution's prestigious name to provide credibility to his totally unsubstantiated and inflammatory claims and, if he wishes to continue to raise criticisms of performance on any of our contracts, you would persuade him to do so as a private individual and not in the name of your respected institution.[54]

The *Construction News* story broke on 6 August 2014 as a front-page exclusive. Rydon was quoted as saying that it had found 'absolutely nothing whatsoever that would suggest these allegations were beyond the scope of operational delivery issues that are not uncommon on such large projects'. Local Labour MP Kate Hoey, however, was also quoted, and she had a very different perspective: 'throughout this process, the rights and views of the residents have been ignored…. The overall management of this project has been surrounded in mistakes and lack of monitoring….'[55]. In response, both public and private sector partners went on a united offensive. On 11 August 2014, Lambeth's head of corporate resilience circulated interim findings from the council's investigation that were later published online and featured in specialist trade press. Instead of focusing on the PFI companies, Lambeth's report appeared more interested in casting doubt on the reliability of the allegations: 'The report … falls short of the technical input that we would normally receive … elucidates the concerns of a handful of residents, based on accounts from previous employees'.[56] Four months later, on 15 December 2014, Lambeth's hatchet job turned to shooting the messenger with the publication and press release of its final report, which found Regenter and co had no case to answer and instead questioned the motives of the authors of the MFN RAMB/University of Leeds report:

> The report and its seven-page covering letter used highly emotive language, and it was unclear whether it was intended to critique Private Finance Initiatives … or highlight legitimate concerns about Lambeth and its MFN residents…. What was clear from Dr Hodkinson's letter and the report is that 14 residents were aggrieved and in that aspect was valuable as a source document about resident dissatisfaction…. The HSE raised some minor points but none that indicated anything remotely close to the level of concern suggested by Dr Hodkinson.[57]

Lambeth's response to the health and safety allegation was not simply disingenuous but also deliberate obfuscation. The council knew full well that this was not about 14 residents or their dissatisfaction, and that many of what it called 'anecdotes' formed part of formal complaints and examples, brought to its attention over several years, that they had failed to investigate. Rather than

finding minor problems, as suggested, the HSE raised a number
of serious concerns with the PFI contractors, including: the lack
of monitoring of their 15 on-site sub-contractors; the absence of
evacuation plans for vulnerable people in the event of a fire; a risk
of fire ignition to wood chippings being stored near to a hoarding
fence; a self-employed sub-contractor on site using a band saw
covered in wood dust not using any protective breathing masks; a
dumper truck unlawfully driving around with no banksman – an
operative trained to direct vehicle movement on or around site;
and a forklift truck carrying too high a load.[58]

While the HSE did write to Regenter with an informal warning
about the need to improve the management of its contractors,
the inspector told me that it was not able to write a formal letter
due to the impact of austerity cuts to the HSE, which meant that
formal notices had to be accompanied by fines to recover the
HSE's costs, and such notices could be triggered only by specific
breaches. Crucially, the HSE site inspector did not inspect any of
Rydon's work – despite Rydon being specifically named in the
report.[59] In reality, Lambeth had already tipped off Regenter and
its contractors in early June 2014 about the allegations as part of
its 'partnership working' approach and the HSE took 33 days to
visit the estate, giving the contractors plenty of time to get their
paperwork in order and to ensure the construction site did not
have any obvious health and safety breaches.

Meanwhile, Rydon continued to write to my University
employer, sending a total of six letters over six months, including
one from its legal department. The letters stopped abruptly after
the University informed them in January 2015 that its investigation had 'concluded unequivocally that Dr Hodkinson had been
acting in the course of his University employment in producing the
June 2014 report ... and ... has raised issues of potential public
interest'.[60]

Nowhere to go

This experience revealed in the starkest possible terms that there
really is nowhere for residents to go when trying to raise issues

of health and safety. The HSE inspector made it clear that it can look at only those unsafe working practices that immediately endanger the lives of the workers and the public on building sites, not at how safe the actual workmanship is behind the front door. Instead, residents should take complaints about poor-quality work or defects to their local council's trading standards department; when the Rydon whistle-blower did this, he was told it was not that department's remit – he should contact the council's environmental health officers or the police. Yet, as I explained in chapter 1, the environmental health avenue is a dead-end for council tenants, as local authorities cannot enforce against themselves, even where they have outsourced housing management to private companies. Nor would the residents I spoke to dream of contacting the police over this kind of matter, seeing it as a waste of their time. The HSE told me that if an FRA was ignored, then the fire brigade should be contacted. But what residents wanted was a single point of contact to investigate all of their health and safety concerns – a joined-up statutory body that simply does not exist. Residents had been led to believe that, under PFI, the local authority would perform this role, as it had contracted out the estate's management and thus could enforce the contract; but when MFN residents went directly to their landlord about their concerns, they were told to contact Regenter, as the council no longer managed the estate.

Conclusion

This chapter has illustrated how residents suffer an enormous loss of democratic accountability over their landlord under de-municipalisation and outsourced regeneration. PFI has involved a shift from a publicly run and publicly accountable housing service to one managed by an opaque network of private companies whose sole interest is to make profit. The public landlord no longer takes direct responsibility for what goes on. Residents in Islington and Lambeth did everything possible, both as individuals and collectively through their residents' bodies and PFI monitoring forums, to raise the long list of problems and get them sorted out. But despite all of this effort, the overall accountability vacuum remained and a certain methodology of evasion was identified. All residents experienced being passed around different contractors without resolution, while elected representatives found their efforts to scrutinise delivery of the contract and contractors' performance continually frustrated by frequent changes of personnel attending meetings and surgeries, and a refusal to disclose information deemed 'commercially confidential'. Finally, we saw how residents like Edward were met with a brick wall of resistance from external auditors when they raised the flagrant waste and possible fraud going on in PFI contracts, with the perception that these accounting firms have deep conflicts of interest through being simultaneously contracted by PFI consortia to advise and audit them. It is to this question of commercial interest and money that we now turn.

Notes

1 D. Whitfield, *PFI/PPP Buyouts, Bailouts, Terminations and Major Problem Contracts in UK*, Research Report No. 9 (Tralee: European Services Strategy Unit, February 2017), at https://www.european-services-strategy. org.uk/wp-content/uploads/2017/02/pfi-ppp-buyouts-bailouts-and-terminations.pdf (accessed 14 October 2018).

2 J. Cole, *Report of the Independent Inquiry into the Construction of Edinburgh Schools* (February 2017), p. 130, at https://www.edinburgh. gov.uk/download/meetings/id/53239/report_of_the_independent_inquiry_ into_the_construction_of_edinburgh_schools (accessed 14 October 2018).

3 *Ibid.*, p. 187.

4 *Ibid.*, p. 131.

5 *Ibid.*, p. 190.

6 Interview with Stephen Boniface, surveyor, 12 June 2013.

7 Interview with Islington housing officers.

8 Interview with former employee of Partners for Improvement in Islington Ltd, 19 April 2018.

9 Social Landlords Mandatory Reduction of Service Charges (England) Directions 1997.

10 Interview with former employee of Partners.

11 Law and Lease, 'London Borough of Lewisham v Luis Rey-Orderes & ors [2013] UKUT 014 (LC): Part I', Law and Lease blogsite (no date), at http:// www.lawandlease.co.uk/2013/02/07/london-borough-of-lewisham-v-luis-rey-ordieres-ors-2013-ukut-014-lc-part-i/ (accessed 14 October 2018).

12 'FOI request made by Mark Pack to LB Islington', July 2013, at https://

www.whatdotheyknow.com/request/partners_for_islington_financial (accessed 14 October 2018).

13 The quote is taken from a transcript of a resident's audio-recording of a meeting with the Lambeth housing officer, June 2013.

14 Gleeds, 'Myatts Field North – repairs audit', Report no.1, 1 May 2013, provided to MFN RAMB.

15 D. Churchill, 'Islington council contractor says it is in the clear after fraud probe', *Islington Gazette*, 15 April 2013, at https://www.islingtongazette. co.uk/news/politics/islington-council-contractor-says-it-is-in-the-clear-after-fraud-probe-1-2019115 (accessed 14 October 2018).

16 Interview with former employee of Partners.

17 London Borough of Lambeth, 'Myatts Field North housing PFI: full business case, version 14', July 2011, p. 64, available at http://peoplevspfi. org.uk/home/myatts-field-north-regeneration (accessed 14 October 2018).

18 Transcript of resident's audio-recording of a meeting.

19 Interview with Islington housing officers.

20 *Ibid.*

21 Interview with former employee of Partners.

22 Interview with PFI advisor 2 (PPP project advisor), 8 March 2010.

23 Interview with Islington housing officers.

24 Notes of telephone conversation with Lambeth housing officer, 26 March 2014.

25 Office of the Deputy Prime Minister, *Tenant Involvement in Housing Management: Supplementary Guidance* (London: The Stationery Office, 2002).

26 Pinsents, 'Agreement for the HRA PFI project Islington street properties project one between LB Islington and Partners for Improvement in Islington', Schedule 2, Output specification, 31 March 2003, p. 26; Eversheds, 'Project agreement in relation to the Myatts Field North Housing HRA PFI project', Schedule 2 (document 5.16, 'Involving residents), 4 May 2012, p. 3, available at https://goo.gl/6EIsoZ (accessed 14 October 2018).

27 Interview with 'Daisy', Islington tenant, 3 June 2013.

28 Interview with 'Harry', Islington leaseholder, 10 June 2013.

29 Interview with Islington housing officers.

30 Interview with 'Daisy'.

31 *Ibid.*

32 Resident Scrutiny Steering Group, 'Confidential – Pilot scrutiny review of communal repairs and customer experience', Islington Street Properties PFI Schemes, January 2013.

33 'FOI request to LB Islington by Stuart Hodkinson "housing PFI decent homes standard"', What Do They Know website, 28 December 2012, at https://www.whatdotheyknow.com/request/housing_pfi_decent_homes_standar#incoming-380872 (accessed 16 October 2018).

34 'Open forums', Partners website, at https://www.partnersislington.net/get-involved/open-forums (accessed 14 October 2018).

35 S. Booth, '"Tsunami of festering" housing works with PFI contract, says housing chief', *Islington Tribune*, 21 September 2018, at http://

islingtontribune.com/article/tsunami-of-festering-housing-works-with-pfi-contract-says-housing-chief (accessed 14 October 2018).

36 Interview with Jacqui Dyer, Lambeth tenant, 27 January 2013.

37 *Ibid.*

38 Interview with Uzoamaka Okafor, Lambeth leaseholder, 10 March 2015.

39 Interview with Jacqui Dyer.

40 Interview with Uzoamaka Okafor.

41 Notes of telephone conversation with Lambeth housing officer, 26 March 2014.

42 *Ibid.*

43 London Borough of Lambeth and Regenter Myatts Field North, 'MFN PFI internal refurbishment programme: response to "resident experiences of internal refurbishment under the Myatts Field North PFI contract"', June 2014 (internal document circulated to residents).

44 Interview with 'Edward', Islington tenant, 5 October 2018.

45 London Borough of Islington – v – Mr [redacted], 'Single joint expert report of Stephen L. Boniface', January 2009, pp. 80–81 (privately held court document).

46 Interview with 'Edward'.

47 Letter from KPMG LLP to 'Edward', 'Your objection to Islington council's statement of accounts 2011/12', 22 October 2013.

48 Email from KPMG LLP auditor to 'Edward', 'RE: RE (objection to the accounts): LB Islington', 8 July 2014.

49 Interview with 'Edward'.

50 The evidence presented in this section is provided in full, with sources, in the following report: S. Hodkinson, C. Essen, U. Okafor, J. Cornillon and S. Hack, *Health and Safety Concerns on the Myatts Field North Estate Under the Private Finance Initiative* (MFN RAMB and University of Leeds, June, 2014), available at http://peoplevspfi.org.uk/wp-content/uploads/2017/07/HealthSafetyReport_REDACTED.pdf (accessed 14 October 2018).

51 *Ibid.*

52 Email from Lambeth's head of corporate resilience to author, 9 June 2014.

53 A. Beard, 'Alex Beard reports on today's protest in Lambeth', London Live website, 25 July 2014, at https://www.londonlive.co.uk/news/alex-beard-reports-on-today-s-protest-in-lambeth (accessed 14 October 2018).

54 Email from Jeff Henton, managing director and co-owner of Rydon Maintenance Ltd, to University of Leeds, 30 July 2014.

55 R. Wilson, 'Exclusive: Health and safety failing alleged on £150m PFI', *Construction News*, 6 August 2014, at https://www.constructionnews.co.uk/markets/sectors/housing/exclusive-safety-failings-alleged-on-150m-pfi/8666839.article (accessed 14 October 2018).

56 Email from London Borough of Lambeth's head of corporate resilience to Lambeth's press office, Regenter, Rydon and the author, 11 August 2014.

57 Regenter Myatts Field North, 'Myatts Field North – health & safety update' (no date), at https://www.regentermyattsfieldnorth.com/media/1397/myatts-field-north-health-and-safety-update-6-.pdf (accessed 14 October 2018).

58 Notes of telephone conversation with HSE inspector, 27 November 2014.
59 *Ibid*.
60 Email from University of Leeds secretary to Jeff Henton, Rydon, 8 January 2015.

6 Follow the money: who profits and how

So far, this book has presented compelling new evidence that the promised land of housing regeneration from the outsourcing of repairs and management to private consortia in England under PFI has instead produced a dystopia of unsafe housing and destroyed lives. The countless examples of rising procurement costs and delays, botched work and poor services, and the accountability vacuum facing residents, have debunked PFI's magic mantra of 'risk transfer', 'payment by results' and 'value for money'. But, as I argued in chapter 2, this magic mantra was part of a wider accounting trick designed to place a veil over what PFI and other forms of privatisation and outsourcing have really always been about: an enormous state-sponsored transfer of wealth from the public sector and individuals to corporations and the 1 per cent – the global elite. This chapter dissects this complex profiteering step by step to show how PFI has transformed some of England's social housing – like other forms of public infrastructure such as hospitals, schools, roads and railways – into a highly lucrative asset class, providing guaranteed and risk-free profitable income streams to private investors. I show who profits and how, by mapping out the long value-extraction chain and following the money from government to the banks, the immediate companies and then their ultimate owners, often offshored in tax havens. The final section then brings the analysis together through an in-depth analysis of profiteering in the MFN scheme. The evidence presented comes from an exhaustive analysis of PFI contracts and data disclosed under the 2000 Freedom of Information Act, the 1998 Audit Act, and its successor, the 2014 Local Audit and Accountability Act, as well as from the annual accounts for each SPV and its holding company in 17 housing PFI schemes where data were freely available on the Companies House website.[1]

PFI's financial extraction wealth machine

As I explained in chapter 2, to build or renew public infrastructure, it is far more expensive to raise investment finance from private financiers than through direct government borrowing. This is for the simple reason that governments can borrow more cheaply than private companies or individuals, due to the security of the return offered by government bonds (governments are largely shielded from bankruptcy by their tax-raising powers). Yet in PFI schemes, it is the private sector that raises the necessary up-front investment finance for the initial construction or refurbishment project. On top of this are the unnecessarily higher costs of outsourcing management and maintenance services for 20–30 years to companies, and these command generous profit margins. There are also the additional costs from public and private sector partners employing special third-party corporate advisors to help them master the complexity of PFI contracts. The PFI companies must also be audited, another cost that would not have arisen if regeneration had remained publicly administered, and another cost that is passed onto the public books by being priced into the PFI financial model.

Overall, these inflated costs and the government-funded payments they attract underpin what Dexter Whitfield calls a global 'wealth machine' for corporate interests.[2] We can get a sense of this largesse in table 6.1. This is the official government valuation of the capital investment being delivered in each contract and its estimate of the total unitary charge payments (the total contract value in nominal terms) for each of the 20 housing PFI schemes.[3] By capital investment value, we do not mean what it actually cost to finance (i.e. the bank interest accrued), but what the effective construction value of the new and refurbished homes is, plus any planned maintenance works over the duration of the contract. As we can see, the total capital investment value across

Table 6.1 Comparing capital investment value to total contract payments in the 20 council housing PFI schemes

Scheme	Year of contract start	Capital investment value (£m)	Total estimated unitary payments (£m)	Ratio of investment to total cost
Islington street properties PFI-1	2003	89.00	356.98	1:4
Manchester, Plymouth Grove	2003	35.16	162.67	1:4.6
Reading, North Whitley	2004	30.70	211.00	1:5.7
Leeds, Swarcliffe	2005	105.00	271.80	1:2.6
Newham, Canning Town	2005	19.40	188.43	1:9.7
Camden, Chalcots Estate	2006	61.00	211.39	1:2.2
Sandwell, Hawthorn Fields	2006	66.18	147.14	1:3.5
Islington street properties PFI-2	2006	153.00	421.32	1:2.8
Oldham, sheltered housing	2006	108.00	439.87	1:4.1
Manchester, Miles Platting	2007	84.86	566.83	1:6.7
Ashford, Stanhope	2007	68.22	129.40	1:1.9
Lewisham, Brockley	2007	96.00	297.09	1:3.1
Newham, Forest Gate	2009	47.13	174.06	1:3.7
Oldham, Gateways to Oldham	2011	77.00	218.53	1:2.8
Kirklees, 'Excellent Homes for Life'	2011	74.81	197.44	1:2.6
Lambeth, Myatts Field North	2012	80.68	272.38	1:3.4
Leeds, Little London/Beeston Holbeck	2013	138.00	335.20	1:2.4
Salford, 'Creating a New Pendleton'	2013	80.70	427.33	1:5.3
Manchester, Brunswick	2013	82.57	273.34	1:3.3
North Tyneside, provision for older people	2014	87.94	272.68	1:3.2
Total		1,585.35	5,574.88	1:3.5

Source: HM Treasury, 'Private Finance Initiative and Private Finance 2 projects': current projects as at 31 March 2017', UK government website, 29 March 2018, at https://www.gov.uk/government/publications/private-finance-initiative-and-private-finance-2-projects-2017-summary-data (accessed 13 October 2018)

the 20 schemes is £1.59 billion, compared with the estimated £5.58 billion total cost of them. While the average contract cost is 3.5 times the value of the capital invested, in nine schemes this was exceeded, with some contracts costing between 5 and nearly 10 times more than the initial investment. It is expected that the contracts will cost more than the capital invested because they include debt charges and long-term maintenance contracts. However, as I will show, a significant part of this difference between the investment and the overall cost is excessive profit being extracted from the public purse for projects and services that could have been far cheaper to undertake in-house.

In the remainder of this chapter, I will unpack how these lucrative spoils are shared among the web of corporate interests in the housing PFI programme. However, the £5.58 billion does not represent the total financial burden of housing PFI to the public purse. It excludes the considerable costs of public authorities hiring private sector consultants to advise them in both the long years of procurement and the even longer years of the PFI contracts. It does not include any additional unplanned payments made to the SPV under so-called 'call-off' clauses of PFI contracts, where the PFI contractor provides specific services on demand without having to go out to tender. For example, in the Islington PFI-2 contract, there are 29 specified call-off events, which cover everything from emergency lighting repair, disability adaptations and missing doors to void dwellings, underground drainage repair, emergency structural repair and communal window cleaning.[4] Some call-off events can include important works or maintenance services that were mistakenly omitted from the contract but which the PFI contractor has the right to provide instead of the council's own in-house team or a more competitive contractor. The self-monitoring system at the heart of PFI enables further profiteering by allowing appalling work to be signed off. In the PFI housing regeneration schemes, financial extraction has also stemmed from the way in which housing and land are financialised, enabling huge windfalls from the transfer of public land to private companies through the development and sale of private housing, which the construction firms, banks and investors all profit from. This privatisation of public land represents an expensive opportunity cost to the public sector, reducing the amount of land available to build affordable social housing, which contributes to greater homelessness, the use of expensive temporary accommodation and higher housing benefit bills from subsidising private landlords.

Feeding the private financiers

Under PFI, the up-front capital investment needed for the main construction or refurbishment phase of a project is sourced from two main sets of private financiers. About 90 per cent of the capital is normally borrowed as 'senior debt' from commercial banks. As I explained in chapter 2, the cost of bank finance under PFI has consistently been found to be double that of government borrowing.[5] Part of this additional cost comes from the need to purchase 'swap deal' financial derivatives that turn the variable rates of interest and inflation at which senior debt is lent into a higher fixed interest rate. The other 10 per cent of the up-front capital investment in PFI schemes is provided by the SPV owners themselves – these are the investors in a PFI scheme, and typically encompass the bank providing the senior debt, the main construction firm and the company providing the long-term management and/or maintenance services. They provide this 10 per cent by injecting a small amount of equity into the SPV (by purchasing shares) and making a larger 'subordinate loan' (also sometimes called an 'equity bridge loan') to the SPV at very high rates of interest. The Treasury's PFI financial model used by local authorities already assumes an internal return on SPV owners' investment of between 14 and 18 per cent, but as we will see below, the actual returns have proven to be much higher. This was confirmed to me by a former PFI project manager who worked on more than 100 PFI and PPP contracts in the UK before setting up a social enterprise aimed at helping the public sector create savings from operational PFI contracts:

> I was working for the PFI sector, negotiating and drawing up contracts, and I saw how the public sector was being fleeced and I wanted to do something about that. The contracts have been

written in ways that enable the PFI consortia to make additional
profits beyond what is reasonable and fair, not the 14 to 18 per cent
normally cited, but returns as high as 70 per cent.[6]

This inflated cost of finance using PFI instead of public borrowing
has enabled the main private financiers of housing PFI schemes –
the banks and other investors – to extract significant wealth from
the public purse. Through forensic examination of 322 SPV
annual reports and audited financial statements – all available in
the public domain via the Companies House website – I was able
to identify key information about the SPVs' senior debt and subordinate debt loan agreements, namely: the original sum borrowed
(the 'principal'), the various interest rates charged, and the length
of the borrowing 'term' (the total period, in years, from the start
of the loan to when it was due for repayment). In 10 housing
PFI schemes, the interest rate on either the senior debt or the
subordinate debt changed after the initial construction period was
over, and in some schemes, there were multiple subordinate loans
issued, with different interest rates. I used all of this information
to estimate the total borrowing cost for each SPV using a simple
loan repayment calculator based on equal monthly payments
of a portion of the initial principal and a portion of the interest
incurred on the outstanding balance (at the start of the loan
period, the interest charges are at their highest but over time they
fall as the total debt comes down).

This method cannot be completely accurate because SPVs do
not normally draw down all of the agreed senior debt at the start of
the PFI contract, but in tranches over the first three to five years as
they need it. Moreover, through their own cost-cutting measures,
some SPVs are also able to avoid drawing down the full amount
of debt they have agreed with the bank, and build up cash reserves
to pay down the debt more quickly than planned. This behaviour
reduces the total amount of interest charged. To complicate
matters further, each SPV has agreed a unique loan agreement with
the bank, with different repayment periods and interest rates and
premiums charged at different stages of the project. In at least two
housing PFI schemes, the SPV has already refinanced to pay back
the original loan plus any early-repayment fees, and taken out a

new loan at a much lower interest rate. This means that, in some schemes, the actual annual interest charges will be less than I have calculated. At the same time, my analysis of the SPVs' accounts reveals that in some schemes, the subordinate debt provided by the SPV owners is not being repaid like a mortgage, but is instead allowed to incur compound interest over some or all of the contract length, incurring much larger interest charges than I have estimated, which I will show below. However, for the purpose of this analysis, it is the *imputed cost* of the SPV's borrowing that matters, because that is what the public sector will be paying. The SPV will then organise its business model so as to minimise the interest charged by its senior debt provider, and maximise the difference between the monthly unitary charge payments and the monthly bank loan repayments. There is also evidence that some SPVs are paying down their bank debt quickly while racking up larger debts and interest payments to their owners, which could be seen as another potential source of profiteering.

Let us first look at the interest earned by banks and bond investors providing the senior debt finance for each of the 17 housing PFI schemes for which data were freely available. The findings are set out in table 6.2. The SPV's annual accounts revealed that a total of £905.17 million was raised in senior debt from banks and bond issues for these 17 schemes. Using the interest rates and terms disclosed, I estimate that these loan agreements will generate £721.73 million in interest income to these financiers. We can also see that some banks have done particularly well, with the Nationwide Building Society and the Bank of Scotland providing senior debt finance in 9 of these 17 schemes.

Now let us look at the estimated interest income earned by the owners of the SPVs across these 17 schemes, which is set out in table 6.3. Overall, these PFI investors have provided £114.82 million of subordinate debt finance at very high interest rates – averaging 10.74 per cent. In the Islington PFI-1 and PFI-2 schemes, Partners' owners receive 14.5 per cent and 13.0 per cent respectively, while in Camden they received 13 per cent; and in the MFN scheme, after 8.02 per cent for the first five years, Regenter is earning 12.5 per cent. If the principal borrowed and interest incurred are paid off together like a simple loan repayment model,

Table 6.2 Estimated PFI senior debt cost in 17 housing PFI schemes

Scheme	Contract start	Senior debt/bond	Loan term (years)	Principal (£m)	Interest rate (%) (construction/ operational)	Total estim- ated interest charged (£m)
Islington street properties PFI-1	1/3/03	Bank of Scotland	30	16.9	6.09	19.93
Manchester, Plymouth Grove	1/3/03	Nationwide	30	29.93	6.06/5.9	36.01
Reading, North Whitley	31/3/04	Nationwide	30	16.3	5.19	15.89
Leeds, Swarcliffe	31/3/05	Bank of Scotland	30	37.01	6.37/5.29	38.23
Newham, Canning Town	3/6/05	Dexia	30	19.6	5.95/5.62	22.48
Camden, Chalcots Estate	2/5/06	Bank of Scotland	14	44	5.20	18.03
Islington street properties PFI-2	15/9/06	Bank of Scotland	15	60	6.6	34.67
Manchester, Miles Platting	22/3/07	Dexia	29	62.85	5.08	57.38
Ashford, Stanhope Estate	14/4/07	Nationwide	30	26	6.18/5.96	29.38
Lewisham, Brockley Housing	4/6/07	SMBC	19	61.77[a]	5.64/6.34	49.53
Oldham, Gateways to Oldham	30/11/11	Barclays, Co-operative Bank, Santander	25	58	5.62	50.10
Kirklees, 'Excellent Homes for Life'	20/12/11	Nord/LB, Co-operative Bank, Nationwide	25	66.22	5.63/5.34[b]	53.78

Scheme	Contract start	Senior debt/bond	Loan term (years)	Principal (£m)	Interest rate (%) (construction/ operational)	Total estimated interest charged (£m)
Lambeth, Myatts Field North	4/5/12	Nord/LB, Co-operative Bank, Nationwide	24	72	3.24	31.68
Leeds, Little London/Beeston Holbeck	5/7/13	SCFL (Finance) PLC bond	19	101.83	5.07	57.00
Salford New Pendleton	17/9/13	FHW Dalmore (Salford Pendleton Housing) – bond	29	82.6	5.82	88.60
Manchester, Brunswick	17/12/13	S4B (issuer) PLC bond	24	73.53	4.93	52.02
North Tyneside, provision for older people	24/3/14	Solutions 4 North Tyneside (Finance) PLC	27	76.63	5.26	67.02
Total/average			18.06	905.17	5.51	721.73

[a] According to Regenter B3 Ltd's accounts, the initial debt facility provided by SMBC for the Lewisham Brockley scheme was £72 million at an interest rate (including swap rate) of 5.64 per cent over 28 years; in 2011, this debt facility reduced to £61.77 million at an interest rate of 6.34 per cent repayable in 2026 (a 19-year term). I calculated the initial interest charges over the first four years using the original loan agreement, and then the remaining 15 years using the new loan agreement.

[b] According to the accounts of JLW Excellent Homes for Life Ltd, the SPV for the Kirklees PFI project, the SPV refinanced in 2016 and the interest rate payable on the senior debt fell to 4.29 per cent. I have not included this refinancing in my calculations.

Source: Author's calculations from the accounts of the SPVs and SPV holding companies, available at Companies House

Table 6.3 Estimated cost of PFI subordinate debt in 17 housing PFI schemes

Scheme	Contract start	Original subordinate debt providers	SPV subordinate loan term (years)	Subordinate principal (£m)	Subordinate loan interest rates (%)	Total estimated interest charged (£m)	Actual interest incurred as of 2017/18 (£m)
Islington street properties PFI-1	1/3/03	United House, Bank of Scotland, Hyde	30	1.88	14.50	6.41	6.38
Manchester, Plymouth Grove	1/3/03	MJ Gleeson; Arena Housing; Nationwide	26	3.77	9.07	6.34	3.05
Reading, North Whitley	31/3/04	Southern Housing, Windsor Housing, Nationwide, Wates	26	3.23	12.00	7.32	4.84
Leeds, Swarcliffe	31/3/05	Carillion, Bank of Scotland, Yorkshire Community Housing	30	4.00	12.00	10.81	3.41
Newham, Canning Town	3/6/05	Regenter	26	2.09	12.00	4.74	1.89
Camden, Chalcots Estate	2/5/06	United House, Bank of Scotland	15	4.80	13.00	6.13	9.66
Islington street properties PFI-2	15/9/06	United House, Bank of Scotland, Hyde	15	6.55	13.00	8.36	14.27
Manchester, Miles Platting	22/3/07	Morgan Sindall, Investors in the Community, Adactus	5/24.5	8.22	5.50/13.00	21.01	6.1
Ashford, Stanhope Estate	14/4/07	Gleeson, Moat, Nationwide	25	2.70	10.50	4.95	2.08
Lewisham, Brockley Housing	4/6/07	Regenter	17	9.33	12.00	12.58	7.08
Oldham, Gateways to Oldham	30/11/11	John Laing	22	8.37	12.01/7.90	15.14	2.90
Kirklees, 'Excellent Homes for Life'	20/12/11	John Laing, Wates	2.5/20	12.64	5.03/10.99–11.93	11.60	3.68

Scheme	Contract start	Original subordinate debt providers	SPV sub-ordinate loan term (years)	Subordinate principal (£m)	Subordinate loan interest rates (%)	Total estimated interest charged (£m)	Actual interest incurred as of 2017/18 (£m)
Lambeth, Myatts Field North	4/5/12	Regenter	5/20	7.99	8.02/12.05	14.93	3.9
Leeds, Little London/Beeston Holbeck	5/7/13	Keepmoat, Equitix, Uberior	20	12.73	11.75	20.37	10.27
Salford New Pendleton	17/9/13	Together Housing	30	12.52	6.00	14.51	5.48
Manchester, Brunswick	17/12/13	Equitix, Contour Homes, Galliford Try	22	6.07	11.5	10.63	Nil
North Tyneside, provision for older people	24/3/14	Miller, Equitix	27/25	7.93	3.6/12.45	12.78	1.73
Total/average			21	114.82	10.74	188.61	86.72

Source: Author's calculations from the accounts of the SPVs and SPV holding companies, available at Companies House

I estimate that this will generate an estimated £191.06 million in interest income over the life of these contracts for the SPV owners. However, in some of the schemes, this is not happening and much higher interest charges are being incurred. This is most obviously the case in the three PFI schemes run by Partners for Improvement in Islington and Camden featured in this book. According to these SPVs' accounts, the actual interest incurred has already far exceeded my estimates – by just under £10 million in total. This strongly suggests that, in those schemes, the SPV owners may in fact be extracting far more profit from the PFI contract than anticipated, and this is set to continue for years, given that the Islington PFI-2 scheme is not due to terminate until 2022 and the PFI-1 scheme until 2033.

Finally, let us compare the interest rates and the overall estimated cost to the public purse of PFI financing with what it would have cost if done via direct government borrowing. To generate this comparison, I used two alternatives: (i) a standard 25-year borrowing term; and (ii) an identical term to the senior debt loan in each housing PFI scheme. To calculate the effective interest rate that government would pay, I first identified the interest rates that would have been charged to local authorities by the government's Public Works Loan Board on the date that each PFI contract was signed using a repayment maturity loan where the interest and principal are paid back together at the end of the borrowing period.[7] As the Treasury charges local authorities a premium for raising finance from the Loan Board – 0.15 per cent on top of the gilts yield rate prior to October 2010, and 1 per cent thereafter – I deducted these premiums to work out the actual cost of borrowing to the public purse (as opposed to local authorities). I then used these alternative interest rates to calculate the interest charges on the total investment capital raised by the SPV – its senior and subordinate debt combined – comparing whichever gave the lower total PFI interest cost.

The results are set out in table 6.4. The analysis first of all confirms the vastly greater expense of investment financing via PFI as opposed to government borrowing. PFI interest rates for senior debt and subordinated debt have averaged 5.51 per cent and 10.74 respectively, with an effective interest rate of 6.01 per cent on average. In contrast, government borrowing rates averaged 3.48 per cent for a 25-year maturity repayment term or 3.70 per cent where the PFI senior debt term was used. Based on these contrasting interest rates, my analysis suggests that the overall additional PFI cost to the public purse of financing £1.59 billion in capital investment for these 17 housing PFI schemes has been in excess of £482 million.

But this is not where the potential profiteering ends for the banks and other investors which set up or have bought shares in the SPVs. Looking at the housing PFI schemes that have finished their construction phase and are now in operational mode, SPVs are paying out handsome dividends to their shareholders from the annual profits they make. Table 6.5 shows that, as of October 2018, an impressive £48.32 million had already been distributed to these investors across just 12 housing PFI schemes. If these annual dividend payments continue at their present rate (with the exception of the Camden Chalcots Estate scheme, which was terminated in 2018), then, by the end of these contracts, I estimate that they will have generated an enormous £165.13 million in dividend payments to their shareholders. Part of these profits comes from the indexing of unitary charge payments to the retail price index after the first year of the contract. For example, in the Islington PFI-2 scheme, 50 per cent of the unitary charge will rise by 2.5 per cent a year (the other 50 per cent remains fixed), with the corresponding figure for the MFN scheme of 33 per cent. In other words, investors are guaranteed inflation-proof revenue streams for up to 30 years.[8] And herein lies another potential hidden cost: should the actual retail price index turn out to be higher than the assumed rate of 2.5 per cent over the course of the contract, the public authority will be liable for the extra cost. The PFI SPV can also make additional profit by earning interest on any available cash surpluses in the form of short-term deposits with banks or other investment vehicles. For example, as of October 2018, Partners for Improvement in Islington had earned some £3.15 million in interest in this way across its two street properties schemes.[9] Finally, in addition to the profitable income streams from interest payments and dividends, the main shareholding companies in the SPV receive a variety of generous director and

Table 6.4 Estimated additional cost to public purse of PFI financing in 17 housing PFI schemes

Scheme	Contract start	Loan term (years)	Total capital borrowed (£m)	Total PFI interest cost (£m)	Effective PFI interest rate (%)	Government borrowing interest rate (25 years) (%)	Total government interest cost (25 years) (£m)	Total government interest cost (PFI term) (£m)	Total government interest cost – cheapest (£m)	Estimated additional cost of PFI (£m)
Islington street properties PFI-1	1/3/03	30	18.78	26.34	7.03	4.40	12.22	15.08	12.22	14.12
Manchester, Plymouth Grove	1/3/03	30	33.70	42.35	6.42	4.40	21.92	27.05	21.92	20.43
Reading, North Whitley	31/3/04	30	19.53	23.21	6.13	4.7/4.8	13.70	16.92	13.70	9.51
Leeds, Swarcliffe	31/3/05	28	41.01	49.04	6.6	4.65	28.42	32.40	28.42	20.62
Newham, Canning Town	3/6/05	30	21.69	27.22	6.41	4.65	15.03	18.57	15.03	12.19
Camden, Chalcots Estate	2/5/06	14	48.80	24.16	6.16	4.4/4.65	31.75	17.69	17.69	6.47
Islington street properties PFI-2	15/9/06	15	66.55	43.03	7.28	4.35/4.55	42.75	25.42	25.42	17.61
Manchester, Miles Platting	22/3/07	29	71.07	78.39	5.96	4.5/4.4	47.39	54.85	47.39	31.00
Ashford, Stanhope Estate	14/4/07	28	28.70	34.33	6.6	4.8/4.60	20.65	22.39	20.65	13.68
Lewisham, Brockley Housing	4/6/07	19	71.08	62.11	7.46	4.9/5.10	52.32	40.05	40.05	22.06
Oldham, Gateways to Oldham	30/11/11	25	66.37	65.24	6.27	2.09/2.15	18.90	19.47	18.90	46.34
Kirklees, 'Excellent Homes for Life'	20/12/11	23	73.24	65.38	6.28	2.17/2.13	21.70	19.46	19.46	45.92

Scheme	Contract start	Loan term (years)	Total capital borrowed (£m)	Total PFI interest cost (£m)	Effective PFI interest rate (%)	Government borrowing interest rate (25 years) (%)	Total government interest cost (25 years) (£m)	Total government interest cost (PFI term) (£m)	Total government interest cost – cheapest (£m)	Estimated additional cost of PFI (£m)
Lambeth, Myatts Field North	4/5/12	24	79.99	46.61	4.16	2.35/2.38	24.79	26.27	24.79	21.82
Leeds, Little London/Beeston Holbeck	5/7/13	19	114.56	77.37	5.98	2.58/2.39	41.00	28.13	28.13	49.24
Salford New Pendleton	17/9/13	29	95.12	103.11	5.87	2.71/2.73	35.88	42.60	35.88	67.23
Manchester, Brunswick	17/12/13	24	79.60	62.65	5.41	2.68	29.67	28.37	28.37	34.28
North Tyneside, provision for older people	24/3/14	27	84.89	79.80	5.59	2.6/2.61	29.41	32.14	29.41	50.39
Total/average		24.94	1014.68	910.34	6.01	4.16	487.51	466.86	427.43	482.91

Source: Author's calculations from accounts of SPVs and SPV holding companies available at Companies House; UK Debt Management Office, 'New Loan Maturity, National Loans Fund Interest Rates– Historical National Loans Fund Rates' (1 April 1994 to previous business date)

Table 6.5 Dividends paid to SPV investors in 12 housing PFI schemes

Scheme	Special purpose vehicle (SPV)	Contract start	Total dividends to October 2018 (£m)	Estimated total dividends by contract end (£m)
Islington street properties PFI-1	Partners for Improvement in Islington Ltd	1/3/03	5.10	15.30
Manchester, Plymouth Grove	Grove Village Ltd	1/3/03	1.16	4.89
Leeds, Swarcliffe	Yorkshire Transformations Ltd	31/3/05	4.64	14.49
Newham, Canning Town	Regenter LCEP Ltd	3/6/05	4.19	16.78
Camden, Chalcots Estate	Partners For Improvement In Camden Ltd	2/5/06	4.50	4.50
Islington street properties PFI-2	Partners for Improvement in Islington 2 Ltd	15/9/06	13.15	26.30
Manchester, Miles Platting	Renaissance Miles Platting Ltd	22/3/07	4.93	24.67
Ashford, Stanhope Estate	Chrysalis (Stanhope) Ltd	14/4/07	0.51	1.94
Lewisham, Brockley Housing	Regenter B3 Ltd	4/6/07	6.15	14.06
Oldham, Gateways to Oldham	Inspiral Oldham Ltd	30/11/11	1.87	13.12
Kirklees, 'Excellent Homes for Life'	JLW Excellent Homes For Life Ltd	20/12/11	1.17	11.12
Lambeth, Myatts Field North	Regenter Myatts Field North Ltd	4/5/12	0.95	17.96
Total			48.32	165.13

Source: Accounts of SPVs and SPV holding companies available at Companies House

management fees over time. For example, in the Manchester Miles Platting scheme, the various investors received over £5.6 million in fees between 2006 and 2017.[10]

Bringing the analysis from tables 6.2 to 6.5 together, I estimate that the unnecessary additional interest charges of PFI financing and the structuring of PFI contracts to maximise profit will enable the private financiers to extract around £648 million in profitable income streams from just 17 housing PFI schemes over their duration. This is an astonishing amount, which, if turned into capital grant funding at the Mayor of London's current offer of £100,000 per social home, would enable local authorities in London to build around 6480 council homes to help address the housing crisis.[11] Instead, this vital supply of public money has gone towards boosting the profits of the PFI financiers. But the profiteering does not even end there.

Following the money offshore: the role of the global secondary market

As should now be clear, PFI has enabled commercial lenders, investors, contractors and consultants to profiteer on the back of the taxpayer. But there is another dimension to this profiteering – the lucrative global secondary market for shares in the SPVs and the huge exit rates of return being earned by the original investors when either selling on their shareholdings or being taken over themselves by other investors.[12] As I argued in chapter 2, these equity stakes are usually bought by specialist infrastructure funds – investment vehicles that provide their owners – whether banks, private equity firms, pension funds, insurance companies or even the odd government – with handsome dividend payments. These profits and those from the trading of equity in PFI schemes are inextricably linked to systematic corporate tax avoidance. Many PFI schemes are owned by companies registered 'offshore', in countries or territories like Jersey, Guernsey, Luxembourg and the Caribbean islands – tax havens as they are more commonly known – where they are normally exempt from paying taxes on income, profit and capital gains.[13]

This picture of a thriving secondary market for equity in PFI schemes is evident in the housing PFI programme. Analysis of the European Services Strategy Unit (ESSU) PPP Equity Database[14] and individual SPV accounts and annual returns data from Companies House shows that, as of October 2018, there had been 21 separate equity transactions, with an estimated value of over £100 million. In relation to the PFI schemes featured in this book, we see that United House Group sold its 45 per cent stakes in Islington PFI-1 and PFI-2 and its 50 per cent stake in Camden Chalcots PFI for £30.5 million in January 2012. In 2017, two private equity firms, Tunstall Real Estate Asset Management and Starwood Capital Group, bought 50 per cent of the equity in the MFN scheme through their purchase (at an estimated £50–£60 million) of Pinnacle Regeneration Group from its previous Hong Kong-based owners.

By analysing each SPV's annual statement of who its shareholders are (called the 'annual return'), and then doing the same for each of the shareholder companies listed, we find that these equity sales and secondary market infrastructure buy-outs have led to the ownership of housing PFI SPVs becoming highly concentrated: four global infrastructure companies with offshore connections now dominate the ownership of 15 of the 20 housing PFI SPVs, with 60 per cent of total equity held; six SPVs are majority-controlled offshore. The most powerful of these is Guernsey-based John Laing Infrastructure Fund (JLIF) Ltd. This was set up by John Laing Group PLC in 2010 and is managed by its subsidiary, John Laing Capital Management, but is owned by a diverse group of wealth managers, multi-asset fund managers and private investors. JLIF is one of the UK's biggest listed infrastructure funds, with major shareholdings in schools, roads and street-lighting PFI schemes, and PPP infrastructure projects around the world, including an 11.8 per cent stake in Barcelona Metro Stations. By acquiring the equity stakes held by its former owner, John Laing Group, and purchasing shares held by United House, Nationwide and Adactus Housing Group, JLIF Ltd now controls or has significant ownership of eight housing PFI schemes and 36 per cent of all equity. The other major owners of housing PFI schemes are: Aberdeen Infrastructure Partners LP

Inc. (Guernsey), which controls or has significant ownership of four schemes (7 per cent); Equitix Investments Ltd (Guernsey), which controls or has significant ownership of three schemes (11 per cent); and MBIA Inc. (Connecticut, USA), which controls or has significant ownership of two schemes through its ownership of TIF Holdco Ltd (8 per cent). However, further digging into the ownership of these companies reveals an even greater concentration of ownership in offshore tax havens. Following the Labour Party's 2017 conference announcement that it would seek to nationalise the SPVs that hold PFI contracts – a policy proposal I will discuss in chapter 7 – JLIF's share price fell dramatically, prompting a successful £1.45 billion cash takeover bid by Jura Acquisition Ltd, owned by infrastructure investors Dalmore Capital Ltd and Equitix.[15] Equitix is in turn owned by Tetragon Financial Group, registered in Guernsey and headquartered in the UK. This means that Tetragon is now the single largest owner of equity in the housing PFI programme, with stakes in 11 housing PFI schemes.

PFI's outsourcing bonanza for construction and maintenance companies

We now turn to the lucrative construction and maintenance contracts available to the companies selected by the SPV as their main sub-contractors, some of whom also happen to be the main investors in the SPV – it's a small world here! These are usually fixed-price contracts and in normal circumstances should reflect industry benchmarks following a competitive procurement; for the top 100 construction firms, these average margins were 4.9 per cent in 1999, 3 per cent in 2011 and around 2 per cent in 2016.[16] But PFI sub-contractors are able to command much higher margins, estimated at between 6 and 12 per cent.[17] The proponents of PFI argue that these higher margins reflect the higher risks they are exposed to in a PFI contract – risks which, as I have shown in chapters 2 and 5, are largely exaggerated. In reality, the high margins that the sub-contractors can earn come in large part from the lack of competition during the procurement process.

This because of the high 'transaction costs' associated with PFI contracts. The European Investment Bank found for PPP deals that the set-up and monitoring costs amount to 'well over 10 per cent of total project capital value'.[18] My research found that bidding costs for housing PFI contracts typically ranged from £1 million to £5 million each, due to the average procurement time of 6.5 years and the sheer complexity of the projects under PFI. With the risk of not winning the contract too great, there tended to be very few serious bidders. One PFI advisor I spoke to implied that the process was rigged by default: 'If you look at who's bidding and you look at who's winning, it's the same. If you're not going to win it you ain't going to bid.'[19]

As we saw in chapter 2, in four housing PFI schemes short-listed bidders pulled out early, leaving only one bidder, and there have been allegations that some schemes have experienced 'phantom' bids – where bidders arrange to go only through the motions on some bids in return for getting a free run at other contracts. This has led to a stark absence of genuine competition for PFI contracts. Large corporations are readily able to fund the employment of advisors to negotiate from a position of power over the local authorities, and this contributes to unnecessarily higher costs for the public purse.

The scale of this unnecessary cost burden from outsourcing is then taken further by the inclusion in every PFI contract of long-term facilities management and maintenance contracts (of up to 30 years) to companies commanding these high profit margins. The National Audit Office estimates that the bulk of a PFI contract's value – around 60 per cent – normally goes to paying for-profit contractors to provide exactly the kinds of repair services that the local authority could have done far cheaper in-house.[20]

Table 6.6 records the impact of this small market on the profile of a selection of the main companies appointed to the 20 housing PFI regeneration schemes and the size of the contracts they have won. There are approximately 60 large sub-contracts across these schemes, and 36 of them are held by just nine companies: Rydon, Pinnacle, Morgan Sindall Group, Wates, Keepmoat, United House, Higgins, Galliford Try and Hyde Housing.

Table 6.6 Selection of the main housing PFI sub-contractors

Contractor	Construc-tion	Service	Total	Examples of contract value
Rydon (Equipe)	3	5	8	£50m (estimated) – Chalcots Estate
Pinnacle		5	5	£23.05m (estimated) – Myatts Field North
Morgan Sindall (Gleeson, Powerminster, Lovell)	2	3	5	£79.8m – Miles Platting
Wates	3	1	4	£68.1m – Gateways to Oldham
Keepmoat	2	2	4	£145.2m – Little London, Beeston/Holbeck
United House	3		3	£217.13m across Islington PFI-1 and PFI-2
Higgins	3		3	£70m – Brockley
Galliford Try	2		2	£69m – North Tyneside
Hyde Housing		2	2	£88.52m across across Islington PFI-1 and PFI-2
Carillion	1		1	£38.86m – Leeds Swarcliffe
Denne	1		1	£27.03m – Reading Brockley
Radian and Southern Housing Groups		1	1	£20.15m (estimated) – Reading Brockley
Yorkshire Community Housing		1	1	£44.08m (estimated) – Leeds Swarcliffe
Jigsaw Group (Adactus)		1	1	£130m (estimated) – Manchester Miles Platting
Moat Housing Group		1	1	£25.2m – Ashford Stanhope
Contour Housing		1	1	£22.58m – Manchester Brunswick
Manchester and District Housing Association (Your Housing Group)		1	1	£23.84m – Manchester Plymouth Grove

Source: Accounts of SPVs and SPV holding companies available at Companies House; author's own data compiled from press releases and the individual companies' project websites

The consultants and auditors gravy train

There are still more profitable income streams available from these
PFI contracts for the corporate consultancy and auditing industry.
Both public and private sectors rely on these special third-party
corporate advisors – lawyers, accountants and other financial
and planning consultants – to master the sheer complexity of PFI,
and perform due diligence checks to mitigate the potential legal
and financial risks to them. Local authorities in particular have
become increasingly dependent on these consultants because of
the hollowing-out effect on their in-house expertise and experience
from decades of privatisation and outsourcing. These consultants
charge eye-watering legal and financial advisors' fees throughout
the pre-contract design and procurement phases, and these fees
form the major part of the PFI procurement cost. Some will then
be retained once a scheme is operational to help trouble-shoot
problems and amend contracts. A partner in one private sector
legal advice firm disclosed that it would expect to earn around
£500,000 (in 2010) to advise a winning consortium.[21] Another
PFI consultant told me that the PFI market entry costs for
companies were so high 'because the advisors have milked it for
huge amounts of money ... all over-charging for unnecessary and
repetitive work'.[22] These costs in turn further inflate the price of
PFI contracts; the winning consortia in housing PFI schemes have
had around 75 per cent of their bid costs reimbursed by the SPV
from unitary charge payments once the contract is signed. For
example, in the Manchester Plymouth Grove PFI scheme, MJ
Gleeson Group received payments totalling £1.36 million over
the period 2003–05; and in the Manchester Miles Platting project,
Lovell Partnerships Ltd received £935,232 towards its bid costs.[23]
These consultancy costs place an additional financial burden on
the public purse, outside of the PFI contract payments.

In the 20 housing PFI schemes, local authorities and winning
PFI consortia collectively awarded at least 157 separate
advisory contracts to 67 different private firms for both procurement and operational phases.[24] But this will understate the
contractual largesse, as many shareholders, banks, contractors
and sub-contractors will have engaged their own advisors as well.

The list is remarkable for three reasons. The first is that it reveals the far greater number of advisors serving on the private sector side of PFI (92 contracts) than on the public side (65 contracts), providing a real power imbalance in the procurement process. Second, it shows that there is an unhealthy revolving door, with some firms alternating between advising the public sector on one scheme and then the private sector on another. Third, when we look at who has won these 157 contracts, almost 50 per cent went to just 12 companies, a list dominated by the powerful legal, financial, accountancy, insurance and surveying firms – PwC, AON, Addleshaw & Goddard, Gleeds, KPMG, Deloitte, Abros, Pinsent Curtis, Sweett Group, Trowers & Hamlins, EY and Gibbs Laidler.

This advisor oligopoly not only strengthens the power of these companies to command very high fees but also creates a remarkable conflict of interest: at the same time as advising the public and private sectors in these PFI schemes, the same powerful accountancy firms are also receiving large sums of money to simultaneously audit the accounts of the SPVs, the main sub-contractors and the local authorities. As table 6.7 shows, for the 20 housing PFI contracts, we see that just seven accountancy firms – Grant Thornton, Deloitte, KPMG, PwC, BDO, EY and PFK – have been auditing the 20 SPVs, so far earning at least £2.6 million in audit fees (table 6.7 only includes audit fees for 17 schemes due to the restricted availability of data). Changes of appointments mean that, as of March 2018, the 20 SPVs were audited by just six firms – Deloitte (5), KPMG (4), Grant Thornton (4), BDO (4), PwC (2) and EY (1).

Things get even cosier when we look at who was paid to audit the annual accounts of the 14 local authorities in 2016–17 that have these housing PFI schemes – KPMG (5), Grant Thornton (5), EY (2) and Mazars (1). With the same concentration of companies both advising the public–private partners involved the PFI schemes and then auditing their accounts, a large number of conflicts of interests are being created, as table 6.7 reveals.

These conflicts of interests are particularly pronounced in the four PFI schemes featured in this book. In Islington and Camden, we see that KPMG advised the winning PFI consortium during the procurement of these schemes and then went on to audit Partners

Table 6.7 Conflicts of interest: the auditors

SPV auditors	Schemes	Payments[a]	Conflicts of interest
Grant Thornton LLP	6	£706,607	Manchester Brunswick: audited SPV and local authority before 2018; Salford New Pendleton: advised the PFI consortium in procurement, then audited both the local authority and the SPV until 2018
Deloitte LLP	6	£650,650	Lambeth Myatts Field North: advised the public sector in procurement and then between 2012 and 2015 audited both the local authority and the SPV
KPMG LLP	5	£536,755	Camden Chalcots: advised the PFI consortium in procurement, audits the local authority, and since 2012 has audited the SPV; Islington PFI-1 and PFI-2: advised the PFI consortium in procurement and audits the local authority; Leeds Swarcliffe: between 2012–16 acted as auditor for both SPV and the local authority; Sandwell Hawthorns: advised the PFI consortium in procurement and now audits Riverside Housing Group, which owns the SPV
PwC	2	£212,886	Manchester Plymouth Grove: advised the PFI consortium in procurement and audits the SPV's accounts; Newham Canning Town: advised the PFI consortium in procurement and prior to 2015 audited the local authority
BDO LLP	4	£185,180	Leeds Little London, Beeston Holbeck: advised the PFI consortium in procurement and now audits SPV
EY LLP	1	£158,260	Ashford Stanhope: advised PFI consortium in procurement and now audits the SPV's accounts
PFK UK LLP	1	£146,000	
Total	25[b]	£2,596,338	

[a] These are the recorded annual payments in the SPV and holding companies' annual accounts for auditing and other services provided by the appointed auditor of the SPV and its parent or subsidiary companies. It includes only 17 PFI schemes as three SPVs are 'industrial provident' companies and data are not freely available

[b] Adds up to more than 17 due to some SPVs changing their auditors

Source: SPV and SPV holding company accounts available at Companies House; local authority websites

for Improvement in Camden, as well as auditing both local authorities' accounts. In Lambeth, Deloitte advised the public sector in procurement and between 2012 and 2015 audited the accounts of both the council and the SPV. While these accountancy firms always claim that their advisory and auditing functions are conducted by separate companies within their group structures, the problem for democratic accountability of these cosy relationships is clear. As we saw in chapter 5 with Edward's fruitless efforts to get the local authority's external auditor, KPMG, to properly investigate his and other residents' experiences at the hand of Partners and Islington, district auditors like KPMG, BDO or Deloitte are unlikely to seriously investigate their own clients and in some cases the role of one of their own sister companies which may have advised either the local authority or the SPV. These conflicts of interest are yet more examples of the social risks that are never taken into account when considering the value for money of PFI.

Bringing it all together: following the money on MFN estate

To understand who profits and how from housing regeneration under PFI, let us focus on the MFN estate in Lambeth, using the same methods described above, again with data from the annual accounts and reports of the various companies.[25] The PFI scheme was awarded in May 2012 to Regenter – a joint venture between John Laing Investments Ltd and Pinnacle Regeneration Group (see box 4.1, pp. 124–125). The PFI contract has a capital value of £80.7 million and a total nominal value of £272.4 million over its 25 years. In common with other PFI schemes, prior to being awarded the contract, John Laing and Pinnacle set up a holding company called Regenter MFN Holding Company Ltd, which in turn set up the SPV that was awarded the PFI contract in May 2012 – Regenter MFN Ltd (RMFN Ltd). As we saw in chapter 4, RMFN Ltd sub-contracted the different elements of this contract to Pinnacle PSG, Higgins, Rydon and E.ON. It also entered into a debt financing agreement with three banks: Nord/LB (Norddeutsche Landesbank, a public corporation owned by North German federal states), the Co-operative Bank PLC and

Nationwide. In addition to this PFI contract but as part of the overall project agreement, Regenter was awarded a separate private development contract of an unknown value to build 503 private homes. RMFN Ltd sub-contracted this development contract to Oval Quarter Developments Ltd, a joint venture between the family-owned UK builder Higgins Homes PLC, and MY8 Development LLP, jointly-owned by Pinnacle and a Singaporean property company, Riverglade Properties Ltd. Let us now break down the estimated value extracted by this chain of companies step by step, starting with the bankers.

Profits for the bankers

Once the PFI contract began in May 2012, RMFN Ltd agreed a senior debt facility of £72 million with Nord/LB, the Co-operative Bank and Nationwide. The loan is charged at 3.24 per cent interest per annum, including the interest rate swap, and is fully repayable by 2036. I estimate that this will bring £31.68 million in interest income to these banks. If the £72 million had instead been raised through direct government borrowing on a 25-year gilt maturity at a rate of 2.35 per cent, it would have cost an estimated £23.23 million. The £8.45 million in unnecessary borrowing costs translates into a profitable income stream for this trio of banks.

Profits for the SPV owners

The £72 million borrowed from the banks represented 90 per cent of the capital investment needed. The remaining 10 per cent of the capital was provided to RMFN Ltd by Regenter's equal owners – John Laing and Pinnacle – through an unsecured loan of £7.99 million. This was charged at 8.023 per cent interest per annum and both the loan and interest had been repaid in full by 29 March 2017. John Laing and Pinnacle then immediately provided a new unsecured loan to RMFN Ltd, again of £7.99 million but this time at 12.5 per cent interest per annum, with the new loan repayable in 2037. Cross-referencing to table 6.3, I estimated that these subordinate loans would earn John Laing and Pinnacle an equal share of £14.93 million over 25 years, made up of £1.73 million for the first loan and £13.19 million for the second loan. However, careful analysis of RMFN Ltd's accounts suggests that the actual total interest income may far exceed this estimate. John Laing and Pinnacle in fact shared £3.64 million in interest from their first loan because no principal repayments were made and interest was allowed to build up on the full debt amount over the five years. If this arrangement is repeated for the second subordinate loan, then I estimate that it will accrue £19.95 million in interest over 20 years. That makes a total of £23.59 million in interest income to be shared by John Laing and Pinnacle. Once again, if the government had borrowed this £7.99 million directly via the gilts market on 4 May 2012 on a 25-year maturity loan, it would have paid an interest rate of 2.35 per cent, generating just £2.58 million in interest charges by 2037.

I estimate that the combined overall unnecessary additional cost of financing the MFN PFI scheme could eventually reach £29.46 million, to be shared by private banks and the SPV investors.

RMFN Ltd's owners will also profit from annual dividends, now that the construction period has ended (on 29 March 2017) along with the major upfront costs and risks. For the year ending December 2017, a dividend of £945,000 (£472,500 for each of the two owners) was paid. However, we can already see from RMFN Ltd's accounts that it is a highly profitable company, having already accumulated £2.22 million in post-tax profit in its first five and half years. This means that we can expect similar-sized dividends each year now for the next 20 years, amounting to an estimated £17.96 million for the owners, a huge return on their original £5,000 equity investment in setting up RMFN Ltd. In addition to these dividends, the owners will receive annual fees and other payments for their services as directors and administrators of the SPV and its holding company. From May 2012 up to October 2018, John Laing received £1.21 million in fees and 'operating costs', while Pinnacle received £32,000.

Finally, John Laing and Pinnacle have made additional profits from the cuts to corporation tax since April 2012. The PFI contract payments agreed by Lambeth were based on corporate tax rates of 25 per cent from 2012. However, the March 2012 budget cut corporation tax to 24 per cent from April 2012, and then to 23 per cent in 2013, and 21 per cent in 2014, 20 per cent in 2015 and 19 per cent in 2017. In the first five and half years, RMFN Ltd has paid just £681,000 in corporation tax on a £2.83 million gross profit, a saving of £119,880 on what it would have paid if the 25 per cent corporation tax rate had remained in place.[26] This is important because part of the estimated value for money 'savings' of using the PFI route compared with the public sector route depends on an assumed sum of tax receipts. As we can see, the cuts to corporation tax mean that the actual tax receipts from profits will be much less than expected.

If we add all of this up, RMFN Ltd's owners will receive an equal share of an estimated £47.42 million in interest and dividend payments over the 25 years of the MFN PFI scheme – this is a remarkable return on the £5,000 of equity they injected into RMFN Ltd upon incorporation and the £7.99 million loan they made to the company. This profitability explains why, during 2018, John Laing PLC and Pinnacle sold their shares in RMFN Ltd to Guernsey-based John Laing Infrastructure Fund (JLIF) Ltd for an estimated £28 million (£14 million each).[27] As I explained earlier in this chapter, JLIF Ltd is now owned independently of John Laing PLC, and was taken over by Tetragon Financial Group, also registered in Guernsey, in 2018.

Profits for the construction, maintenance, advisors and accountancy firms

When we add together the aforementioned debt repayments, interest charges, fees, and dividends estimated to be paid to the banks and the main investors in the MFN PFI scheme over 25 years, we arrive at an estimated £154.37 million. With a nominal contract value of £272.4 million, this leaves an estimated £118.03 million in contractual payments to be shared between the construction, maintenance, advisory and accountancy firms involved in the PFI consortium. There are four main PFI sub-contractors in the MFN scheme – Higgins Construction PLC, Pinnacle PSG Ltd, Rydon Maintenance Ltd and E.ON UK PLC. We must also include PRP, which was the main architect for the regeneration masterplan, Sweett Group which acted as the independent certifier, BBS Building Control Ltd, which was contracted to perform inspections to ensure building regulations were adhered to, PwC and Nabarro, which both provided legal and financial advice to the SPV, and Deloitte LLP, which audited the SPV's accounts.

Although the precise contract values and profit margins are subject to commercial confidentiality, we know that PFI sub-contractors typically command 6–12 per cent margins in these schemes. There is some information on the various MFN sub-contracts in the public domain. Higgins has put the total contract value for its construction of 808 homes – the majority outside of the PFI contract – at £142 million,[28] which would give a probable PFI contract value of around £55 million. Rydon has publicly stated that its refurbishment contract was worth £9.8 million and its 25-year maintenance contract is likely to be worth upwards of £25 million; Pinnacle PSG had received £5.53 million for its housing management contract up to December 2017, which if continued over the remaining 20 years suggests a contract value of approximately £23.05 million (based on a staggered management fee at the start of the contract). It is not possible to estimate what E.ON is earning directly from the PFI contract, but it is likely to be relatively small as it will make most of its money on this project through the 40-year energy services contract that grants it a monopoly on heat and hot water supply to approximately 980 individual customers. Finally, Deloitte LLP should receive around £350,000 in auditing fees related to RMFN Ltd over the 25-year period. All of these companies are extremely profitable in their own right. For example, in 2017, Rydon Group made a post-tax profit of £7.4 million, Higgins Group PLC made £6.6 million, Pinnacle Group made £5.9 million, E.ON made £629 million and Deloitte £388 million.[29]

Profiting from the private development on the MFN estate

Pinnacle, Higgins and other private investors have also profited from the Oval Quarter private residential development, which has

seen 503 homes built for sale, of which 146 are for shared ownership, within and around the MFN estate. The developer, Oval
Quarter Developments Ltd, is a joint venture between Higgins
Homes PLC and MY8 Development LLP. MY8 is itself a joint
venture between Pinnacle and Riverglade Properties Ltd, which is
owned by Hasetrale Holdings PTE Ltd, a Singapore construction
company ultimately owned by Choon Keat Tan, a major property
developer in Singapore involved in building private hospitals
and shopping centres.[30] Around a third of the 503 homes were
sold to investors prior to construction beginning. Somewhat
mysteriously, during the year August 2012–July 2013, Quick Hero
LLP, a company set up in April 2013 by, among others, Pinnacle
directors Godfrey Blott and Perry Lloyd, contracted to buy five
homes from Oval Quarter Developments Ltd for an undisclosed
amount.[31] According to Quick Hero's accounts, it paid £84,870 in
'property deposits' during the financial year ending 30 April 2014
and had no income or other expenditure.[32] Quick Hero LLP was
voluntarily dissolved in January 2017.

In May 2012, Oval Quarter Developments Ltd received a
£10.66 million loan from Higgins Group and a £4.57 million
loan from MY8.[33] From May 2012 to July 2017, Oval Quarter
Developments Ltd contracted Higgins Construction PLC to build
the 503 homes, a mix of one-bed, two-bed and three-bed apartments. Sale prices ranged from £286,500 for one-bed flats to over
£600,000 for three-beds. As detailed in chapter 4, Oval Quarter
Developments Ltd paid Regenter an estimated £8 million for
125-year leases to all 17 private development sites. The resulting
financials for Oval Quarter Development Ltd from August 2012
to July 2017 are remarkable. Over this period, the company had
a turnover of £167.88 million and made a gross profit of £63.45
million. This was turned into a pre-tax profit of £33.71 million
after a very large 'management charge' (of £24.86 million) was
added to its 'administrative expenses' during the financial year
ending July 2017. As a result, Oval Quarter Developments paid
just £7.18 million in corporation tax while paying out dividends
of £10 million to each of its two owners, Higgins Homes PLC and
MY8 Development LLP (meaning £5 million each to Pinnacle and
Riverglade Properties). It is important to remember that some of

these profits came from Oval Quarter Developments Ltd selling the 14 homes not taken up by those homeowners who were unable to port their existing mortgage or to remortgage, as explained in chapter 4. For every 'like-for-like' property not taken up by an existing resident, Lambeth sold them on to Oval Quarters Development Ltd for a sum rumoured to be £240,000 each, and the private developer then sold on the open market for as much as £550,000 each.[34]

The leasehold scandal

One way in which Higgins, Pinnacle and Riverglade Properties were able to make so much profit from the Oval Quarter development was by selling on the head-leases to some of the 17 development sites to property management companies once the homes had been bought. These head-leases were granted to Oval Quarter Developments Ltd by Lambeth council, giving the developer a 125-year lease on the land. Under its legal powers granted by these land titles, Oval Quarter Developments Ltd was permitted to develop these sites with new housing, and then sell 99-year sub-leases to every new homeowner who bought a property in the development. While these sub-leases grant the homeowners title to their new apartment, they also come with obligations to pay annual ground rent and service charges to the head-lease owner. As such, these head-leases can prove to be lucrative for whoever owns them. Land Registry sales and title records, combined with information provided by Oval Quarter leaseholders, show that, as of 2017, Oval Quarter Developments Ltd had sold on its 125-year head-leases to sites encompassing 261 flats for a total of £7.05 million to three new owners, giving them the right to collect the annual ground rents and service charges from the individual homeowners.[35]

One of these new owners is Notting Hill Home Ownership Ltd, which was always part of the affordable shared-ownership housing deal. However, the two other new owners are A&N Real Estates Ltd and E&J Ground Rents No. 15 Ltd. Scratch the surface and we find that E&J Ground Rents No. 15 Ltd is part of a property empire controlled by James Edward Tuttiett. Since 1991, Tuttiett has acquired the freeholds of over 40,000 properties, including houses, schools, health clubs and petrol stations in almost every city in England and Wales, through a web of 85 ground rent companies he controls.[36] The freeholds on thousands of homes are now at the centre of controversy over spiralling ground rents that double in value every 10 to 15 years, making the properties virtually unsellable. In 2016, one of these 85 companies, SF Funding Ltd, recorded an £80 million increase in the value of its ground rents from the year before, to £267.4 million. The financing of Tuttiett's property empire is helped by low-interest loans totalling £336 million, made by an insurance company, Rothesay Life, spun out of Goldman Sachs, in which the US investment bank remains the largest shareholder.[37]

When some residents of Oval Quarter made the link between their homes and Tuttiett, they realised that their leases also contained the same controversial spiralling ground rent charges. The ground rent for a private one-bed flat is £300 per annum and for a two-bed flat is £375 per annum, and doubles every 15 years. To illustrate just how profitable these head-leases are, let us look at what E&J Ground Rents can expect to earn from the ground rents it has acquired in Oval Quarter. By October 2016, E&J had purchased the head-lease to 129 flats for £2.28 million. These will be mostly a mix of one- and two-bedroom flats, for which the data are not available, but let us assume that they are in the proportions of the overall development, so 70 two-bedroom and 59 one-bedroom units. Over the 99 years of these 129 flats' sub-lease, E&J will have collected an enormous £33.83 million in ground rent – a cool £262,273 per flat. All it has to do to 'earn' this is to send out a bill every six months and watch the cash roll in. This is not all – E&J will be entitled to collect ground rent for any car parking spaces, as well as annual service charges for management and maintenance, with a generous profit margin built in.

As the MFN regeneration scheme clearly shows, PFI is not simply the outsourcing of public housing regeneration and management – it is about turning over people's homes, communities, services and the very land on which they reside to a den of profit-hungry rentiers getting rich on their backs.

Conclusion

This chapter has clearly shown how public money is plundered through housing PFI schemes. In the first instance, these contracts are extremely expensive to develop, procure and then monitor, feeding the trough of corporate accountants, lawyers and construction advisors. They then saddle the public authority and taxpayers with excessive long-term debt repayments – further swelling the big banks' balance sheets – that would have been much cheaper if the public sector had directly borrowed the investment capital. The shareholders of the PFI SPV and its sub-contractors then make huge returns on their minimal investment, due to extravagant internal rates of return and the extremely low risk of construction failure that these projects enjoy, allowing bigger profits to be made from both refinancing and selling on equity stakes. These profits to the SPV investors and sub-contractors are then maximised by minimising costs of delivery, by doing poor-quality work and even on occasions failing to do agreed work. Then comes the added sting in the tail – tax avoidance through a complex system of corporate vehicles ultimately owned offshore in tax havens. And yet every penny invested and made in profit from a PFI scheme in reality comes from a twofold process of extraction and value creation from the public purse. This super-profiteering is not only a huge burden to the public sector and the taxpayer, it represents a major opportunity cost – we could be spending the money on the same or different projects and getting far more infrastructure and services for it; or we could be re-routing that money elsewhere. In the concluding chapter we turn to what we can do about this rampant financialisation and the deregulation policies that enabled it.

Notes

1 The Companies House trial service 'Search the register', at https://beta. companieshouse.gov.uk (accessed 16 October 2018).
2 D. Whitfield, *PPP Wealth Machine: UK and Global Trends in Trading Project Ownership*, ESSU Research Report No. 6 (Tralee: European Services Strategy Unit, 13 December 2012), at https://www.

european-services-strategy.org.uk/publications/essu-research-reports/
essu-research-report-no-6-ppp-wealth-machine-u (accessed 11 December
2018).

3   HM Treasury, 'Private Finance Initiative and Private Finance 2 projects:
current projects as at 31 March 2017', UK government website, 29 March
2018, at https://www.gov.uk/government/publications/private-finance-
initiative-and-private-finance-2-projects-2017-summary-data (accessed 13
October 2018).

4   'Response to request made by E. Hockenjos re: "Islington council
housing – rates for PFI unitary charge"', What Do They Know website,
24 January 2011, at https://www.whatdotheyknow.com/request/islington_
council_housing_rates (accessed 16 October 2018).

5   L. Booth and V. Starodubtseva, 'PFI costs and benefits', House of Commons
Library Briefing Paper No. 6007, 13 May 2015, at http://researchbriefings.
files.parliament.uk/documents/SN06007/SN06007.pdf (accessed 16
October 2018).

6   Interview with former PFI project manager, 24 November 2014.

7   UK Debt Management Office, 'New loan maturity', National loans fund
interest rates – Historical national loans fund rates (1 April 1994 to
previous business date), Public Works Loan Board, at http://www.dmo.
gov.uk/dmo_scheduled_reports/nlfnewmat.xls (accessed 16 October 208).

8   These figures are taken from parts of these PFI contracts and other project
documentation disclosed under freedom of information requests.

9   This figure comes from an analysis of the annual accounts for Partners
for Improvement in Islington Ltd from 2003 to 2017 and Partners for
Improvement in Islington 2 Ltd from 2006 to 2017 available from
Companies House, at https://beta.companieshouse.gov.uk (accessed 16
October 2018).

10 This figure comes from an analysis of Renaissance Miles Planning
Ltd annual accounts 2006–17, at https://beta.companieshouse.gov.uk/
company/05598459/filing-history (accessed 16 October 2018).

11 Mayor of London, 'Building council homes for Londoners: funding
prospectus', Greater London Authority website, May 2018, at https://
www.london.gov.uk/sites/default/files/building_council_homes_for_
londoners_16_may.pdf (accessed 16 October 2018).

12 D. Whitfield, 'New evidence of the scale of UK PFI/PPP equity offshoring
and tax avoidance', European Services Strategy Unit website, 27 October
2017, at https://www.european-services-strategy.org.uk/news/2017/new-
evidence-of-the-scale-of-uk-pfippp-equity-offshoring-and-tax-avoidance
(accessed 14 October 2018).

13 Helen Mercer, *The Private Finance Initiative (PFI): How Come We're Still
Paying For This?* (London: People versus PFI, 2017), at http://peoplevspfi.
org.uk/exhibition-how-come-were-still-paying-for-this (accessed 13
October 2018).

14 D. Whitfield, PPP Equity Database: update ESSU PPP Equity Database
1998–2016, European Services Strategy Unit website, at https://www.
european-services-strategy.org.uk/ppp-database/ppp-equity-database
(accessed 18 October 2018).

15 J. Thompson, 'John Laing Infrastructure Fund takeover approved', *Financial Times*, 24 September 2018, at https://www.ft.com/content/42e8a288-c013-11e8-8d55-54197280d3f7 (accessed 17 October 2018).

16 D. White and M. Hewes, 'Top hundred contractors and housebuilders by turnover', *Building*, 28 July 2000, at https://www.building.co.uk/focus/top-100-contractors-and-housebuilders-by-turnover/1001326.article (accessed 16 October 2018); EY, *UK Construction: Margin Pressure* (London, EYGM, 2017), at https://www.ey.com/Publication/vwLUAssets/UK_Construction_Industry_-_Margin_matters/$FILE/ATTJK7IP.pdf (accessed 16 October 2018).

17 H. Mercer and D. Whitfield, *Nationalising Special Purpose Vehicles to End PFI: A Discussion of the Costs and Benefits* (Greenwich: Public Services International Research Unit, 2018), p. 39, at http://gala.gre.ac.uk/20016/1/20016%20MERCER_Nationalising_Special_Purpose_Vehicles_to_End_PFI%20_2018.pdf (accessed 16 October 2018).

18 G. Dudkin and T. Välilä, *Transaction Costs in Public–Private Partnerships: A First Look at the Evidence*, Economic and Financial Report 2005/03 (Kirchberg: European Investment Bank, 2005), at http://www.eib.org/attachments/efs/efr_2005_v03_en.pdf (accessed 16 October 2018).

19 Interview with PFI advisor 1 (partner in a major global law firm), 18 March 2010.

20 National Audit Office, *The Choice of Finance for Capital Investment* (London: National Audit Office, March 2015), at https://www.nao.org.uk/wp-content/uploads/2015/03/The-choice-of-finance-for-capital-investment.pdf (accessed 16 October 2018).

21 Interview with PFI advisor 3 (partner in a major global financial law firm), 28 February 2010.

22 Interview with PFI advisor 2 (PPP project advisor), 8 March 2010.

23 Annual accounts of Grove Village Ltd and Renaissance Miles Platting Ltd, seen at beta.companieshouse.gov.uk.

24 Data were collected from individual press releases of winning consortia and the now defunct Partnerships UK website. A scraped version (subset only) is available at https://docs.google.com/spreadsheets/d/1RBf8VefQ1XoVO_v9e1PM4yx59qej04SAcxMjp9rHIVI (accessed 16 October 2018).

25 See https://beta.companieshouse.gov.uk/company/07489177/filing-history (accessed 16 October 2018).

26 These figures come from my analysis of Regenter Myatts Field North Ltd's annual accounts from 2012 to 2017 available at https://beta.companieshouse.gov.uk/company/07489177 (accessed 16 October 2018).

27 This estimated sale price comes from comparing financial data from two sources: John Laing Group PLC's results for the six months ended 30 June 2018, London Stock Exchange website, 23 August 2018, at https://www.londonstockexchange.com/exchange/news/market-news/market-news-detail/JLG/13765321.html (accessed 19 November 2018); and 'John Laing sells Intercity Express Programme stake', *Railway Gazette*, 19 March 2018, at https://www.railwaygazette.com/news/business/single-view/view/john-laing-sells-intercity-express-programme-stake.html (accessed 19 November 2018).

28 'Myatts Field North, Lambeth' (not dated), Higgins website, at https://
    www.higginsconstruction.co.uk/current-projects/featured-past-projects/
    myatts-field-north (accessed 16 October 2018).

29 These figures come from my analysis of the companies' annual reports
    available at the Companies House website, at https://beta.companieshouse.
    gov.uk (accessed 18 October 2018).

30 'Company overview of Pure Beauty Investments Limited' (not dated),
    Bloomberg website, at https://www.bloomberg.com/research/stocks/
    private/person.asp?personId=8360393&privcapId=253027943 (accessed
    18 October 2018).

31 Oval Quarter Developments Ltd, 'Directors' report and financial statements
    for the year ended July 31, 2013', p. 10, at https://beta.companieshouse.
    gov.uk/company/07875412/filing-history (accessed 16 October 2018).

32 Quick Hero LLP, Unaudited abbreviated accounts for the periods ended
    30 April 2014 and 30 April 2015, at https://beta.companieshouse.gov.uk/
    company/OC384635/filing-history (accessed 16 October 2018).

33 Analysis of the accounts of Higgins PLC, 2012–17, at https://www.
    higgins-group.co.uk/group/financial-information (accessed 16 October
    2018).

34 Z. Williams, 'The real cost of regeneration', Guardian, 21 July 2017,
    at https://www.theguardian.com/society/2017/jul/21/the-real-cost-of-
    regeneration-social-housing-private-developers-pfi (accessed 16 October
    2018).

35 Sources: 'MFN asset schedule handed over' spreadsheet disclosed by
    Pinnacle to Oval Quarter resident, 24 October 2016; and the Land Registry
    website, at https://eservices.landregistry.gov.uk/eservices/FindAProperty/
    view/QuickEnquiryInit.do?id=p_search_link (accessed 16 October 2018).
    For example, see Title Numbers: TGL369438, TGL372702, TGL390387.

36 P. Collinson, 'Leasehold tycoon: man whose firms control 40,000 UK
    homes', Guardian, 29 July 2017, at https://www.theguardian.com/
    money/2017/jul/29/leasehold-tycoon-man-whose-firms-control-40000-
    uk-homes (accessed 16 October 2018).

37 Ibid.

7 After Grenfell: safe and secure homes for all

This book has presented compelling new evidence from out-sourced public housing regeneration schemes under PFI to show that the Grenfell disaster of June 2017 was no accident. Rather, it was the inevitable outcome of a privatised, deregulated and unaccountable system of housing provision, developed over 40 years of neoliberal policies that fed the insatiable greed of private interests at the expense of resident safety. If Grenfell was a disaster foretold, not just by the residents but also by the long lineage of neoliberalism's discontents, then it must also mark the moment in history when policy changed course, to put housing safety and need before profit and greed. In this concluding chapter, I will draw on my research findings to put forward ideas for both the immediate and the gradual reforms needed to tackle the growing problem of unsafe and insecure housing provision in England and the rest of the UK. The chapter begins by discussing the scale of the challenge that confronts us. It then sets out three policy lessons raised by Grenfell and my own research on outsourced regeneration under PFI, lessons that are still being ignored by government: the need to restore accountability and power to residents; the need to re-regulate construction and housing provision in the interests of safety; and the need to end the privatisation disaster through a programme of reforms that will gradually phase out PFI and outsourcing, push back the financialisation of housing and land, and restore a reinvented public housing model based on the Bevanite principle of treating housing as 'a social service' and not a commodity, as outlined in chapter 1.

The housing safety and insecurity crisis

At the time of writing this book, the enormous scale of the safety time bomb left in the wake of the Grenfell fire was still being revealed. In the 15 months after the disaster, over 6,000 high-rise buildings were inspected and the number officially deemed unsafe more than doubled, to 468 – nearly 1 in 10 of the total – with the majority in the private sector.[1] However, this under-estimates the potential scale of the safety challenge because of the narrow focus on both cladding and buildings over 18 metres high, which ignores other flammable building parts and fire safety problems[2] in the majority of England's 1,584 social housing tower blocks, and which excludes the tens of thousands of smaller multi-storey buildings believed to be covered in some form of cladding.[3] Then there are the wider health and safety threats from dangerous housing and disempowered tenants. In 2015, 8.4 million homes in England were said to have a 'significant' hazard to residents' health, costing the NHS an estimated £2 billion each year.[4] While some social landlords are clearly guilty of providing unsafe housing, the vast majority of dangerous homes are privately owned and in the deregulated private sector, where over a quarter of properties fail the 'decency standard'.[5]

Despite these growing safety problems, tenants and lease-holders are hitting the same accountability vacuum experienced by the residents of Grenfell Tower and by the residents in the PFI schemes documented in this book. As of September 2018, just 32 of the 468 high-rise buildings found to have flammable cladding had been successfully repaired, while the owners of 124 private buildings had so far refused to inform government of their safety plans.[6] The government eventually agreed to fund in full the removal and replacement of dangerous cladding on social housing blocks, at an estimated cost of £400 million (but taking money from the affordable-housing budget to do so). However, the government has told private building owners that they are legally and financially responsible for making their properties safe. As a result, up to 20,000 leaseholders living in private high-rise blocks face being trapped in unsafe, uninsurable and unsellable homes, and liable for the huge repair bills, ranging from £10,000 to £60,000 per flat, as these costs are being passed down by the building owners under the terms of their leases.[7] Moreover, local authorities with PFI schemes covering properties found to have flammable cladding have been told that they do not qualify for the government funding while the tower blocks remain the responsibility of the PFI contractor.

This is the situation facing residents living in nine tower blocks managed under the Creating a New Pendleton PFI project in Salford, run by the SPV Pendleton Together Operating Ltd, which is wholly owned by the Together Housing Group. The government even blocked Salford's attempt to use its own borrowing powers to lend the SPV money, while the council declared that it could not 'step in and end the contract without significant delays and further financial penalties'.[8] Hundreds of residents at the time of writing had already been waiting more than a year to have the unsafe cladding removed and replaced. Salford council stated that it had been unable to inform residents about the reasons for the delay, for fears of what it could do to the share price of one of the SPV investors.[9] But just as at Grenfell, flammable cladding is only the tip of the iceberg at Salford. In December 2018, Phil Murphy, the former firefighter we met in chapter 1, teamed up with Channel 4 News to inspect one of the Salford PFI tower blocks upon the invitation of a worried tenant called 'Bill'. What happened is shocking:

> We were 40 metres away when, out of nowhere, four large men in yellow jackets came rushing at us, shouting at us to stop filming. They were really aggressive and one of them physically assaulted me. In the melee, I managed to get into ['Bill']'s block and up to his flat where he told me that these men were the 'Fire Safety Team' supposedly employed to keep people safe while the cladding was still in place but were routinely intimidating and interrogating visitors to the blocks. They had even stopped him leafleting his neighbours about setting up a residents' fire safety group. Pendleton Together later warned him that if he continued the police would be asked to issue an ASBO [anti-social behavioural order] on him and another mark on his tenancy file could see him evicted. When I inspected the flat I could understand why the landlord was so keen to keep a lid on the problems. There were two plastic and

non-compartmented vent ducts – one in the kitchen and one in the lounge – leading directly on to the combustible cladding. If there was a fire, these vents would be perfect routes for flames to either enter or leave the flat and onto cladding, as has been identified by the public inquiry into the Grenfell disaster. There was also a complete lack of clarity about what the fire safety routine is in the event of a fire and the fire alarms that have been installed in the tower block communal areas do not actually alert residents to the presence of a fire. Once we were back outside we could see big holes in the cladding structure right above where the communal bins are, a clear fire hazard.[10]

More generally, as I argued in chapter 1, renters are too afraid to make repair requests or take their landlords to court because of 'retaliatory evictions'. Feeling unable to speak out about dangerous housing for fear of losing one's home is underpinned by the wider crisis of housing insecurity that is seeing landlords once again developing monopoly power over tenants.

Learning the lessons from Grenfell and outsourced regeneration

Tackling this housing safety and insecurity crisis means learning the lessons of the Grenfell disaster. The various investigations into the causes of the fire and my own research into outsourced housing regeneration under PFI suggest three such lessons that can inform the principles of public policy reform and campaigns.

Lesson 1: we need to re-empower residents and restore accountability in housing

As the book has made clear, the production of unsafe housing at Grenfell, the MFN estate, the Chalcots Estate and across Islington is fundamentally rooted in the erosion of tenants' rights and the accountability vacuum they face in both the social and the private rented sectors in England. Part of this disempowerment stems from the decades of privatisation, demunicipalisation and outsourcing policies on public housing that have turned a once clear line of accountability between landlord and resident into a highly fragmented set of relationships between multiple actors, with residents routinely being passed around from contractor to contractor, ignored, harassed and even threatened. At the same time, waves of deregulation ensured that landlords have been under no legal obligation to make sure their tenants live in conditions fit for human habitation.

After 2015, the Conservative government put in place some new regulatory measures in the private rented sector to try to prevent retaliatory evictions and improve safety. 'Section 21' eviction notices are now invalid if the landlord has not provided tenants with an energy performance or gas safety certificate, or if issued within six months of the landlord being served an improvement notice or emergency remedial action notice by the council. The 2016 Housing and Planning Act introduced minimum 12-month banning orders and a national database of 'rogue' landlords or property agents who commit one of 41 separate offences, including unlawful eviction, breach of gas and fire safety regulations, and failure to comply with overcrowding and improvement notices or prohibition orders. In practice, however, the legal process for preventing retaliatory evictions against tenants who complain about unsafe housing process remains in the landlords' favour. Should court eviction hearings take place before the local authority's inspectors have visited the property and issued a notice, the tenant has no defence and is likely to be evicted. Given the stretched nature of councils' environmental health services, it can take months for an inspection to take place, and local authorities increasingly engage informally with landlords, thus removing tenants' protection against retaliatory eviction.

None of these changes helps council tenants to force their landlord to keep their homes fit for habitation. Having opposed it prior to Grenfell, the government agreed to support the passage of Labour MP Karen Buck's private member's bill into law as the 2018 Homes (Fitness for Human Habitation) Act. This will legally oblige all landlords to keep their property in a condition fit for human habitation; where local authority enforcement is unable or unwilling to act, tenants will be able to take their landlord to court. However, with the slashing of legal aid, the ability of tenants to use these new rights will remain restricted. Since Grenfell, the government has also published a social housing green paper that puts forward vague ideas about stronger powers for the existing social housing regulator to empower residents and linking social landlords' access to future government subsidy to their performance on repair and resident satisfaction in league tables.[11] As chapter 5 of this book has made clear, such PFI-style KPI monitoring is not the answer, as the standards and measures used are typically meaningless and compliance with them is easy to fiddle. Nor will any of this help residential leaseholders in either social or private tower blocks covered in combustible cladding to challenge their landlords to make their homes safe without landing the huge cost back on to the residents.

In order to really empower residents, two key reforms are needed: to reinstate residents' rights; and to create a new independent enforcement body accountable to residents.

Reinstate residents' rights: legal aid and security of tenure

The cuts to legal aid since 2013 must be urgently reversed to enable low-income tenants and leaseholders to take their landlord, freeholder or other parties like private builders and maintenance firms to court for letting or selling homes in disrepair or with safety hazards and defects (including defective cladding). This would also empower tenants to fight unlawful evictions, bullying and intimidation by their landlord. It would send a very powerful message to landlords that their tenants could once again take them on, and this would be a powerful incentive for them to obey the law and let homes fit for human habitation. However, restoring and expanding legal aid must be accompanied by changing the rules on compensation awards. As we saw in chapter 5, a tenant in Islington was prevented from continuing his claim for compensation because legal aid rules stipulated that funding could be granted only if the potential compensation awarded to a legally aided applicant was four times the court costs incurred. We need higher compensation awards and a lower multiple of compensation to legal cost so that tenants are empowered and incentivised to take their landlords or contractors to court in search of damages, and not denied justice.

Alongside legal aid, government must reinstate the statutory right of all tenants to a secure tenancy. Long-term security of tenure was introduced for most social housing tenants by the Housing Act 1980, followed by the assured tenancy regime of the Housing Act 1988 that has applied to most new housing association tenancies created since 15 January 1989. Private tenants also once enjoyed security of tenure courtesy of the 1977 Rent Act, which regulated rents and tenancies. The security of tenure from these Acts of Parliament meant that, with some limited exceptions, if secure or assured tenants did not breach the conditions of their tenancy agreement they could not be evicted. Having this legal right to remain is a powerful tool for ensuring that landlords do not respond to repair requests and complaints with retaliatory eviction. While the majority of existing social housing tenants still enjoy security of tenure, as we saw in chapter 1, new social housing tenants since April 2012 are reliant on the goodwill of their social landlord for such security. Since 1989, any new private tenancies created have typically had just six months' statutory protection. While many campaigners advocate three-year or five-year secure tenancies for private renters, if we really want to empower private tenants to resist unsafe housing, then they too should have lifetime tenancies, with rents regulated once again.

Create a new independent enforcement body accountable to residents

Even with these legal rights restored, tenants (and leaseholders) in both social and private sectors need a simpler and speedier non-court-based route to redress serious health and safety conditions in their homes that removes completely the ability of landlords, building owners and local authority environmental health enforcement teams to ignore these issues. Council tenants also face ongoing conflicts of interest where local authority building control teams are inspecting works carried out on behalf of the local authority landlord, as the fires at Lakanal and Grenfell exposed. A more radical solution proposed here is the creation of a new national housing safety and fitness inspectorate that would be accountable to residents and be independent of government, local authorities, landlords, companies and industry bodies. This national housing safety inspectorate would in effect be a new emergency service that residents, as well as building workers, professionals, trade unions and the general public could contact to raise urgent concerns about the poor quality of ongoing or recent construction or refurbishment, or rental housing conditions, where it is deemed to pose a threat to health or life. This is an area that currently falls outside the jurisdiction of the Health and Safety Executive, which considers only workplace safety and the immediate health and safety of workers. The proposed inspectorate would have strong legal powers to rapidly investigate these concerns independently of the landlord or developer, and where necessary enforce building, housing and fire safety regulations by issuing an immediate enforcement notice on the responsible party. The costs of the inspectorate could be met by levying fines against those deemed responsible. Should landlords or developers contest the notices and fines, they would have to take the inspectorate, not the resident, to court. If landlords refused to take action, the inspectorate would be legally empowered to directly make homes safe by temporarily taking over the building. Sanctions for landlords or building owners refusing to comply, or blocking the inspectorate from carrying out the work, would include banning orders, being placed on the government's new 'rogue landlords' database, and ultimately facing a compulsory purchase order (CPO).

Lesson 2: we need to re-regulate the building and landlord sectors

The second lesson we must learn is that giving residents and other bodies more power to tackle unsafe housing will succeed only if it is accompanied by measures to strengthen both the legal standards governing building work and the systems by which they are enforced. This book has clearly shown the devastating consequences of decades of deregulation that has replaced a once-rigorous and prescriptive system of building standards with a more flexible environment in which developers, builders and landlords are able to find cheaper and ultimately less safe routes to compliance. More flexible regulations have gone hand in hand with the building industry's dirty war against trade unionists to casualise building sites. Corporate interests have been allowed to capture and undermine the systems of safety testing and certification. A system of self-regulation has been introduced, reducing the number of national regulatory bodies and removing the 'burden' of inspection from most businesses, which have instead been tasked with self-monitoring their own safety compliance, secure in the knowledge that the chances of being caught are now negligible. Developers and construction companies have been further empowered by the gradual liberalisation and commercialisation of building control services that were previously the preserve of local authorities, and the roll-out of self-certification for most building work, diluting the quality and quantity of external inspection and enforcement. In social housing, work done almost exclusively by private contractors and their long, badly monitored sub-contracting chains is rarely properly checked. Meanwhile, responsibility for assessing whether rented housing meets the health, safety and fire standards has been largely passed from local authorities and fire service authorities to building owners or landlords, who also operate in a deregulated and self-regulating environment.

To make the health and safety of residents the overriding priority of building regulation, two key reforms are needed: to introduce more 'green tape' to regulate building safety; and to end self-regulation and re-empower independent building inspectors.

Introduce more 'green tape' to regulate building safety

A first step is to completely overhaul the regulatory framework in favour of more 'green tape' – seeing regulation in terms of life-saving standards as opposed to the financial burden of red tape. Such green tape should be aimed at preventing future deadly fires and other hazards. Following the public backlash against the initial refusal of the government-commissioned review of building regulations under Dame Judith Hackitt to recommend a ban on all forms of flammable cladding, the government confirmed in October 2018 that it would ban all combustible materials, including that used in cladding, on the outside of all new residential buildings, hospitals, care homes and student accommodation over

18 metres high. However, the ban does not go far enough – we should outlaw flammable materials on all buildings, whether new or existing, irrespective of height and use. The law in England must also change to ensure that sprinkler systems are mandatory in all new and existing residential care homes, purpose-built residential apartment blocks, single-family homes converted into flats ('houses in multiple occupation' – HMOs), and all housing featuring open-plan layouts that provide insufficient compartmentation to prevent the spread of fire and smoke. Residential buildings with a large number of occupiers (say, 60 or more) should also have a second means of escape.

End self-regulation, re-empower independent building inspectors

A second step is to introduce a new regulatory enforcement system to ensure that stricter safety standards are enforced in the construction and housing sectors for all existing and new homes of all tenures. Despite its many problems, the Hackitt review did produce a useful blueprint for how a new enforcement regime could work for high-rise residential buildings that could be extended to the entire built environment. It called for private sector building inspectors to be completely independent of building companies and for an end to the false division between the regulation of safety in existing homes and those in construction, by creating a joined-up system that requires building companies and owners to continuously prove fire and structural safety compliance before, during and after construction. Arguably the most interesting proposal was for a new 'Joint Competent Authority' (JCA), comprising local authority building control, fire and rescue authorities and the HSE, which would work together to maximise safety throughout a building's entire life, while recovering all of its costs by fining those in breach of building safety. The building owner or landlord would have to conduct FRAs at least annually and after any significant alterations to the building; the results of those FRAs would have to be shared with residents and the fire and rescue authority. The JCA would inspect buildings to verify compliance and would be able to issue statutory enforcement notices, fines and, ultimately, criminal sanctions.[12] In December 2018, the Conservative government announced it would implement the

Hackitt recommendations in full as well as launch a full review of fire safety guidance within building regulations.

While Hackitt's proposals provide a basis for reform, they need to go further if the conflicts of interest in the current enforcement system are to be rooted out. The competitive market for building control and fire risk assessors must end with the monopoly on checking building work and compliance, with fire safety restored to local authorities and the fire brigade service through a properly funded inspection system that is financially independent of the firms whose work is being evaluated for its legal safety compliance. That means local authorities should not be paid by a builder to inspect that builder's work; instead, all building and maintenance companies as well as landlords should pay annual fees to be licensed by a national government body – such as Hackitt's JCA – with their legal ability to operate dependent on their safety record. These fees would be used to fund local authority building control work and fire brigade inspections. The scope of self-certification must also be rolled back to ensure that any building work that could undermine residents' safety is subject to local authority inspection once again. Crucially, local authority building control departments should not be allowed to inspect and approve any work carried out on their own behalf, such as new council housing or regeneration schemes in which they are a partner. Wherever conflicts of interest like this are present, another local authority should carry out the inspection and approval role.

Lesson 3: we need to push back the rentiers and reboot public housing again

The final and arguably most important lesson we must learn is that restoring residents' rights and re-regulating the built environment will not address the problem of unsafe and insecure housing if we leave the present system of housing provision untouched. As I argued in chapter 1, during the 20th century public housing performed a vital decommodifying role as a form of *common property* that protected working-class people from the social murder and exploitation of rentier capitalism. As part of capitalism's long-term response to falling profitability, since 1979 neoliberal policies of privatisation, demunicipalisation and outsourcing have been purposely transforming housing and land, plus other public infrastructure such as schools and hospitals, into a financial asset class for wealth extraction. The end of mass public housing has left the supply of new homes in the hands of for-profit developers and speculative housebuilders with a vested interest in rising housing and land prices, as well as in lowering construction standards. In the process, what remains of social housing has seen its use value as affordable, safe and secure shelter relegated in importance to its potential exchange value. This has turned what was once an imperfectly managed common resource into an increasingly financialised world of 'assets' from which landlords, contractors, investors and financiers seek to maximise income and profit.

The use of PFI in housing has taken this model to new extremes, enriching construction firms, banks and global investors, while endangering residents' lives. Since Grenfell, the wider disaster of public sector outsourcing has become even more apparent with the collapse in 2018 of one major PFI contractor, Carillion, which has highlighted the loss of democratic control and accountability in the provision of public infrastructure. The overall policy implications are clear: the provision of safe and secure homes for all means a return to Bevan's principles (seen in the 1951 Conservative manifesto) and a reframing of housing as a 'social service' and not a private commodity. This means ending the privatisation and outsourcing disaster, bringing social housing management and maintenance back under democratic control, and replacing the profit motive with the public good as the central organising principle of housing provision. Central to this decommodification agenda is the need for a new era of public housing, based on the main principles set out in chapter 1. However, in practice, rolling back housing privatisation and demunicipalisation, and rolling out new public housing, face enormous practical challenges, as well as resistance from politicians, investors, banks and the private outsourcing industry. This means that any government committed to real change will have to operate on a gradual and strategic basis. With this in mind, I outline the following principles of reforms, and give some concrete proposals for how the reforms could be implemented.

End the ongoing privatisation of social housing

We need to stop the ongoing privatisation and marketisation of the existing council and social housing stock. The first step is to abolish – not suspend as the Labour Party currently proposes – the RTB in England as has been done in Scotland and Wales, saving just under 20,000 homes a year from privatisation. Similarly, councils and RSLs must no longer be allowed to demolish, sell or dispose of social housing (and land attached to it) without the consent of both the immediate resident body affected and central government, and demolition must be seen as the last resort. Social landlords must also no longer be permitted to convert social rent properties – normally let at an average of 60 per cent below the market rent – into so-called 'affordable rent' – set at up to 80 per cent of local market values.

Bring council housing back in-house by gradually ending PFI and outsourcing

At the same time as stemming the flow of privatisation, we need to take measures to end PFI and similar outsourcing arrangements, and again make in-house local authority provision the preferred option for council housing management and maintenance. However, this cannot be done overnight, as local councils currently lack the technical, financial and human capacity. For short-term outsourcing contracts (of, say, 5–10 years), one strategy is to wait for these individual contracts to reach the end of their lives and then bring the services back in-house. The danger with this, of course, is that private contractors would have every incentive to renege on agreed service delivery standards and milk the public purse for all they can, knowing their contracts were not going to be renewed. This therefore requires a two-stage approach, with the long-term objective of in-house provision accompanied by ongoing efforts to subject contractors to far more stringent performance scrutiny, financial deductions and adherence to terms and conditions comparable to those in public sector employment, such as trade union recognition and negotiating rights. This would either improve the quality and safety of these contractors' work, or create the legal ammunition required for terminating contracts early. An important mechanism to this end would be to extend the 2000 Freedom of Information Act to all RSLs and private sector contractors (including all sub-contractors) of public services and recipients of public funding, and change its provisions so as to make all public sector contracts publicly available, with redactions permissible only in relation to personal data. This would enable residents and other public servicer users to monitor contractors' compliance with contractual obligations and challenge contracts that are not in the public interest.

However, for the 20 housing PFI schemes featured in this book, bringing services back in-house at the end of the contract would mean residents waiting between another 17 and 24 years. Ending PFI thus requires a different approach. One solution gaining support is the proposal by the 'People versus PFI' campaign to nationalise all PFI SPVs as the starting point for ending these disastrous contracts and bringing the services back into the public sector.[13] This would require one or more Acts of Parliament to acquire the assets and accounts of the SPVs and vest their ownership in a government-owned company. In return for losing their equity, the SPV owners would receive government bonds. This would immediately end the profiteering by the PFI investors, saving huge sums of public money that could be used for the provision of local services by the public authority holding the PFI contract. The government would be able to use its ownership of these PFI contracts to renegotiate the service sub-contracts within them. At the same time, it could investigate whether the PFI build-ings meet building standards and agreed contractual performance levels as a means of triggering greater financial penalties or early termination. Helen Mercer and Dexter Whitfield estimate that the initial cost of compensating the shareholders of the 715 PFI SPVs would be between £2.3 billion and £2.5 billion, but that annual savings of £1.4 billion from the renegotiation of service contracts would mean that nationalisation would be self-financing within two years.[14] This is before account is taken of any savings from refinancing senior debt terms with banks and operating a far more stringent performance monitoring regime that could generate more income from financial penalties.

Build public housing again

The most effective way of making all renting genuinely affordable, safe, decent and secure, while addressing the wider shortage of housing, is for councils to resume their historic role as producers of mass public housing. To do this, we need to abolish the so-called 'affordable rent' programme and cut the strings of the financial straitjacket on local authorities so they can build high-quality, zero-carbon public housing to more generous space standards, as well as repair, modernise and make safe their existing homes. Following growing political pressure to allow councils to build again, in October 2018 the Conservative government announced its intention to lift local authority borrowing caps for housing investment and allow councils to raise finance within their prudential borrowing limits. While a welcome and remarkable policy change given the decades of tight fiscal control over councils to prevent them building housing, the government needs to go further and provide an appropriate subsidy to support the capital costs of building and make this available to other not-for-profit providers building secure and genuinely affordable homes to rent.

However, turning the tap of public investment back on will not mean a huge and sudden increase in public and social housing, as there is currently insufficient capacity within the municipal and housing association sector. Local authorities built just 990 homes in 2016–17, and in the 20 years since 1998 housing associations have managed to build on average only 22,000 homes a year. Around half of all councils now have no housing revenue account, so no conventional council housing assets against which to borrow or staff involved in housing management, and hardly any councils have a direct labour organisation (DLO) that could build new homes itself instead of having to contract construction out to the private sector. Another obstacle is land supply: this has been decimated by the privatisation of around 2 million hectares of public land since 1979 – some 10 per cent of the entire British land mass, and about half of all the land owned by public bodies when Thatcher assumed power.[15] While many local authorities do have land banks, they are not always in the best areas for building new homes, and the huge cost of buying overpriced land from private owners is a major barrier to building at volume again.

Capacity will have to be developed in multiple ways over time. Councils will in effect have to learn to build and manage housing again. Re-establishing in-house council building teams will require a major building programme with a long pipeline of work and a long-term local construction training centre; the London Borough of Southwark is currently doing just this. An idea that is gathering support across the political mainstream is for local authorities to be given powers to compulsorily purchase land at a price closer to existing use value, including by changing the rules governing the compensation paid to landowners. This should be complemented by a ban on selling or gifting existing public land to private owners and developers if it could instead be redeveloped for public housing. But the focus on the new-build misses the enormous potential for expanding secure public housing *from the existing stock of homes*. Ending the disaster caused by speculation in housing means starting to seriously address the iniquitous effects of ownership of multiple homes and the treatment of homes as financial assets. One idea is to look to what many councils were doing in the 1960s and 1970s when they municipalised tens of thousands of homes from the private sector that were in slum conditions, and turned them into council housing. The same could be done today: private landlords that consistently fail decency and safety standards could face compulsory purchase at less than market value.

However, the revival of public housing should not be based on simply reinstating the old public housing model, which was often technocratic, not always based on what people wanted, and for some produced a form of 'municipal serfdom'. Beyond the ravages of Thatcherism, Blairism and austerity, tenants have lacked the kind of 'dweller control' that property ownership confers and this experience of council housing has pushed many tenants over the years to take up the RTB, to escape from their municipal landlord. We need a new model of public housing, based on democratic citizenship and social rights that enable tenants to have greater ownership and control of their homes. This is not just greater rights to repair, improve, decorate, amend, adapt and use as a homeowner would (with permission and support from the landlord). Council and social tenants should be treated as joint owners of their local authority or housing association's stock, giving them an equal voting right to make decisions with other tenants about the future management and maintenance of their homes. Such equality of status and power would be one of the most potent ways of ensuring that Grenfell never happens again.

Notes

1 Ministry of Housing, Communities and Local Government, 'Building safety programme monthly data release', 20 September 2018, at https:// assets.publishing.service.gov.uk/government/uploads/system/uploads/ attachment_data/file/741971/Building_Safety_Datatina_Release_ September_2018.pdf (accessed 16 October 2018).

2 P. Apps, 'The forgotten threat to high-rise tenants', 30 August 2018, *Inside Housing*, Shorthand Stories website, 30 August 2018, at http:// shorthandstories.insidehousing.co.uk/index.html (accessed 16 October 2018); S. Barnes, 'The biggest ever survey of fire risk assessments has revealed widespread safety problems', *Inside Housing*, 13 June 2018, at https://www.insidehousing.co.uk/insight/insight/the-biggest-ever-survey- of-fire-risk-assessments-has-revealed-widespread-safety-problems-56774 (accessed 16 October 2018).

3 'Grenfell sprinkler systems in just 2pc of social housing tower blocks, investigation finds', *Telegraph*, 13 September 2017, at https://www. telegraph.co.uk/news/2017/09/13/grenfell-sprinkler-systems-just-2pc- social-housing-tower-blocks (accessed 16 October 2018).

4 S. Battersby, *The Challenge of Tackling Unsafe and Unhealthy Housing*, Report of a survey of local authorities for Karen Buck MP, December 2015, at http://sabattersby.co.uk/documents/KBReport2.pdf (accessed 16 October 2018).

5 See English Housing Survey 2016–17, at https://www.gov.uk/government/ collections/english-housing-survey (accessed 16 October 2018).

6 Ministry of Housing, Communities and Local Government, 'Building safety programme monthly data release'.

7 H. Dixon and S. Barnes, 'Homeowners face six-figure cladding bills', *Telegraph*, 1 September 2018, at https://www.telegraph.co.uk/news/ 2018/08/31/trapped-homeowners-face-six-figure-bills-grenfell-style- cladding (accessed 18 October 2018).

8 Salford City Council, 'Government restrictions holding up works to tower blocks', Salford City Council website, 21 September 2018, at https://www. salford.gov.uk/your-council/news/news-archive/news-from- september-2018/government-restrictions-holding-up-works-to-tower-blocks (accessed 15 October 2018).

9 'Salford city mayor and deputy rail against government on cladding delays', *Salford Star*, 11 October 2018, at http://www.salfordstar.com/article.asp?id=4758 (accessed 16 October 2018).

10 Interview with Phil Murphy, former firefighter, 14 December 2018.

11 Ministry of Housing, Communities and Local Government, *A New Deal for Social Housing*, social housing green paper (London: Ministry of Housing, Communities and Local Government, August 2018), at https://assets.publishing.service.gov.uk/government/uploads/system/uploads/attachment_data/file/733605/A_new_deal_for_social_housing_web_accessible.pdf (accessed 16 October 2018).

12 J. Hackitt, *Building a Safer Future: Independent Review of Building Regulations and Fire Safety: Final Report*, Presented to Parliament by the Secretary of State for Housing, Communities and Local Government, May 2018, at https://assets.publishing.service.gov.uk/government/uploads/system/uploads/attachment_data/file/707785/Building_a_Safer_Future_-_web.pdf (accessed 16 October 2018).

13 People vs Barts PFI, 'The Private Finance Initiative: nationalise the special purpose vehicles and end profiteering from public assets', 7 December 2015, at https://peoplevsbartspfi.files.wordpress.com/2016/02/pfi-nationalise-the-spvs-pple-vs-barts-pfi-version-1.pdf (accessed 16 October 2018).

14 H. Mercer and D. Whitfield, *Nationalising Special Purpose Vehicles to End PFI: A Discussion of the Costs and Benefits* (Greenwich: Public Services International Research Unit, 2018), at http://gala.gre.ac.uk/20016/1/20016%20MERCER_Nationalising_Special_Purpose_Vehicles_to_End_PFI%20_2018.pdf (accessed 16 October 2018).

15 B. Christophers, *The New Enclosure: The Appropriation of Public Land in Neoliberal Britain* (London: Verso, 2018).

Appendix. List of formal interviews cited in the book

Over the course of the research featured in this book, I conducted approximately 100 recorded interviews with politicians, public officials, private sector employees and residents. Listed below, in chronological order, are all the interviews that are directly quoted from in the book.

Leeds City Council senior councillor, 11 December 2008

Nick Raynsford, former Labour MP and Housing Minister (1999–2001), 16 February 2010

PFI advisor 3 (partner in major global financial law firm), 28 February 2010

PFI advisor 2 (PPP project advisor), 8 March 2010

PFI advisor 1 (partner in major global law firm), 18 March 2010

Keith Hill, former Labour MP and Housing and Planning Minister (2004–05), 18 March 2010

Civil servant involved in the housing PFI programme, 19 March 2010

'Edward', Islington tenant, series of interviews recorded during visits to his home between 2011 and 2018

Danny Moriati, Kirklees Federation of Tenants and Residents Associations, 3 August 2012

'Dec', Lambeth tenant, 31 October 2012

'Winston', Lambeth tenant, 1 November 2012

Jacqui Dyer, Lambeth tenant, 27 January 2013

'Daisy', Islington tenant, 3 June 2013

Dr Brian Potter, Chair of Islington Leaseholders Association, 3 June 2013

'Frank', Islington leaseholder, 4 June 2013

'Harry', Islington leaseholder, 10 June 2013
Islington housing officers, 11 June 2013
Stephen Boniface, surveyor, 12 June 2013
'Jenny', Islington tenant, 13 June 2013 and 17 July 2018
Elected officers of MFN RAMB, 30 June 2013
'Femi', Lambeth leaseholder, 10 October 2014
Former PFI project manager, 24 November 2014
'Gillian', Lambeth tenant, 9 March 2015
Uzoamaka Okafor, Lambeth leaseholder, 10 March 2015
Nigel Rumble, Camden leaseholder, 7 July 2017
Former employee of Partners for Improvement in Islington Ltd, 19 April 2018
'Michael', Camden leaseholder, 1 August 2018
Phil Murphy, former firefighter, 17 September 2018 and 14 December 2018

Index